BLOOD ON THE SNOW

BLOOD ON THE SNOW

THE KILLING OF OLOF PALME

JAN BONDESON

CORNELL UNIVERSITY PRESS
Ithaca and London

Title page illustration: Murder scene on March 1, 1986. Reproduced by permission of the Swedish National Police Board.

First published 2005 by Cornell University Press

Printed in the United States of America

Design by Scott Levine

Library of Congress Cataloging-in-Publication Data

Bondeson, Jan.
   Blood on the snow : the killing of Olof Palme / Jan Bondeson.
      p.   cm.
   Includes bibliographical references and index.
   ISBN 0-8014-4211-7 (cloth : alk. paper)
   1. Palme, Olof, 1927—Assassination. 2. Prime ministers—Sweden—
Death. 3. Assassination—Investigation—Sweden. I. Title.
   DL876.P3B66   2005
   364.152'4'0948509048—dc22
                                                    2004028249

Cornell University Press strives to use environmentally responsible suppliers and materials to the fullest extent possible in the publishing of its books. Such materials include vegetable-based, low-VOC inks and acid-free papers that are recycled, totally chlorine-free, or partly composed of nonwood fibers. For further information, visit our website at www.cornellpress.cornell.edu.

Cloth printing   10 9 8 7 6 5 4 3 2 1

CONTENTS

ILLUSTRATIONS

PREFACE: THE EIGHTY-NINE STEPS

The murder of Prime Minister Olof Palme, in the late evening of February 28, 1986, was a cataclysmic event in twentieth-century Swedish history. It shocked the nation profoundly, forced social and political change, and had an impact similar to that of the murder of President John F. Kennedy in Dallas twenty-one years earlier. The murder of Olof Palme is still unsolved and likely to remain so. The official police investigation is not making any headway, and most Swedes have accepted that the truth about the death of their prime minister, shot in the back after going to the cinema without bodyguards, will never be known.

There are already more books about Palme dead than about Palme alive, and the number of weird theories and urban legends about the murder is steadily growing. Some commentators have wondered whether the actual intention of the establishment and police was to spread disinformation and thereby shield the real culprits from justice, and others speculate about an elaborate conspiracy to assassinate Palme, involving some of the most prominent in the land. Similar mystery and suspicion surround the arrest of Christer Pettersson, a down-and-out alcoholic, as Palme's murderer. Pettersson was freed after two dramatic trials and continued to live in the Swedish capital until his sudden death in September 2004. Had the authorities intended this Swedish Lee Harvey Oswald to be the "ideal murderer," an unprepossessing figure whom no one would have missed? Was it vainly hoped that the conviction of Pettersson would resolve Sweden's national trauma?

This book is the first in English to present the full history of this extraordinary case. In it, I investigate the witness testimony, suspects, and trials, and suggest a new theory to solve the mystery.[1] Compared with the Kennedy assassination, the murder of Olof Palme is much more enigmatic and obscure with regard to motive, the identity of the killer, and the possibility of a larger organization behind the act. The story of the murder and its investigation also reveals extraordinary scenes of incompetence, deceit, and political corruption, resembling a Swedish Watergate.

When you visit Stockholm on a bright summer day, you gain full view of one of the most beautiful cities in Europe. The historic Old Town, where Olof Palme lived; the Royal Castle; the Vasa Museum, which houses an authentic seventeenth-century ship, are among its many attractions, where countless tourists flock each year. On a gloomy February night, however, the impression of Stockholm is very different. By that time of year, darkness sets in at 4 p.m., and the weather is bitterly cold and damp. On the Sveavägen, the busy thoroughfare where Olof Palme was murdered, people walk by like automata, wrapped up warm against the cold and minding their own business. Indeed, Stockholm might be some dire Russian town were it not for the obvious signs of wealth typical of an overconsuming Western state: brand new cars in the street, shop windows full of luxury goods. This is an old part of Stockholm, just by the steep Brunkeberg ridge, but little trace of the older buildings remains: the houses are modern, monotonously sterile, and forbidding-looking.

At the intersection of the Sveavägen and the Tunnelgatan, a crossroads leading to a pedestrian tunnel under the Brunkeberg ridge, a small plaque in the pavement commemorates the murder of Olof Palme. In the months after the murder, this area was covered with red roses as a sign of national grief and outrage. Now, feelings about Sweden's great unsolved mystery are more ambivalent. Some people still make a gesture of reverence when passing the plaque, but the vast majority simply ignore it. Palme remains as controversial in death as he was in life: hooligans and right-wing extremists occasionally urinate on the plaque or deface his gravestone. The police are well aware of these despicable activities: by the tenth anniversary of the murder, they had installed CCTV surveillance nearby, hoping to catch the murderer returning to the scene of the crime. They did see one sinister-looking body of men congregating around the plaque, but under questioning, they turned out to be a group of earnest, religious workmen who had come to honor their hero, the great socialist prime minister.

When you walk up the killer's escape route, eighty-nine steps up the Tunnelgatan stairs, ascending the old Brunkeberg ridge, yet another image emerges. The houses are older, the streets narrower, and the street layout somewhat erratic due to the steep hill. On a dark, cold February night, a psychic might see a crowd of specters lurking nearby, attracted by the blood of the murdered prime minister crying out from the ground. The Phantom, the Shadow, the Grand Man, the Dekorima Man, and other real and imaginary murder suspects hover round the Tunnelgatan stairs in an endless dance macabre . . .

BLOOD ON THE SNOW

DEATH IN STOCKHOLM

Olof Palme was a key player in European politics in the 1970s and 1980s.[1] Born in 1928 to a wealthy and distinguished upper-class family, he was educated at a leading private school, where his superior intelligence soon became apparent. Educated at Kenyon College in Ohio and at Stockholm University, Palme dabbled in law and journalism before becoming a leading member of the European student league. He then joined the ruling Social Democratic party and became parliamentary secretary to Prime Minister Tage Erlander in 1953. It has been speculated that Palme's conversion to socialism was prompted by careerism, although it is fair to point out, as Palme did himself, that his travels as a student leader broadened his views and exposed him to what he called the evils of capitalism and imperialism.

Since the 1930s, the Social Democrats had been in charge of Swedish politics. During these years, the country steadily grew wealthier, poverty was largely abolished, and Sweden's middle-of-the-road socialism was held up as an example for the rest of Europe. After maintaining a frightened neutrality, Sweden emerged from the Second World War with its industry intact. During the 1950s and 1960s, exports were doing very well, and Swedish steel, paper, cars, and telephones made their impact all around the globe. Taxation was gradually increased, and the money was used to construct an impressive national health service and the most generous social services in the world.

Olof Palme soon became indispensable to Erlander: he acted as a lobbyist and spin doctor, wrote speeches and pamphlets, and spoke in parliament with talent and conviction. Already in the early 1960s, many predicted that he would succeed Erlander. He was hated by the conservatives as a class traitor, and even among his own party colleagues, the distrust of his upper-class origin and university education never completely disappeared. The Swedish parliament at the time was probably the most lackluster in Europe. It recruited its members through central electoral lists rather than through individual elections in the constituencies, and people of outstanding talent and intelligence were few and far between. Through his wealth, intellect, and ambition, Palme stood out as a red carnation among his dull party comrades; he spoke six foreign languages fluently while they could barely express themselves literately in their own awkward tongue. Palme knew well that one of the chief motivating forces for his own electorate was envy and distrust of those who stood out from the crowd. As an antidote, he decided to live very frugally. He bought a small terraced house in a Stockholm suburb and commuted to work on a scooter. His wife, the noblewoman Lisbet Beck-Friis, who shared her husband's socialist views, supervised him as he washed dishes and ironed laundry. They had three sons and lived a happy family life.

Palme advanced to minister of education, an area where he held strong socialist views. He made drastic changes to the education system, requiring that most Swedes spend eleven or twelve years in school and lowering university standards to accommodate more students. In 1968, as in the rest of Europe, left-wing student uprisings occurred in Sweden, and distrust of the United States, due to the ongoing war in Vietnam, was widespread. Palme feared that this would lead to the rise of the Swedish communist party (subsidized by the Soviet Union, as Palme knew) and took action accordingly. He managed to monopolize the opposition to the Vietnam War by making a series of hostile remarks about the United States, branding the U.S. Army as murderers and likening the war to the Nazi genocide. These ill-judged comments brought him lasting notoriety in the United States, where conservative politicians considered him a dangerous crypto-communist. A photograph of him with the North Vietnamese ambassador in a torch-lit antiwar protest caused more ill will. But it was an oversimplification by his American critics, for Palme was actually a firm admirer of the United States, albeit unimpressed with many of its presidents. He always considered Sweden part of the Western world and was well aware of the Soviet threat.

In 1969, Palme smoothly took over the leadership of the Social Democrats and succeeded Erlander as prime minister. He upheld the view of Sweden as "the People's Home," where social classes were abolished, poverty a distant memory, and egalitarianism taken to its logical extreme. The state could always be trusted, the laws were just, and everything could be planned. In the People's Home, individuals were cared for from cradle to grave by the strong centralized government, whether they wanted it or not. A vast bureaucracy governed the incredibly complicated taxation system; another one, the similarly complex social benefits system. Tax evasion was branded a heinous

Olof Palme in 1969, an autographed photo.

crime, and accusations of capitalism or profiteering ruined the career of many a promising politician, some of them Palme's own friends. When Palme was offered the use of a large flat in Stockholm's historic Old Town by supporters who thought his tiny suburban house wholly inadequate for a distinguished politician, he did not accept it until a lawyer drew up a rental contract that absolved him from any suspicion of undue profiteering.

On the international front, Palme was among the first European leaders to advocate solidarity between the rich, overconsuming Western countries and the third world. He became recognized as an international authority on peace, disarmament, and redistribution of wealth. Sweden was (and still is) a neutral country, wedged between what was then the Western and Eastern blocs, and Palme wanted to make Northern Europe free of nuclear armaments. As an able spokesman against South American dictators and South African apartheid, he gained prestige in socialist circles throughout the world. Almost single-handedly, he made Sweden known throughout the world as a wealthy, advanced democracy that stood for equality, compassion, and humanitarian values. His support for Castro's Cuba and the communist regime in Nicaragua further blackened his name in the United States, however.

In the mid-1970s, Swedish conservative and liberal parties unleashed a backlash against Palme. Ignoring his international ambitions, they depicted him as personifying a system of rigid socialism and ineffective bureaucracy, a system that rewarded indolence and parasitism while punishing industry and enterprise. Taxation was a key issue, since a middle-class Swede paid seventy percent of his income in tax. Small businesses were literally taxed out of existence. When the celebrated children's book author Astrid Lindgren questioned whether it was really right that she should pay more than one hundred percent tax on her foreign earnings, Palme's minister of finance retorted that she should concentrate on writing books and leave matters of state to those who understood them better. Not long after, the minister was himself accused of tax evasion. Sweden had a monopoly on radio and television, and the two state television channels were widely considered the dullest in the world outside the Eastern bloc. More children were taken into care in Sweden than anywhere else, by an army of assiduous social workers. In the state schools (there were almost no private initiatives) the curriculum was experimental in the extreme, to the detriment of general education. And was it really right that young people should earn more on social security than when employed as an apprentice? In the 1976 election, Palme was defeated by a coalition of liberal and conservative parties; he would remain in opposition for six years.

It is a testament to Palme's strong position within his own party that even after two successive election defeats, there was never any serious debate whether he should resign. Through constant internal bickering, trouble with the powerful trade unions, and various other calamities, the coalition of liberal and conservative parties gradually lost their credibility, and people began to long for Olof Palme's return: the strong, competent leader and respected international statesman. In 1982, Palme did return to power, and in 1985, he won another convincing victory. At a time when most of Europe's socialist leaders had been ousted from power, Palme and his Social Democrats appeared stronger than ever. Not a few of these electoral successes were due to Palme's realization that the rigid socialism of the 1970s had become outdated. He knew that to stay in power, he needed to win the middle-of-the-road vote from the liberals. Despite murmurings among Social Democratic zealots that Palme was tearing down the People's Home, he appointed a minister of finance with liberal views on taxation, Kjell-Olof Feldt, and some modest tax cuts and other reforms took place. When Feldt and Palme wanted to allow private day-care nurseries as an alternative to the state-run system, another furious debate resulted, from which Palme again emerged unscathed. Another Swedish sacred cow, the immensely powerful trade unions, was a more difficult matter. Wholly unconvinced by Palme's new liberal policies and provided with ample funds, they openly challenged the government, but Palme did not budge.

Already in the 1970s, Palme had been detested by his conservative opponents; his return to power infuriated these enemies even further. Using his intellectual advantage to mock and taunt his political rivals, Palme had introduced elements of controversy and hatred that had previously been lacking in the quiet pond of Swedish politics. Although popular among his own supporters, and not lacking the common touch, Palme's arrogant manner and radical socialist rhetoric made him the most hated man in Sweden among right-wing elements. His enemies organized a campaign of vilification against him and delighted in spreading the most extravagant rumors: Palme had extramarital affairs or, alternatively, he was a homosexual. His alleged truckling to the Soviets was particularly unpopular and led to speculation that he took bribes or was a KGB agent. One rumor held that Palme was leading a life of luxury from the ill-gotten gains of wholesale tax evasion, and that his tiny suburban house was connected to vast underground chambers where he sat counting his banknotes. Another ludicrous rumor said that Palme suffered from schizophrenia and that he drove by the lunatic asylum in the morning, before the government meetings, to receive electroconvulsive treatment. The prime minister had really been driving past the asylum, it turned out, to visit his elderly mother in the geriatric ward. Although toughened by years of experience as a controversial politician, Palme was quite upset by this venomous campaign of hatred, particularly when it spilled over on members of his family.

February 28, 1986, began like any other day for Olof Palme.[2] He played tennis with his friend Harry Schein in the morning and won a tough game, which pleased him. He then personally went into a haberdashery to exchange a suit he had bought off the rack the day before, because his wife Lisbet had objected to it. His bodyguards accompanied him on both these expeditions and then to Rosenbad, the Swedish government building. Palme then told the bodyguards to make themselves scarce; he would call if he needed them later during the day. He often wanted to maintain his privacy when walking in central Stockholm and disliked the presence of the bodyguards. Had there been any serious threat against him, the bodyguards would have argued for stricter surveillance, but they did not do so.

As Olof Palme arrived at work on February 28, no person noticed anything particular. If anything, Palme seemed quite jolly, as if he was looking forward to the coming weekend. Palme spent the day meeting various diplomats, journalists, and party officials. Just before lunch, he met with the Iraqi ambassador to discuss the ongoing war between Iran and Iraq, in which Palme had the thankless task of being the UN official arbitrator. The ambassador left at 12:00, and Palme briefly met some colleagues before sitting alone in his room until the official government luncheon at 1:00 p.m. It is not known what he did during this time, or whom he might have contacted, since his secretary was herself at lunch. It surprised many people that when Palme at length came into the Rosenbad dining room, he was nearly twenty minutes late and in a furious temper, completely distraught for some unknown reason, and unwilling to tell anyone why. One of the ministers advised him to resort to the traditional Swedish custom of having a "snaps" of aquavit to steady his nerves, but the prime minister angrily declined. In the afternoon, Palme gradually recovered his usual calm and professional manner. A journalist who interviewed him for a trade union magazine even thought that he was in rather a good mood. But when Palme was asked to pose by the window for a photograph, he moodily declined, saying, "You never know what may be waiting for me out there." This comment struck the journalist as being out of character and in marked contrast to the prime minister's attitude during the interview.

At the end of the day, Olof Palme walks home to his elegant apartment in the Old Town, not far from the government building. He had previously spoken to Lisbet about going to the cinema in the evening, but they had not decided which film to see. Lisbet originally wanted to see *My Life as a Dog*, screening at the Spegeln cinema. At 6:30 Olof phones his son Mårten to discuss various things, among them the plans for the evening. It turns out that young Palme is also going to the cinema that evening, to see a film called *The Brothers Mozart* at the Grand cinema. The Palmes debate whether they should join him. Although Lisbet is still keen on seeing *My Life as a Dog*, the promise of Mårten's company might change her mind. They make no promise they will join Mårten, however, and reserve no tickets for either film. In the evening, the Palmes have a bite to eat before going out. During these hours, Palme receives several telephone calls. Two of them, from old party colleagues, have been identified, but there may well have been others. The Palme apartment has only one phone line, and, like any other citizen, Palme answers the phone when it rings, without any secretary or switchboard monitoring the calls. Former party secretary Sven Aspling calls just as Olof is preparing to leave, and Olof ends the discussion by saying that Lisbet is waiting in the hallway, wearing her coat.

As the Palmes step out of the house at about 8:35 p.m., they have finally decided on *The Brothers Mozart*. A young couple are just passing by the front door. They recognize the prime minister but note nothing untoward, except that when they laugh at some joke, Lisbet looks frightened and surprised, as if she thought they were laughing at her. Neither this young couple, nor several other people who meet the Palmes on their way to the Old Town subway station, notice any person following the prime minister and his wife. Almost everyone who meets him recognizes Olof's aquiline features, since they have

Olof and Lisbet Palme after the election victory of 1985.

been depicted on the front pages of the Swedish newspapers for more than two decades. Lisbet is much less known among the general public, however. The very antithesis of the glamorous Jacqueline Kennedy, she is short, ordinary looking, and not noted for sartorial elegance. At the subway station, the ticket agent politely wishes Olof Palme a pleasant journey. He finds it odd that no bodyguards are following the prime minister. As the Palmes stand on the platform waiting for the northbound train, quite a few people recognize Olof. Most of them shyly look away, but one or two say hello to the prime minister, who politely returns their greetings. A jolly drunk shouts, "Hey there, Palme, are you taking the subway today?" A man who sees Palme close up marvels at the prime minister's plain and inelegant clothes, in particular his very creased and baggy trousers. He also gets the impression that Palme is worried about something, since he is moving around nervously on the platform.

Finally the train comes in, and Olof and Lisbet enter the third of four subway cars. The train is quite full, and at first the Palmes have to stand; although

Olof Palme at the government building in Stockholm.

quite a few people recognize Olof and Lisbet, none of them is chivalrous enough to offer them a seat. A man notices that Palme moves around nervously, as if he were curious about the construction of the subway car. The short subway journey is eventless, and the Palmes emerge from the train at the Rådmansgatan station. As they make their way up the stairs, a mischievous youth recognizes them and decides to walk up behind the prime minister in a threatening manner, to see what the bodyguards will do. He is surprised when nothing happens; not even Palme himself notices him. Neither this youth nor any other witness sees any person following the Palmes as they walk the short distance from the subway station to the Grand cinema.[3] Outside the cinema entrance, Olof and Lisbet are joined by Mårten and his girlfriend. Seeing that the queue in front of the ticket office is a formidable one, the prime minister makes a move as to pull rank and pass it by. A bystander is amused when Lisbet brusquely tells him off, and Olof obediently shuffles off to join the back of the long queue. As he is patiently waiting for his turn, several people recognize him. Since the Palmes have made no reservation, all the good seats are sold when Olof finally reaches the ticket office. Fortunately for him, the ticket seller is a political sympathizer and sells the prime minister and his wife two tickets reserved for one of the cinema directors since he thinks it a pity if the Palmes would not get good seats. He thinks Palme looks just like his photograph but fails to recognize Lisbet, who appears nervous and worried. As

Olof and Lisbet take their seats, a trade union leader walks up to his friend the prime minister, sits down in the seat behind them, and starts talking politics. Lisbet firmly tells him that this evening there should be no political discussions; Olof is going to have a good time and enjoy himself. It is not known whether there was a general hush in the theater after these fateful words, as there would have been in a Greek tragedy.

The Brothers Mozart, by the left-wing director Suzanne Osten, is a rather silly and pretentiously intellectual film, but the Palmes appear to have rather liked it. The film ends a few minutes after 11:00 p.m., but Olof and Lisbet do not join the throng of young people impatient to leave; they stay a bit longer, listening to the music along with Mårten and his girlfriend. Without any hurry, the two couples make their way out of the cinema, and Olof puts on his thick overcoat and his fur hat. As they stand on the sidewalk outside, discussing the film, Olof walks up to a brightly lit bookshop display window to look up the name of one of the actresses in the program. But just as he approaches the window, the lights go out. Olof becomes quite upset and suspects someone in the shop deliberately turned off the lights to annoy him. Mårten thinks his father's reaction to this trivial incident a little odd, but he also goes up to have a look. A woman walking by notices that they seem to be quarreling, although this may be a misinterpretation of their debate about what is going on inside the shop.

Mårten suggests that they all go for a cup of tea, but the others decline, saying it is too late. The time is now 11:15. The group briefly debates how Olof and Lisbet should travel home. Although Lisbet has just announced that she feels tired, Olof makes it clear that he does not want to take the subway but instead to walk all the way home to the Old Town, a distance of nearly a mile and a half. This is a surprising decision, since not only is the weather windy and freezing cold (−7°C), but it is now late on a Friday night, and quite a few rowdy, drunken youths are at large. As the aforementioned trade union leader sees Olof and Lisbet leave the cinema just before 11:17, he remarks to his wife what a marvelous country Sweden is, where the Prime Minister can walk home unescorted late at night, just like any ordinary citizen. It is hard not to draw a parallel to Governor Connolly's wife exclaiming to John F. Kennedy, moments before the fatal shots were fired, how much the people of Dallas loved their president.

As the Palmes walk down the Sveavägen, nothing appears to be wrong.[4] The streets are covered with a thin layer of snow and ice, but Olof and Lisbet are used to these perilous walking conditions and use appropriate footwear. They pass a hot dog stand and walk by a few people going in the opposite direction, but even the hardy Swedes have a reluctance to go for nocturnal walks

The Grand cinema in Stockholm.

in subzero temperatures, and the streets are emptying of people. The Palmes cross the Sveavägen, and Lisbet wants to look at an Indian gown in a shop window display. Olof seems reluctant to stop, but they stand for five or ten seconds admiring the gown. They then continue walking on the same side of the Sveavägen, opposite the side they would eventually need to be on to get home, toward a paint shop called "Dekorima," where the window displays are brilliantly lit.

A music teacher named Inge Morelius, who is sitting in a car nearby, gives a good account of what happens next.[5] He has parked his vehicle near some traffic lights, while his friends withdraw money from an ATM. Morelius has been observing a tall man dressed in a dark overcoat, who hastily walked up to the Dekorima entrance some minutes earlier. This man appears concentrated and alert, and anxiously looks up and down the Sveavägen as if he were waiting for someone. There is something sinister about him, and Morelius suspects he might be planning a robbery or a drug deal. Morelius says to one of his friends in the back seat, "Check out that weird dude over there! He is waiting to do something!"

Although several other things occupy the music teacher's interest, among them the banking transactions of his friends and the fact that his car is illegally parked and that he has to look out for the police and traffic wardens, he keeps looking at the dark-coated man at intervals to see what he is doing. As Morelius watches a man and a woman (the Palmes) walking toward Dekorima, the dark-coated man goes up to them. The music teacher calls out to two friends of his, who are sitting in the back seat of the car, "Hell, now he's going to snatch the old lady's handbag!" At first nothing happens, but just as Morelius turns his eyes back toward the three people outside Dekorima, the man grabs Olof Palme's shoulder, pulls out a large handgun, and fires two shots into the back of the prime minister. "My God, he's shooting!" Morelius cries out. The assassin stands for some seconds looking at his victim to make sure he is really dead, calmly holsters the gun, and quickly runs away up the Tunnelgatan, past some building site barracks.

A bit inside the Tunnelgatan, hidden by the barracks, is a man named Lars Jeppsson. He hears the shots, and sees a man collapse in the street. A woman then comes into view and bends over him; when she becomes aware what has happened, she screams, "No! What are you doing!" in a terrible voice. Jeppsson then hears running footsteps approaching him and correctly deduces that the gunman is heading his way. Fortunately for Jeppsson, he himself is hidden behind the building site barracks, and the gunman, a tall, well-built man wearing a dark overcoat or jacket and a dark cap, runs quickly past him without observing this potential witness. There is a flight of eighty-nine steps up the steep Brunkeberg ridge, and Jeppsson sees the gunman bound up these stairs with agility, two or three at a time. On the top of the stairs, the gunman looks over his shoulder to check for possible pursuers, and then he is gone.

Lars Jeppsson is a short, thin man in his mid-twenties, and his job in the municipal archives has not made him accustomed to chasing armed criminals late at night. He indecisively looks down the Sveavägen, where people are now gathering, wondering if he should go there to try to help the man who has just been shot in the street. He then gathers up his courage and pursues the gunman up the Tunnelgatan stairs, in the hope of observing where he is heading. At the top of the stairs, he meets a woman named Yvonne Nieminen and her friend Ahmed Zahir and asks them where the man has gone.[6] It turns out that they have both also seen the gunman: a tall man in a black overcoat that fluttered around his legs as he ran past them. He was still running after having negotiated the eighty-nine steps, but not very quickly since the road is covered with snow, and he came close to slipping more than once. He once or twice looked behind him as if checking for pursuers. Interestingly, Nieminen later added that he looked like a Scandinavian and that he was carrying a

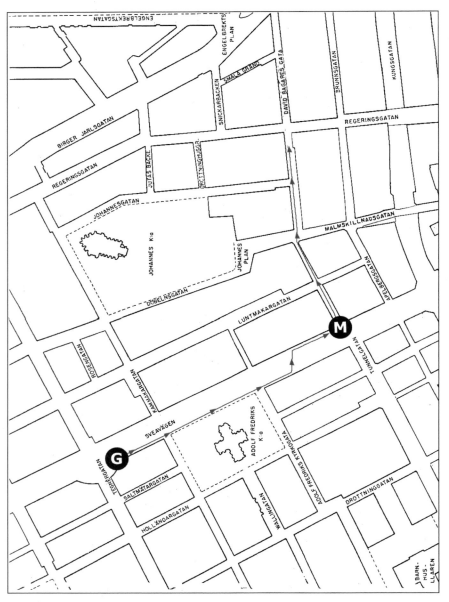

Map of the murder scene, showing the killer's escape route. *G* marks the Grand cinema, *M* the murder site.

small clutch bag, about four by six inches in size, which he seemed to be opening or closing as he ran.

Nieminen directs Jeppsson toward David Bagares Gata, a continuation of the Tunnelgatan; she saw the gunman just five yards from the crossing with Johannesgatan. Jeppsson runs off hoping to see where the man is going. Having run a block down David Bagares Gata, he can only just glimpse what he presumes to be the disappearing gunman quite some distance away. The man seems aware that Jeppsson is in pursuit and suddenly veers off between some parked cars. Jeppsson does not see him emerge or hear a car door slamming, and he thinks that the man might be dodging behind the parked cars to keep out of sight. Rather half-heartedly, Jeppsson walks down David Bagares Gata and looks behind some tarpaulins covering the facade of a house that is being rebuilt. With some relief, he then gives up his pursuit, presuming that the man must be far away, and walks back to the Tunnelgatan steps. These are the last certain observations of the man who murdered Olof Palme.

BLOOD ON THE SNOW

After hearing the shots, building contractor Leif Ljungqvist turns his Chevrolet van around on the Sveavägen and drives up to the crime scene. He is only just able to catch a glimpse of the fugitive gunman: a tall, dark-haired man in a dark overcoat running up the Tunnelgatan. Ljungqvist sees that the victim is bleeding badly, and although some people are running up to try to resuscitate him, Ljungqvist's impression is that the man's life is lost. He grabs his car telephone and in his second attempt manages to dial the Swedish equivalent of 911, telling the operator that someone has just been murdered in the Sveavägen. His call is received at 23:22:07, just 45 or so seconds after the murder. The emergency service switchboard transfers his call to the police at 23:22:25, but the seconds tick by without anyone lifting the receiver at the other end. As the frustrated Ljungqvist waits for the police to respond, he asks his passenger whether he has any description of the killer, and someone says that the man was wearing a blue cap or hood. Finally, after waiting at least ninety seconds, Ljungqvist puts the phone down.

It is amazing that the police do not answer an urgent call within a minute and a half, and even more amazing that the telephone operator does not prompt them to do so, in keeping with her instructions for a call concerning a serious crime.[1] Looking around, Ljungqvist sees a cab driver speaking on the phone nearby, and correctly guesses that this man has been more successful in alarming the authorities. Had Ljungqvist's original phone call been answered by the police, and a prompt alert radioed out, the gunman would almost have run into a squad of five young policemen, who were sitting talking in their police van in the Malmskillnadsgatan, not far from the Tunnelgatan. As things were, the killer probably saw the rear lights of the van, as it slowly drove off, during his mad dash up the Tunnelgatan steps.

A tape recording is made of all calls to the Swedish emergency services, and this night's recording tells us that just as Ljungqvist puts the phone down, someone vainly tries to answer the call at police headquarters. The time is exactly 11:23:40. Ljungqvist steps out of his van to see what he can do to help. He sees that two teenage girls have knelt beside the fallen man: one of them, Anna Hage, tries to revive him with vigorous chest compressions. A young man valiantly attempts mouth-to-mouth resuscitation. Seeing that he is not needed to take care of the man who has been shot, Ljungqvist instead walks up to the woman who accompanied the victim and asks her, "Please Ma'am, why did he shoot?" The blood-spattered woman stares blankly ahead and does not reply. Ljungqvist later said that he had never before seen such a profoundly shocked and distraught human being.

As Mrs. Palme becomes aware of Anna Hage doing chest compressions, she furiously screams at the girl to leave her husband alone; only a qualified doctor should make such resuscitation attempts. Instead, someone should call an ambulance and alert the hospital to prepare an operating room. Anna Hage tries to ignore Mrs. Palme, continuing her attempts at resuscitation, but the hysterical woman attacks her, slaps her face, and tries to pull her away from the lifeless body of her husband. The girl pushes Mrs. Palme away and yells that unless heart activity is restarted, there is no point getting an ambulance at all. Hage's friend Karin Johansson comes up and tries to calm the woman down, but with little success: Mrs. Palme keeps running around the crime scene screaming incoherently about doctors, ambulances, and operations, and even runs out into the street trying to stop cars driving by.

Shortly after 11:22, cab driver Anders Delsborn phones the headquarters of his cab company, which is located in the suburb Järfälla. He calls out, "Someone has just been shot! Call the police and an ambulance! A man is lying in the street and he is not moving!" Switchboard operator Ann-Louise Paulsson asks if an ambulance is really needed, and Delsborn replies that he is sure it is, since the man who has been shot is down and is not moving. Paulsson then promptly alerts the police. Detective Ulf Helin answers her call. In circumstances like these, police standing orders require that the telephone line with the crime scene be kept open, that a senior officer be called, and that a record be kept of all police activity. Helin does none of these things, but puts the phone down after just twenty seconds.[2] He later admitted that although he grasped the essential fact, namely that a man had been shot in the crossing of Sveavägen and Tunnelgatan, he thought the switchboard operator seemed confused and it might be best for a police patrol to verify that someone had really been shot before any action was taken. Some youths might have been playing a prank with fireworks, he reasoned, or a car might have backfired. In the recording of Ann-Louise Paulsson's later telephone conversation with the emergency services switchboard, she does not sound confused in the slightest, but resolutely requests that an ambulance be sent to the crime scene. This turns out to be fortunate, since Helin has not even taken that simple action!

The chronology of the murder of Olof Palme will be looked into in detail later in this chapter, since it is clear that an unexplained delay occurs from the time the police are alerted until the alarm is radioed out. This delay at police headquarters means that the first police car on the scene is one that has not been called into action by Helin. Police lieutenant Gösta Söderström is the senior officer in charge of uniformed police in central Stockholm that fateful night. A veteran officer with thirty-nine years of police experience, he is patrolling the Kungsgatan not far from Sveavägen with his driver. Suddenly, an excited cab driver, who has heard the Järfälla taxi switchboard operator's conversation with the police on his own cab radio, comes running to tell them what has happened. As soon as he understands that a man has been shot, Söderström orders his driver to floor the accelerator. He does not switch on the siren, in order not to warn the gunman of his approach.

As they arrive at the scene, Söderström sees that the man who has been shot is most likely dead. Neither he nor any other person is able to recognize the victim as Olof Palme. A crowd of people are milling about at the scene, and the persistent young people are still trying to resuscitate the victim, although the only apparent effect is that for each attempt at heart compression, blood gushes out of the mouth of the murdered man, rendering the task of the young man attempting mouth-to-mouth resuscitation extremely unpleasant. When he succeeds in blowing air down the victim's windpipe, it escapes with a dreadful hissing sound through the mutilated chest cavity.

Seconds later, the police van that had been so close to cutting off the murderer's escape route arrives with screeching tires, and Sergeant Kjell Östling and his four officers jump out. A blood-spattered woman runs toward them, screaming hysterically. For about a minute or so, the officers try to get some information out of her, but without success; none of them recognize her as Lisbet Palme, nor is she herself able to tell them who she is. Söderström then takes charge. He loudly shouts a question, asking where the gunman went, and a witness (we do still not know who) replies, "They ran that way!" pointing up the Tunnelgatan.[3] Söderström then orders the four officers to pursue the fugitive killer. One of them pipes up, saying that this might be dangerous, and they have no bulletproof vests. Another officer adds that it might be advantageous if they knew what the gunman looks like. Söderström gruffly orders them to hurry up, adding that he will radio the killer's description to them later if he can get any information out of the shocked and confused witnesses.

Without further ado, all four officers draw their pistols and run up the Tunnelgatan steps. Yvonne Nieminen and her boyfriend, who are now on their way down the stairs, have to flatten themselves against the railings to avoid being run down by this unexpected police stampede. One of the officers, who has just drunk a large can of Coke, has to stop and vomit after a while, but the other three carry on running. Reaching David Bagares Gata, they can see the witness Jeppsson and another police car, containing lieutenant Christian Dalsgaard, Söderström's second in command, and his driver. Dalsgaard heard the alarm and volunteered to try to cut off the gunman's escape route, arriving just in time to see Jeppsson return from his pursuit down David Bagares Gata. It is odd that Dalsgaard makes no effort to stop or question Jeppsson, until the witness himself flags down the police car and meekly asks the lieutenant whether he might be pursuing the man who just shot someone down in the Sveavägen.

The four officers then come pounding up, and Dalsgaard is amazed that they have no clear idea what has happened; they think someone might have been shot, they say, and have been ordered to pursue the gunman without knowing what he looks like. At the same time, Dalsgaard hears Söderström's voice on the police radio saying, "Do you know it is Palme?" but he does not connect this message with the incident in question. Jeppsson tells Dalsgaard about the killer's probable escape route, but the cop still does not act decisively. Suspicious that Jeppsson might have been involved in the crime, he decides to have one of the officers escort this witness back to the crime scene. It is not until this officer returns that a proper pursuit is made down David Bagares Gata. The police squad splits up into two teams to search the nearby streets and the large Johannes churchyard. Dalsgaard, the only one having access to a motor vehicle, does not take part in the pursuit but orders his driver to take him down to the crime scene.

Two other young officers in a squad car hear the police alarm and have the excellent idea of trying to intercept the killer at the Birger Jarlsgatan, a likely escape route. After lying in wait for some minutes, they hear running footsteps approaching. One of the cops jumps out, but is dismayed to be facing one of the officers from the police van. Panting and exhausted, waving his pistol around in a dangerous manner, he yells, "Where the hell did he go?" and the officer thinks himself lucky not to have been inadvertently shot dead by one of his own colleagues.[4]

At the crime scene, confusion still reigns supreme. Söderström valiantly tries to find witnesses, and finally somebody tells him that the killer might have been wearing a blue parka. Söderström promptly radios this information to his colleagues, also informing police headquarters that a man has indeed been shot and that the gunman has escaped up the Tunnelgatan steps. He is annoyed to find that just moments later, a officer is radioing out a completely different description of the killer, a man wearing a gray overcoat and a flat cap. In the meantime, the hysterical woman is still screaming desperately for help. Söderström sees that although her face and hair are bloodstained, as if she had tried to sweep back her hair with a bloody hand, she does not seem to be badly injured. In some strange way, he feels that he has seen her before. As she rushes toward him, screaming that he must save her husband's life, Söderström counters by asking for her identification documents. It takes several attempts for him to get through to her with this request, but finally she glares at him and screams, "Are you crazy? Don't you recognize me? I am Lisbet Palme, damn it, and there [pointing] lies my husband Olof!"

The veteran lieutenant later eloquently described his acute feelings of surprise and dismay on hearing this singular announcement. He first responds with an incredulous remark but then walks over to make a closer inspection of the mangled body on the sidewalk. The ambulance has now arrived, and the paramedics are taking over the futile resuscitation attempts. Although the victim's head and body are bloody, and the eyes staring and bloodshot, Söderström recognizes Olof Palme's features, and realizes that he is standing next to the corpse of the prime minister of Sweden. The witness Ljungqvist sees Söderström clasp his forehead and exclaim the Swedish equivalent of "Oh dear! Oh dear!" as he staggers back to his police car. Sinking into the front seat, he sits for a short while trying to decide what to do. He then makes an open radio call to police headquarters and all patrol cars that the prime minister of Sweden has just been shot down in the street. After some moments of stunned radio silence, a confused voice from police headquarters calls out, "For God's sake, Gösta, you're not saying that Olof Palme has been shot, are you?" "The answer is yes!" Söderström replies.[5]

The ambulance arriving at the scene is not the one alarmed by the authorities, but a suburban one whose crew decided to cruise through central Stockholm to have a burger and "take a look at the girls" before returning to their own precinct. But if they wanted excitement that fateful night, they get more than they bargained for when the witness Ljungqvist flags them down at the crime scene. The two paramedics quickly fasten an oxygen mask over Palme's face and insert a pharyngeal tube to clear the upper airways. They then open Palme's coat and jacket, and cut his shirt open with scissors to inspect the wound. They can see only the exit wound, a small hole in the chest cavity. They then swiftly lift the badly bleeding victim onto a stretcher and wheel it into the ambulance.

Just at that moment, the second ambulance arrives, and the paramedics gesture to Lisbet Palme that she should follow her husband in that vehicle. She angrily screams back that she is not under any circumstances leaving her husband. The ubiquitous Ljungqvist chivalrously opens the passenger door of the first ambulance for her, and she sits down next to the driver. Just before 11:28, the shaken ambulance driver makes a hurried radio call to the emergency services switchboard, saying that they are leaving for nearby Sabbatsberg Hospital; he adds that the victim is badly injured, with a gunshot wound to the chest, and is a famous person. In the background of the tape recording of this radio call, Lisbet Palme can be heard saying, "Palme . . . has . . . fallen" in a low, groaning voice. The paramedics know the identity of the victim and are in a state of shock. The driver almost fails to find his way to the hospital, taking at least one wrong turn along the way; he would later describe this nightmare experience, with Mrs. Palme sitting next to him screaming furiously, as the worst in his life.

At the Sabbatsberg Hospital, the emergency department has been alerted by the emergency services switchboard, and the anesthetist and surgeon on duty are standing by as the ambulance arrives at 11:30. They both see that life is extinct, but at Mrs. Palme's insistence that everything possible be done for her husband, the surgeon cuts the corpse's thorax open, bares the heart, and massages it with his gloved hand. Intravenous access is established, and for some minutes, the doctors and nurses work intensely to resuscitate Palme, but without eliciting any response. Mrs. Palme is taken into another room by a nurse. As her coat is taken off, she complains that her back hurts. The nurse can see that the killer's second shot penetrated all of Mrs. Palme's clothing and left a red line on the skin of the upper part of her back, but without causing any injury. Mrs. Palme does not permit a doctor or a forensic technician to see her injury, saying it is just a trifling matter.

Olof Palme is officially declared dead at 12:06 a.m., and a few minutes later the doctors let Mrs. Palme know that her husband is dead. The kindly nurse feels sorry for the distraught Lisbet Palme and helps her to telephone her sons Joakim and Mårten. She can overhear Mrs. Palme saying, "Now it has happened, what we so long sought to avoid." Mrs. Palme and the nurse also try to contact the Swedish Embassy in Paris, since the Palmes' youngest son Mattias is in Chamonix for a skiing holiday, and Lisbet Palme wants him to be informed by ambassador Carl Lidbom, a friend to the Palme family.

The exact chronology of the murder of Olof Palme has been the subject of much debate.[6] It is well established, from the timing of the telephone calls of Delsborn and Ljungqvist, and the bank withdrawals of the friends of Inge Morelius, that Palme was murdered between 11:21:10 and 11:21:30. More controversial questions are when the police alarm was sent out and when the first police patrol reached the murder scene. The early police chronology says that the police alarm was made at 11:23:00 and that the first police car arrived at 11:23:10. But according to the timed tape recording of all calls reaching the Stockholm emergency services, it is notable that when Ljungqvist put down the phone at 11:23:40, there was still no police presence. Thus the official chronology must be wrong.

The murder scene witnesses have given variable estimations of the time between the shots and the arrival of the first police car: three minutes (Delsborn and Johansson), three or four minutes (Svensson), and three to five minutes (Wallin). Ljungqvist and his passenger independently stated that it took three or four minutes from the time Ljungqvist stepped out of the car (about 11:23:50) until the police arrived. The two girls who helped to resuscitate Palme thought that it took at least seven minutes from the shots until the police arrived.[7] In a nightmare situation like this, it is very difficult to estimate the time correctly, however, and the witness who is eagerly waiting for help to arrive usually exaggerates the time he or she had to wait. Nevertheless, the testimony of Ljungqvist and his passenger must be taken seriously, since they have a later, fixed reference point (11:23:40) that can be verified by independent means. Thus it probably took at least a minute or two from 11:23:40 until the police arrived, and thus the first police car arrived after 11:24:40.

The second key time point from the timed tape recordings is the departure of the ambulance at 11:27:50. The two paramedics later agreed they had been at the murder scene between two and four minutes. It is a pity that neither of these men, nor any of the police officers, seems to have made a note of the exact time they arrived at the scene. In contrast to the vague estimate made by the two ambulance men, the three young people who tried to resuscitate Palme independently estimated that the ambulance remained stationary between sixty and ninety seconds.[8] Several other witnesses remarked that the paramedics worked very swiftly, wasting no time before wheeling the stretcher into the ambulance. In my opinion, it would normally take trained paramedics less than two minutes to perform the simple tasks outlined above. In this case, one has to make allowances firstly for them being taken completely unaware when flagged down at the scene and secondly for the delay caused by the debate about Lisbet Palme's mode of transportation. Thus it is reasonable to suggest that the ambulance stayed at the scene between two and three minutes, and that it arrived between 11:24:50 and 11:25:50.

A third clue comes from the evidence given by the cab driver who alerted Lieutenant Söderström.[9] He said that he had heard Delsborn's call to the taxi switchboard and about sixty to ninety seconds later heard the confirmation of Paulsson, the switchboard operator, that she had phoned the police. This agrees with what we know about her call for an ambulance, which is timed at

11:23:40 on the aforementioned tape recording: Paulsson's confirmation of the alarm was likely radioed out between 11:23:20 and 11:23:35. Shortly after hearing the confirmation, the cab driver looked around and saw a police car on the other side of the road. He estimated that it took him between thirty and ninety seconds to cross the road, hail the police car, and explain what had happened. If Paulsson's confirmation of the alarm was radioed out at 11:23:30, it would be reasonable to suppose that the cab driver hailed the police car at 11:24:10 and that the cops drove off at 11:24:20. The drive to the murder site would take Söderström thirty to forty seconds, meaning that he would arrive shortly before 11:25:00.

All accounts agree that Söderström's police car arrived first, that the first police van came second, and that the ambulance arrived after the police van. Since the policemen in the van said that they saw Söderström's car in front of them as they sped toward the scene, it is reasonable to suggest that they arrived ten seconds later, just as Söderström himself later testified. The ambulance driver later said that as he was stopping at the traffic lights at the crossing of Kungsgatan and Sveavägen, he saw the police van racing past, and then himself drove after it without any urgency. This would imply that the ambulance arrived twenty to forty seconds after the van, probably at the lower end of this interval, since several witnesses commented that it came very shortly after the police van had stopped at the scene. If Söderström arrived at 11:25:00 and the first police van at 11:25:10, this would mean that the ambulance arrived about 11:25:35, and thus that the paramedics would have two minutes and fifteen seconds to perform their duties at the scene.

Söderström himself said that he heard the police alarm not long after driving off, thus probably between 11:24:30 and 11:24:40. This agrees with the estimated time for the first police van to reach the murder scene: the drive took about thirty seconds (or slightly less), as estimated by the police driver as well as by others, and if the van arrived at 11:25:10 the alarm would have been radioed out at 11:24:40. It is recorded that at 11:26, one of the officers in the van confirmed to police headquarters that a man had really been shot, and this again supports the scenario outlined here: it would take him forty to fifty seconds to have a look around before radioing out this information. Newspaper photographer Ulf Karlsson, who was monitoring the police radio traffic in his car, later calculated that it took five to six minutes from Helin's alert until Söderström confirmed that the victim was Olof Palme at 11:30, again indicating that the police alarm was made between 11:24 and 11:25.[10]

A second police van was patrolling in central Stockholm that night. It is recorded to have arrived at the murder scene as late as 11:27:20, just in time for the officers to see the paramedics wheel the stretcher into the ambulance.[11] The officers were only about a minute and a half away from the murder scene, however. The only official explanation for their tardiness is that they had just been refueling, and that one of the officers had to wait in a line to pay! Still, had the police alarm been made at 11:23, these officers would have had ample time to refuel, pay, and eat several doughnuts each before driving off at a stately pace to reach the murder scene. But when questioned later, several of the officers said that apart from the delay caused by paying for their gas, they had acted swiftly and driven at speed using the siren and blue flashing lights. If we assume the police alarm was made at 11:24:40, the scenario becomes far more likely: it would take the officers a little more than a minute to finish refueling and pay for their gas, and then a minute and a half to reach the murder scene.

Evidence shows that Helin must have been alerted at about 11:22:50. In the official version of events, he swiftly sends out the police alarm at 11:23:00. This version of events has some much-needed support from the police computer system, where it is stated that an alarm was made at 11:23, meaning any time from 11:23:00 until 11:23:59. The police clock is not synchronized with standard time, and might well be up to a minute wrong, according to evidence from people visiting police headquarters after the murder. This further element of uncertainty would place the alarm in the interval 11:22:00 to 11:24:59. The official chronology leaves it unexplained why, at 11:24:40, another police detective, Jan Hedlund, denied any knowledge of the shooting and said that no police alarm had been made.[12] At 23:26:10, Hedlund reported that news of the incident at the corner of Sveavägen and Tunnelgatan had just reached the police and that patrols in the field had been alerted.

These remarkable conversations—which, unlike the very slack documentation created by the police themselves, are recorded on tape with a speaking clock making a running report of the correct time—strongly suggest that the police alarm was delayed, either by accident or by stratagem. Helin has claimed that the computers used by the police were so unreliable that one operator at Stockholm police headquarters could not see what alarms and emergency calls his colleague had made until after several minutes; and this excuse was accepted by the 1999 commission looking into the police investigation of the Palme murder. But these whitewashers ignored that in the commission hearings, a police computer expert resolutely testified that if there was a lag period for the computer equipment, it was at most three seconds![13] As we have seen, the late arrival of the police patrol alerted by Helin also indicates that the alarm was delayed by about a minute and a half. Conspiracy theorists have suggested that Helin and his colleagues at police headquarters were part of a sinister plot to assassinate Palme, and that Helin was deliberately helping the murderer to escape. However, as will be discussed later in this book, there is insufficient evidence to support the existence of such a plot.

Helin's mistake may well have a perfectly natural explanation. The cab company was based in Järfälla, a suburb of Stockholm. On the aforementioned tape recording of calls to and from the emergency services, it is notable that the operator phoned the taxi switchboard to make sure the shooting had taken place in central Stockholm and not in Järfälla. There might be a Sveavägen in Järfälla, just as there was one in central Stockholm, he reasoned, and he wanted to make sure he got the right one. It seemed difficult for both him and Detective Hedlund to accept that a cab from this suburban company was in central Stockholm. The situation may have been the same when Helin was to radio out the police alarm: the time it took him to ascertain which Sveavägen was being referred to, by means that are unknown, since no recording was made of police telephone calls, may explain the delay.

Gösta Söderström told a journalist that he later spoke to the boyfriend of the Järfälla taxi radio operator and learned that she had been amazed when the police called her back five minutes later, objecting that they could not find any Sveavägen in Järfälla.[14] There is also a curious note that "it took several phone calls" to establish that the murder had not taken place in Järfälla.[15] At 11:24, one of the police vans allegedly dispatched to the Sveavägen shooting one minute earlier was ordered to help another police car arrest a drunk. The hapless Helin, who was again involved, has explained this as a mere mistake. It is also recorded that in first hour after the murder, police headquarters twice asked the emergency services for the exact time when the ambulance was alerted. This is certainly not normal police procedure, and an uncharitable mind would suspect that the purpose of these calls was to establish exactly when the murder scene witnesses alerted the emergency services, in an attempt to cover up the delay at police headquarters.[16]

The Minutes after the Murder of Olof Palme

(A) HANS HOLMÉR'S VERSION

11:21:20	The murder.
11:23:00	The police alarm.
11:23:10	The first police car reaches the scene of crime.
11:28:00	The ambulance drives off.

(B) THE VERSION CONSTRUCTED BY THE AUTHOR
(BOLD: CERTAIN TIME POINTS)

11:21:20	**The murder.**
11:22:10	Anders Delsborn alerts his switchboard.
11:22:07	**Leif Ljungqvist calls the emergency services.**
11:22:50	Ann-Louise Paulsson phones the police.

11:23:10	Detective Helin puts the phone down.
11:23:30	Paulsson confirms the alarm over the taxi radio.
11:23:40	Ljungqvist puts the phone down without his call being answered. At this time, there is no police presence.
11:23:40	**Paulsson calls for an ambulance.**
11:24:00	Ljungqvist tries to speak to Lisbet Palme. There is still no police presence.
11:24:20	The cab driver Anders A. alerts Gösta Söderström.
11:24:40	**Detective Jan Hedlund denies that the police know anything about the murder.**
11:24:40	The police alarm.
11:25:00	Söderström arrives at the crime scene.
11:25:10	The first police van arrives.
11:25:35	The ambulance arrives.
11:26:10	**Detective Hedlund verifies that he knows about the police alarm.**
11:27:20	The second police van arrives.
11:27:40	Söderström radios out that the victim is Olof Palme.
11:27:50	**The ambulance leaves.**

A KILLER ON THE LOOSE

If the crime scene is nightmarish and chaotic, the situation in police head-quarters is complete pandemonium.[1] This nerve center of the Stockholm po-lice, situated in modern facilities, is staffed by ten radio operators, led by three sergeants and a lieutenant on duty. But in spite of all their high-tech equip-ment, both the officer in charge, Lieutenant Hans Koci, and many of his sub-ordinates seem to become completely dumbstruck when Söderström's fateful news reaches them and Koci's second in command, sergeant Anders Thornestedt, yells out, "It is Palme!" None of them even take the simple step of alerting all the police precincts in Stockholm, a procedure that is followed for even the most trivial of offences. For example, such an alarm is radioed out at exactly 11:23 about a green Volvo being driven erratically; one would think that the murder of the prime minister would merit similar action. It was to take several hours before this basic step is taken.

By 11:30, the telephones are ringing furiously at police headquarters, as journalists seek confirmation that the prime minister has been shot. Koci himself takes most of these calls, along with one of the sergeants. Thus the in-dividuals supposed to be leading the hunt for the killer are tied up on the tele-phone most of the time. The plainclothes detectives on duty, based outside police headquarters, show praiseworthy initiative in radioing all bus and cab drivers in central Stockholm, informing them of the murder and the rudi-mentary description of the killer. Amazed that Koci and his men have not sent out a general alert for the Swedish police, the detectives several times telephone headquarters to remind them of this vital step, but the reply is that there must be a better description of the killer before any alert can be sent out.

The police presence in Stockholm that night is considerable: at least seventy police cars, thirty of them in the central part of town. Before midnight, fourteen of these vehicles are involved in the hunt for the killer; by 1:00 a.m., the number has grown to four police vans and seventeen patrol cars. The problem is that Koci and his men offer little in the way of leadership, and any initiative in the initial hunt for the murderer is left to individual officers and detectives in the field. Many police cars and foot patrol officers search restaurants and bars, questioning any person who appears suspicious, but police headquarters gives no instructions, and the grid for the systematic searching of inner Stockholm is never used. The absence of a clear description of the killer is another drawback: some officers look for a man in a blue parka, others have heard that the killer is wearing a long dark coat, yet others seek a scruffy-looking man in a floppy cap. Rather than receiving orders and instructions from police headquarters, they report to headquarters what steps they have taken. The officers later eloquently described their anger and frustration as they ran around in circles that fateful night, chasing a mere phantom.[2]

Koci desperately telephones for senior officers to come in and take charge. Commissioner Hans Holmér is in northern Sweden to take part in a ski race, and Hans Wranghult, the assistant commissioner who also serves as chief of detectives, is also away. At 11:50, Koci manages to reach assistant commissioner Sune Sandström, the chief of uniformed police, and Sandström phones deputy commissioner Gösta Welander, who decides to come in to police headquarters to take command. A police car is dispatched to pick up these two senior officers, neither of whom has basic police training nor experience in handling emergencies or commanding a large police force in the field.

Just before midnight, Koci decides that the police command center is to be manned. This is a spacious room with high-tech computer facilities, specially adapted for serious emergencies and disasters. The problem is, however, that the command center has not been used for quite some time, and none of the officers is able to connect the wiring for the computer terminals. Koci later said that he himself could easily have done it, had he not been tied up by the frantically ringing telephones. For a horrible twenty-five minutes, the radio operators uselessly stand around, waiting for a specialist in police computer equipment to connect the terminals. They are finally connected around 12:25 a.m. Shortly thereafter, Welander and Sandström arrive, and the former takes command of operations. Koci is greatly relieved, and seems to presume that this gives him permission to take care of other business than the hunt for Olof Palme's killer for the rest of the night. Welander and Sandström believe that he is still the officer in charge, however, and that they themselves are merely "observers"; the misunderstanding is caused by either lack of communication skills or simply wishful thinking, since they are themselves completely out of their depth. Just thirty minutes later, Koci's second in command, sergeant Anders Thornestedt, "feels unwell" and asks permission to step down: he thinks he is still capable of working as an ordinary radio operator, but asks not to have any responsibility in the hunt for the killer of the prime minister. This leave is granted him, although it means that the person who is at the time the most knowledgeable about the early police response to the murder is left to deal with nonurgent matters for the rest of the night.

There seems to have been a very uneasy feeling in police headquarters that night, and it is difficult not to link the eagerness among the officers to distance themselves from the murder investigation to some kind of awareness that serious mistakes had been committed in the initial police response. It is probably no coincidence that along with Koci and Thornestedt, Helin himself asks for and receives permission to work on other police business that night. It is also notable that Helin later claimed to have worked on the Palme murder just for a few minutes, although he was proven wrong when it was demonstrated that he had taken action as late as 12:13 a.m. The result of this reluctance on the part of the officers at police headquarters is that only two radio operators, compared with the minimum of three prescribed by standard police procedure for serious crimes, are actually working on the murder of Olof Palme. A third operator stands by to assist with searches in police files but does little work.[3]

As the night goes on, the dismal list of police mistakes grows even longer. The cop who is supposed to keep a written record of police activities uses the wrong form (there are just four to choose from), and her notes are rudimentary in the extreme, particularly concerning the vital period before midnight. Nor does she use the standard police checklist of important tasks to be completed in the case of a serious crime. It would have been relatively easy to put up road-blocks around central Stockholm, or at least on the major highways out of the capital, but amazingly, this is never done. The police precincts bordering Stockholm are never appealed to for extra officers; indeed, they are left in the dark that a murder has happened at all. Teams of skilled narcotics detectives are kept on standby but never used. About an hour after the murder, someone realizes that it might be a good idea to search the trains leaving the central station, but in that hour, several trains have already left. Another hour later, similar precautions are taken with regard to the main Stockholm airports. Throughout the night, the great ferries from Stockholm to Finland, not an entirely illogical escape route for the killer, leave their terminals without any police presence. Lieutenant Arne Ivrell, the head of the Stockholm murder squad, is never called in, since the senior officers at police headquarters think he would benefit from a full night's sleep before tackling the case in the morning.

Back at the murder scene, Söderström is taking charge of putting up police cordons. Only a very small area, about 11 x 11 yards, is cordoned off, since

The murder site. An early police photo showing police lines and blood on the snow. Reproduced by permission of the Swedish National Police Board.

Söderström considers this to be enough. Lieutenant Dalsgaard then arrives, and Söderström tells him that Olof Palme has been shot, and that he is in charge of the crime scene. At 11:36, a police canine unit arrives at the scene, and Söderström shows the dog handler the killer's escape route. But just as the handler is about to unleash the police dog, Dalsgaard orders him not to, believing the track has gone cold already. He may well have been right, although no harm would have been done if the beast had been sent off to see what results could be accomplished.

The officers in the late-arriving second police van are put to work questioning the remaining witnesses. Söderström would later claim that he thought they were doing a good job, but the witnesses tend to disagree. The ubiquitous Leif Ljungqvist approaches a officer and tells him that he saw everything and how distraught he is that Olof Palme was shot. "But Palme wasn't shot!" the astonished officer replies. "Say what you want, but I just helped to get the body of the prime minister of Sweden into an ambulance!" Ljungqvist snaps back. Completely flabbergasted, the officer staggers off to tell his colleagues, without bothering to get the name and address of this important witness. The aforementioned Yvonne Nieminen, who clearly saw the killer escape, eagerly approaches one of the officers, saying that she has vital information as to the direction in which the gunman fled. The confused cop takes her name and telephone number without bothering to question her further. The young man who tried to resuscitate Palme with artificial respiration is given a cloth to wipe his bloody face, but the officers show no interest at all in hearing what he has to say, and he leaves the murder scene in disgust.

Detective sergeant Dan Andersson, a plainclothes police officer in central Stockholm, by accident comes past the murder scene about 11:40 and approaches Dalsgaard, asking whether he and his colleagues could do anything to help, but he receives no clear answer. He can see the dazed Söderström sitting in his police car and Dalsgaard walking about the scene. Two female witnesses are surrounded by inquisitive journalists, and the detective urges the feeble, shocked police officers at least to make the effort to question them.[4]

Lieutenant Dalsgaard and another senior officer, lieutenant Lars Christianson, both ask Söderström whether he needs any help at the murder scene, but the veteran lieutenant thinks he and his men are doing fine. Christianson is instead dispatched to Sabbatsberg Hospital to see Mrs. Palme and try to get a better description of the killer. Dalsgaard phones Koci and volunteers to join the police command center, where he has previously worked for eight years, but Koci replies that Dalsgaard is not needed, since the situation is under control. Dalsgaard leaves the scene to go to a nearby police station.

Söderström remains sitting in his car, listening to the police radio. He is appalled that the police are not conducting a systematic search for the killer according to the grid he knows has been used to good effect in the past. He arranges for detectives to take some of the key witnesses to police headquarters for further questioning. At 12:15, Söderström himself goes off to police headquarters to make a formal report of the crime, taking two more witnesses with him in his car. He orders the officers in the second police van to stay behind to guard the crime scene. At the command center, Söderström hands over the formal report of the crime, written by his young police driver, to Welander and Sandström. They ask the veteran lieutenant some questions and then order him to command a police strike force—a van and two police cars—but Söderström and his men spend the rest of the night in idleness, awaiting further orders.

The murder site. An early police photo showing the stairs up the Tunnelgatan. Reproduced by permission of the Swedish National Police Board.

At 1:10 in the morning, two police forensic experts begin their examination of the murder scene. Their boss, captain Wincent Lange, appears at 1:30. He is disgusted when he sees the tiny area that has been cordoned off and even more annoyed upon perceiving that many people have been walking up to the murder scene to throw flowers near the pool of blood on the snowy sidewalk. He realizes that little can be done under these conditions, and orders his men to withdraw. Although understandable, this may not have been a wise decision.[5] At 1:30, Lieutenant Christianson orders the crew of the police van to return to police headquarters to be part of a strike force. These officers then spend the entire night sitting around uselessly. A patrol of just two officers is left to guard the crime scene, which is cordoned off with thin plastic tape.

Throughout the night, this pathetic police cordon is surreptitiously broken through, either by mourners wanting to put flowers on the murder site or by drunken hooligans who tear down the tape for the fun of it and walk all over the place. At 3:15, the officers, who have arrested one of the hooligans, ask for help from police headquarters, and the crew of a police van takes over the vigil. Although six policemen now guard the crime scene, people still have little respect for the police cordon, and the police squad orders proper fencing to be brought and erected. This being done, they complacently drive off, leaving just two officers on guard. As the morning comes, large heaps of flowers can be seen inside the police cordon.

As we know, Lieutenant Christianson was sent to Sabbatsberg Hospital by Söderström to question Lisbet Palme. Another officer, Sergeant Åke Rimborn, is independently dispatched to the hospital by police headquarters at an earlier stage, arriving as the doctors are trying to resuscitate Palme. Rimborn can see that Palme is badly injured and unlikely to survive. Lisbet Palme is very shocked, and her face and hair are so stained with blood that Rimborn hardly recognizes her. He briefly speaks to her, and she says she thinks the Ustasja (or Mustafa, Rimborn could not say which) is responsible for what happened. Rimborn arranges for the hospital to be guarded by a large police squad. The entire emergency department is closed, the Palmes being the only patients there. Rimborn returns to headquarters to report to Welander and confirm that it is really Olof Palme who has been murdered.

Later, around 1:00 a.m., one of the policemen at the hospital calls Rimborn to say that Lisbet Palme has refused to speak to any detective, or even a policewoman or police psychologist. The only person she is willing to meet with is Rimborn himself, and he drives off to the hospital in the hope of obtaining a better description of the killer. This time, Mrs. Palme is more collected and manages to convey to Rimborn that she saw nothing of the murderer except that he was wearing a blue jacket. Around Christmas the previous year, she had seen two men loitering outside the Palme house in the Old Town, and the killer might be one of them. She suspects they belong to the Ustasja movement of Croatian separatists, but does not say why. She clearly tells Rimborn, "The men who did this were those who were in the Old Town. One of them was the man who shot Olof."[6]

Rimborn promptly goes back to the chaotic police headquarters, where a general alert for the Swedish police force is drawn up. It takes until 2:05 a.m., almost three hours after the murder, for this alert to be telexed out. Until then, provincial police, customs officials, and the border patrol know nothing of the murder. The alert states that there are two murderers, one of them a very tall man, the other wearing a blue parka; both are forty to forty-five years old and possibly belong to the Ustasja movement. It is surprising that Rimborn's version with two killers is allowed to prevail over the accounts from several murder scene witnesses that there was only one killer. And where did the police get the strangely precise age interval of forty to forty-five years old? After this alert has been telexed out, Welander goes to visit Lisbet Palme himself and later to meet with several the government ministers. For several critical hours, no one leads the hunt for the murderer, and no worthwhile initiatives are taken. When Welander returns to police headquarters, he orders that the sentence about Ustasja be taken out of the alert, since this is obviously Mrs. Palme's own speculation, but the paragraph about the two killers remains. It is again surprising that no determined attempts seem to have been made to persuade Lisbet Palme to speak to an experienced senior detective, particularly since the earlier interviews had been handled by two uniformed cops who had been selected for this task by coincidence alone.

Ten or twenty minutes after the shooting, rumors are already spreading among Stockholm journalists that something extraordinary is happening before their eyes. Some of them have overheard Söderström's open radio call on their police radio monitors, and the news spreads like wildfire. The journalists desperately try to telephone various people in the government and police to obtain further information. One of them phones one of Palme's bodyguards and relates the rumor that the prime minister has been shot. The bodyguard replies that this rumor is certainly unfounded, since he himself saw Palme alive earlier that day. This answer persuades the journalist that he must try someone higher up in the secret service hierarchy. When he finally manages to reach a senior officer, he receives another incredulous reply, but the journalist is adamant that Palme has really been shot. The officer then groans, "My God, what am I to do?" "Maybe you should go to work," the journalist suggests.[7] Around 11:30, another enterprising journalist contacts Palme's private secretary, Anne-Marie Willsson, telling her that Palme has been shot. She phones another bodyguard, who confidently tells her to go back to sleep: if anything untoward happened, he would know about it.

The journalist then contacts the government press secretary, Kjell Lindström, and informs him of the shooting. Lindström first thinks it is a hoax, but other journalists keep calling to tell him the same thing. He alerts Ulf Dahlsten, the government political secretary, who in turn phones the deputy prime minister, Ingvar Carlsson. Dahlsten is ordered to scramble together the majority of the government ministers for an emergency meeting. But as the ministers reach the Rosenbad government building, in taxis or private cars, they are aghast to find that there is no police presence at all. Had the murder of Olof Palme heralded an invasion or a coup d'état, a few gunmen could have mowed down the entire government as the ministers blearily arrived from whatever activities they had been up to this fateful Friday night. Kjell-Olof Feldt, the minister of finance, is clearly aware of this danger: trembling and ashen faced, he races past the few confused journalists who have gathered outside Rosenbad, muttering, "No comments! No comments!" Ingvar Carlsson's first official action as prime minister is to alert the Rosenbad security guards and tell them for God's sake to call for police backup.[8]

At 12:20 a.m., the state news service sends out an alert that the acting prime minister has been murdered. This alert reaches all Swedish newspapers that can afford to employ a night editor and all major international news services. At this time, only one man, the night DJ, is at work at the Swedish state radio station. Normally, a flasher signal would have lit up when this kind of breaking news was received, but this particular night the contraption has not been plugged in. Nor does any person at police headquarters think of alerting the radio station about what happened; another disastrous mistake, since an early radio bulletin would have done much to spread the news among police forces around the country, as well as emergency services and customs officials.

More than ninety minutes after the murder of Olof Palme, the state radio station is still blaring out pop music interspersed with lighthearted commentary from the DJ. By this time, the BBC and many American television stations have already spread the news of the murder. Some enterprising British and American journalists phone the Swedish state radio station to find someone who knows more about the murder. They are put through to the DJ, who does not know there has been a murder at all. His first responses are incredulous—this kind of thing does not happen in Sweden!—but the journalists are persistent. One American journalist from ABC television firmly demands to speak to the news reporter in charge. When the DJ tells her that he is the only person working at the radio station, she thinks he is joking and angrily hangs up. The BBC is the next to call, and then Radio Nippon from Japan.

The DJ begins to realize that something momentous and terrible is happening, and that he is sitting right in the middle of things. He calls the director of state radio, hoping the latter will use his authority and take decisive action. But the director tells the DJ that the whole thing is probably a hoax, and that he should do nothing until the news has been confirmed by official sources. But the phones keep ringing and the desperate DJ feels that he needs to act. He smashes the pane of a glass cabinet containing the keys to a safe in which there is a parcel marked "KD" for "The King is Dead"; it includes a list of people to call and a cassette with mournful classical music. The latter is used to good effect, but nearly all the phone numbers are out of date, since the parcel was put away many years earlier. It is not until 1:10, almost two hours after the murder, that a radio bulletin is finally transmitted, curtly informing the citizens of the bare facts about the murder. As the London *Times* correspondent Chris Mosey later remarked, like a nation of cuckolded husbands, the Swedes were the last to know.[9]

Similar shambolic scenes take place at the state television station. As the news of the murder reaches the station, quite a few journalists and technical staff are still at work, and the Friday night movie is still on. In fact, a television team has been making a documentary about street violence in central Stockholm that very night. Passing by the crime scene in their van, just twenty minutes or so after the murder, they ask one of the officers what has happened and receive the curt reply that someone might have been shot. The van then slowly drives away from the scoop of the century. As the news of the murder reaches the state television building, someone suggests that it might be advisable to do an extra news bulletin, but this suggestion is turned down by the technical staff. Trade union regulations forbid them to work after 1:00 a.m., they say, whether or not the prime minister has been shot! It is not until 4:00 a.m., when almost every other television station in the world has told the news of the murder, that Swedish television finally transmits an emergency news bulletin; the news anchorwoman, having been alerted by her daughter, who lives in London, has come in to work in the middle of the night.[10] The Swedish military chiefs of staff get the news from the Swedish military attaché in Washington, who hears it on American television. The king of Sweden, who is on a skiing vacation, is not informed at all until the following morning.

In the meantime, the Swedish government has its emergency meeting, and Palme's friend and longtime colleague Ingvar Carlsson takes charge. At 2:00 a.m., Mrs. Palme summons the ministers to the hospital "to acquaint them with certain suspicions regarding the murder." Ingvar Carlsson, Kjell-Olof Feldt, and three others go to Sabbatsberg Hospital to see Lisbet Palme and to meet with deputy commissioner Welander about the progress in the hunt for the murderer. We do not know what Lisbet Palme told the ministers that fateful night, but it would be most interesting to know. Dahlsten later said he was affected by her obvious distress and the sound of the blood squishing in her boots.

Where all this blood could have come from is yet another minor mystery. The two nurses who inspected Lisbet Palme's injury described it as a "branding" across the back. Mrs. Palme's brother-in-law Dr. Åke Nilzén, who also saw it, agreed that it was just a slight reddening of the skin. In contrast, Lieutenant Christianson described the injury as a wound two or three millimeters deep; but according to the nurses, he never saw the injury, instead making his own interpretation based on what they told him.[11] Since Mrs. Palme steadfastly refused to have her injury seen by a doctor or police technician, or to have it photographed or documented, we will never know for sure.

The clothes of both Olof and Lisbet Palme are taken for forensic analysis by the police technicians, before the bereaved widow and her sons are escorted home in a cortege of police cars at 4:00 a.m. Worried that terrorists may be lurking nearby, intent on wiping out the entire Palme family, the police clear the surrounding streets before quickly escorting Lisbet Palme and her sons inside.

The politicians meanwhile have returned to Rosenbad, where the government meets at 3:07. After a press conference at 5:00, they head home for some much-needed rest. As they emerge from Rosenbad, an odd-looking little man makes a loud grunting noise and runs up to Feldt, nearly pushing the startled minister over. This time, there is a massive police presence outside Rosenbad, and two officers promptly grab the attacker and haul him into a police van. They cannot fail to notice that he is wearing a parka and a flat cap. They then search his pockets and find a sketch of the murder site. The man has no explanation either for his behavior or for the sketch; indeed, he does not say a single word, although he gesticulates wildly. Triumphantly, the officers drive off to police headquarters with their captive, after sending a radio message to their superiors that they have just arrested a man fitting the description of the killer, who may well have been intent on further violent action against another government minister. This message is intercepted by some journalists listening to the police radio, and an international news bulletin is cabled out that the police already have a suspect in custody. When questioned by detectives, the man is still stubbornly silent. In another farcical turn of events, it is discovered that he is actually a deaf-mute, thus explaining both his persistent silence and the sketch some kind person drew to show him what happened. He has a perfect alibi, having been hard at work as a cleaner until well after midnight.[12]

The initial response to the murder of Olof Palme makes dismal reading. There have been three state commissions appointed to scrutinize the murder investigation, and their verdicts on the early police response have been scathing. In particular, the large and well-staffed command center, furnished with high-tech equipment and led by some very senior officers, was clearly unable to do its job properly. Yet the commissions cautiously stand clear of naming any factors that might explain these remarkable failings. They hint at a lack of training and competence among the police, pointing out that much more is required from a sergeant or lieutenant when on duty at the command center than when commanding a squad of officers on beat patrol. Commissioner Hans Holmér added that Koci's team was known as one of the least competent of those who took turns being on duty at police headquarters, and he may well have been right. A fair amount of criticism has also been directed against the senior officers Welander and Sandström: they were ignorant of police procedure and showed a culpable lack of enterprise and leadership.

In most other countries, the murder of the head of state would have resulted in a series of senior officials losing their jobs. In particular, the person responsible for the leader's security would have found it very difficult to explain why he had been allowed to walk the streets without any bodyguards. This was the aforementioned Social Democratic politician Ulf Dahlsten. Commissioner Hans Holmér wrote that in spite of Palme's formidable intelligence, he still needed advice on how to manage his own security. He should certainly not have been allowed to dismiss his bodyguards whenever he felt like it. Dahlsten lacked knowledge in police and security matters, and as the person ultimately responsible for Olof Palme's personal safety, he had clearly neglected his duties.[13] But this was Sweden, and there was no chance of Dahlsten suffering any indignity: he had support from his fellow Social Democrats and was soon promoted to become the postmaster general, one of the most prestigious and highly paid state officials in Sweden. Both the chief of national police, Holger Romander, and the chief of the secret police, Sven-Åke Hjälmroth, kept their jobs and their reputations intact. Amazingly, both Welander and Sandström also survived to fight another day. Welander kept his job as deputy commissioner of the Stockholm police until his retirement. When a swift police response was needed after several people were killed at a Stockholm nightclub in 1994, Welander was again found wanting. Sandström was actually promoted to become head of the secret police, and we will encounter him again in this book, in far from flattering circumstances.

It is recorded that within sixty minutes, 90 percent of Americans knew that John F. Kennedy had been assassinated. Within ninety minutes, the same percentage of Americans had been made aware of the assassination attempt on president Ronald Reagan. The situation was very different with regard to the murder of Olof Palme, partly due to the late hour at which the murder took place, partly due to the obvious incompetence at the state radio and television stations. Journalists from the large Swedish evening newspapers showed praiseworthy alertness and diligence in following up on the news of the suspected shooting. Without the efforts of these reporters, it would have been much longer before the central government became aware of what had happened. Five newspapers and the state news agency knew what had happened before midnight. The news flash at 12:20 a.m. was observed by thirty-five out of ninety-seven Swedish newspapers, and thirty-three more were able to grasp what had happened before 3:00 a.m. But the Swedish morning newspapers were already being printed as the news of the murder came in; some of them stopped the presses, others did not. Some newspaper editors thought the news might be a hoax instigated by a hacker or a drunk and switched on the radio; when they heard only raucous rock music, they naturally chose to disbelieve the rumor. Many provincial newspapers made the compromise to "break" the front page, inserting the words "OLOF PALME IS MURDERED" or just "PALME DEAD" in place of some unimportant advertisement or article. The effect was sometimes ludicrous, as the crime of the century was announced curtly beneath a detailed and well-illustrated report on the Social Democratic pensioners' rally or the local boy scout meeting. Even the biggest morning newspapers caught only the bare details, and some errors at the same time: Olof Palme had been shot in the chest or in the belly, a force of two hundred policemen were chasing two men aged between forty and forty-five, the hospital staff answered no questions, and the police were looking out for a blue Volkswagen Passat heading for the suburb of Tensta. More than nine hours had passed before 90 percent of Swedes knew that Olof Palme had been murdered.[14]

Most Swedish people, including the present author, became aware of what had happened between 7:00 and 9:00 a.m., as the morning newspapers were delivered. Almost everyone then turned on the television, where hour-long special news programs were aired about the early hunt for the murderer. In the 8:00 a.m. news, Welander repeated that there had been two killers, although he was surprised that the witnesses on the scene could describe only one of them. The Swedish evening newspapers are printed in the early morning hours, but they have the advantage of being privately owned, and thus free from the numbing effects of state bureaucracy; their go-getting journalists seized this great opportunity with gusto. The two big evening papers, *Expressen* and *Aftonbladet*, devoted most of their March 1 editions to the murder. These early snapshots of the murder investigation contain many interesting details, some of which have since been conveniently forgotten.

The *Expressen* interviewed Sergeant Kjell Östling, who said that when he and his men arrived at the crime scene, Lisbet Palme was running around in a state of shock. The only thing he knew about the killer was that he had been wearing a knee-length dark brown overcoat. The officers had been running around all night looking for someone fitting this description but found nothing. Both papers quoted other murder scene witnesses giving a similar description of the killer: a tall man wearing a dark trench coat. In contrast, Captain Nils Linder, speaking to the *Aftonbladet*, said that the ten witnesses questioned so far had told highly divergent stories. Sandström told the *Expressen* that the killer had acted with great determination. He was puzzled that Palme had been shot at such close range. Both papers contained an interview with cab driver Anders Delsborn, who told the journalists, in no uncertain terms, that the Palmes had stood talking to the killer for some time before the murder took place. The *Aftonbladet* reported that several eye witnesses "said that Olof and Lisbet had stopped to talk with the unknown man. The conversation went on for some time—exactly how long is unknown—before the man suddenly drew the gun."

All British and French newspapers ran the murder of Olof Palme as front-page news, and papers as far away as Africa, Chile, and Nicaragua mourned the death of the last decent left-wing democrat in European politics. The response of the American newspapers was more mixed. In the *New York Times*, columnist Anthony Lewis wrote a very fair appreciation of the fallen prime minister: as the leader of a very small country, he had captured imaginations all over the world. Henry Kissinger had called Palme a warm friend with whom he often disagreed but whom he greatly respected. Lewis praised Palme's efforts for peace, economic development, and particularly the reversal of the nuclear arms race, but treaded lightly when discussing the Swedish taxation policy and the tensions of egalitarianism. He ended with the words: "The terrible irony is that he died by unreasoning violence. No death since John F. Kennedy's has been more fearful witness of the kind of world this has become. But Olof Palme left us the example of caring." Another influential columnist, William F. Buckley Jr., bluntly wrote that during Palme's long career, he had done his best to make Sweden uninhabitable with his relentless socialist policies. Mounting one bold accusation on another, he jeered Palme's unwise comments about the Vietnam War and denounced his Socialist International as a crypto-communist enterprise, aimed to placate the Soviet Union, with its aggressive nuclear arms policy. Palme left behind a Sweden where one-third of all business was done in the black-market economy, to avoid the savage taxation with which he punished any Swede who was antisocial enough to succeed in commercial enterprise. Buckley ended his obituary by saying that even if Palme's death was a personal tragedy, his life remained a public tragedy, and must be regarded as such.[15] This condemnation of Palme's policies did not escape uncensored by the Swedish newspapers, and Buckley was blasted as having denigrated a dead man.

HANS HOLMÉR TAKES CHARGE

At the time of the murder of Olof Palme, the police commissioner in the county of Stockholm was a certain Hans Holmér. Born in Stockholm in 1930, the son of a celebrated athlete, he started his career as a lawyer and later became a police administrator. In the 1960s, he was already known as an up-and-comer, loyal to the Social Democrats. In 1970, he became head of SÄPO, the civilian secret police. He firmly allied himself with political power, and the chief of national police, Carl Persson, wrote in his memoirs that he noted a change in his former protégé Holmér during these years. From having been a competent and loyal colleague, he became a scheming undercover operator, often disposed to be untruthful and secretive about his intrigues.[1] Holmér's position as head of the secret police gradually became untenable, since he was distrusted by many of his subordinates, who considered him a government stooge, and the Social Democrats had to remove him. In 1976, they made sure he was promoted to become police-master (an archaic Swedish term for police commissioner) in Stockholm. Here he was more successful and developed a reputation as a tough but straight police chief who cracked down on violent crime and drug trafficking. In 1982, his friend Olof Palme appointed him chairman of the state commission on drug-related crimes. Two years later, he was promoted to become police commissioner for the entire county of Stockholm. Holger Romander, the chief of national police, was going to retire in a few years, and Holmér was considered his obvious successor.

In the late 1970s, there was an increase in street violence in central Stockholm, and Holmér founded a police task force to combat street hooliganism. Young, muscular officers were recruited to this unit; their habit of wearing scruffy civilian attire and baseball caps back to front earned them the nickname the "Baseball Gang." They were successful in their given task, and put many a hooligan and street robber behind bars, but at the price of introducing some very undesirable features into Swedish policing. The Baseball Gang consisted of the good, the bad, and the ugly: most of them were decent hard-working policemen who were fed up with the customary mollycoddling of young offenders, some were themselves vicious thugs who liked beating people up more than anything, yet others were racists and right-wing extremists. Their dislike for criminal immigrants often resulted in unprovoked violence: not a few innocent people were beaten up, and the list of police complaints grew steadily until it reached several hundred. Finally, Holmér had to disband the Baseball Gang, but evidence shows he was actually quite pleased with his elite task force. None of the officers received any disciplinary action, and they all remained within the police force, although they were transferred to other units.

In Sweden at this time, the most senior rank an ordinary police officer could aspire to was that of captain. The vast majority of higher police officials were not trained policemen, but lawyers who had specialized in police administration. Some of them took pains to learn the practical side of police work, but others did not. Nor can the possibility be ruled out that during the long hegemony of the Social Democrats, political affiliation sometimes meant more than competence and enterprise in the selection of senior police administrators. There were more than a few of these so-called turkeys in senior posts within the Swedish police, and large police forces were led by people who themselves knew little about practical police work. As we have seen, this system must carry a fair part of the blame for the slack and indecisive police response to the murder of Olof Palme.

Hans Holmér was not one of these "turkeys," however. Although political favor undoubtedly had facilitated his career, Holmér soon became known as an efficient leader, popular among the uniformed police for his hard line on street crime. He more than once personally led large police operations, and liked to portray himself as a dashing man of action. Some much-publicized successes inflated the police-master's already prominent ego, and made him think he could handle any police emergency. Like in an American cop movie, the tough police chief would personally arrive at the crime scene to take charge and find the killer.

At the time of the murder, Hans Holmér was traveling to take part in the Vasaloppet, a famous skiing race in northern Sweden. With him was his mistress, a young policewoman. Stockholm police headquarters desperately tried to reach Holmér that fateful night, but the commissioner had made a nocturnal visit to the officer's hotel room, and thus could not hear the phone ringing in his own empty room. It was not until Saturday morning that he heard the

fateful news from Stockholm. Dashing to the nearest phone, Holmér contacted police headquarters in Stockholm, where the foolish Welander told
him that he could go ahead with the ski race as planned, since everything was
under control in the capital. Eschewing such misplaced complacency, Holmér
returned to Stockholm right away, driving at breakneck speed on icy, haz-
ardous roads.[2] It would have been ironic if he had been arrested for speeding
by some of his own colleagues, but the dashing commissioner was spared this
indignity. He must have ground his teeth when he heard the early radio bulletins about the hunt for the killer: the disastrous police mistakes were obvious to him, as was the absence of leadership on the part of Welander and
Sandström. Holmér later said that if he had been in Stockholm to direct operations than night, much would have been different, and he may well have
been right. After the police-master had chivalrously driven his police mistress
home, he continued to police headquarters, walking through the doors at
10:50 on Saturday morning. He immediately announced that he was taking
charge of the hunt for the killer.

Hans Holmér had had ample time to plan his strategy during the lengthy
drive down to Stockholm. He appreciated the need for swift action, and after
spending little more than an hour at police headquarters, he gave his first
press conference at noon. Holmér later wrote a 274–page book about his part
in the hunt for Palme's killer, but although this book contains many interesting tidbits from the murder investigation and much trivia about the police-
master's personal life, it is silent on how he prepared for this press conference.
It is clear, however, that at the police briefing that must have taken place
around 11:00 a.m., a large amount of rather contradictory data was at the
commissioner's disposal, and some extremely vital decisions had to be made in
a very short period of time. It cannot have helped matters that Holmér must
have been uneasily aware that some very serious mistakes had been committed in the early police response to the murder. It was of course imperative for
him to get the newspapers on his side, and the best way to do so was to appear
calm, confident, and on top of the situation. He must convince the media that
the killer would be caught very soon by the efficient Swedish police, and the
national trauma of the murder of Olof Palme would soon be ended.

With regard to the murder scene witnesses, it is likely that Holmér had access to the succinct testimony of Morelius and Jeppsson, which has already
been given in some detail. Two other important witnesses were the teenage
girls Anna Hage and Karin Johansson, who had tried to resuscitate Palme.[3]
They had both been questioned by a detective shortly after midnight. The
two girls had been traveling past the murder scene in a car along with three
other young people. The car stereo was blaring out loud music, and neither of

the girls actually heard the shots. When she saw Palme collapse, Anna thought he might have suffered a heart attack or an epileptic seizure. Since she was a student nurse, she did not hesitate to run up to see what she could do to help. For a few seconds, she saw a broad-shouldered, dark-haired man, wearing a knee-length dark overcoat, running away into the Tunnelgatan. As she reached Palme, a young man was already there, and together they attempted to resuscitate him, although with little success. Anna once thought she could feel the victim's pulse, but she must have felt her own by mistake. The other girl, Karin, who had tried to calm down the distraught Mrs. Palme, said that she had not seen the gunman escape, although she heard other people on the scene describe a dark-haired man around thirty-five years old, wearing a dark overcoat.

Another important witness was cab driver Anders Delsborn, who had actually been clear-headed enough to phone for help.[4] He, too, was questioned shortly after midnight. He told the police that as he had been waiting at the traffic lights at the intersection of the Sveavägen and Tunnelgatan, he had clearly seen three people standing talking on the sidewalk. Two of them, a man and a woman, had their backs toward Delsborn's car; the man they were talking to was facing them. The traffic light changed, and Delsborn took his eyes off the three people as he drove into the intersection. A loud bang came from where the three people had been standing, and just as Delsborn turned to look another bang followed. The startled cab driver saw that the man who had been facing the Palmes was holding a large handgun with a long barrel; he could even see the puff of gun smoke after the second shot. Delsborn described the killer as a tall, broad-shouldered man wearing a darkish gray ulster coat and a gray cap or hat. The killer stood for a while looking at his victim, as if unsure which way to escape. Unlike most other witnesses, Delsborn thought that the killer did not run particularly quickly: instead, he seemed a bit clumsy and slow taking off from the scene.

The person closest to the Palmes at the time of the murder was designer Anders Björkman.[5] He was walking immediately behind the Palmes, and as the shots rang out, he quickly dodged into the Dekorima doorway to take cover. He emerged from his hiding place a few minutes later, briefly spoke to Ljungqvist, and gave his name and address to one of the police officers before going home. Two hours later, he was woken up by a detective for some further questioning. This turned out to be time well spent, since Björkman's story was a remarkable one. Previously that evening, he had been to a rather raucous office party, where he had drunk two or three glasses of beer, three slugs of vodka, and perhaps also a small whisky. He had then joined some friends who wanted to go to a nightclub, and waited outside as they withdrew money from an ATM. But Björkman had had quite a lot to drink, and he began to doubt whether further partying that night was going to agree with him. He decided to go home. As he was walking along the Sveavägen, he observed a party of three people in front of him. To the far right was a short woman. To the far left was a taller man, who had his arm around the person in the middle. Björkman thought this person walking in the middle must be a woman, since he found it unnatural for a man to embrace another man in such a manner. The three people "were talking together and having a good time." All of a sudden, two muffled bangs rang out. At first, the startled Björkman thought it was firecrackers, and looked around to see who might be playing such a prank. He then saw the person walking in the middle collapse to the ground and realized that he or she must have been shot. The short woman screamed something in a foreign language. The tall man, who was wearing a long dark overcoat and a dark blue knitted cap, ran off with alacrity into the Tunnelgatan, and the stunned Björkman, who had hidden in the Dekorima doorway, lost sight of him. When Björkman went home, he told his wife that the whole thing had been very confusing: here is a party of three people walking and talking together perfectly innocuously, and then one of them pulls a gun, shoots one of the others, and calmly takes off.

At the press conference at noon on Saturday, Hans Holmér would have the attention of every journalist in Sweden and a large posse of foreign correspondents. He had quite a few difficult decisions to make. Firstly, the public would want to know whether the murder had been the result of a conspiracy or the action of a lone avenger. Holmér chose not to make any definitive statement with regard to this crucial question, although he was convinced that such an accomplished murder and swift escape could only be the result of a carefully planned assassination. Another central point was whether any credence should be given to the early report that Lisbet Palme had seen two men at the murder scene. Here, Holmér chose to act decisively. He bluntly declared that there had been only one killer, giving no explanation for the police alert about the two assassins previously seen outside the Palme apartment in the Old Town.

Later, Holmér would declare that this was a misinterpretation of what Lisbet Palme had really been saying at the hospital. Holmér had access to a report made by lieutenant Lars Christianson, another officer who had gone to the hospital that night. Christianson had spoken to Lisbet Palme, and she had said nothing about there being two gunmen. She described the killer as a tall, well-built man with dark hair, wearing a short blue parka. She said nothing about his face. It is not known why Christianson's information was not taken into account when the national police alert was drawn up during the night. Nor is it known what other supporting evidence made Holmér credit Christianson's version of events over that of Sergeant Rimborn. It must have been of some importance that Christianson clearly distinguished between Mrs. Palme's observation of one gunman and her previous observation of two men acting suspiciously outside the Palme apartment; the implication was that either Rimborn or some foolish individual at police headquarters mistakenly linked these two separate events. Holmér also knew that none of the murder scene witness had seen more than one killer running away, and some of them were very well placed to make such an observation.[6]

More difficult decisions remained for the police-master, including whether to say that Palme had met and spoken to his killer, as suggested by the testimony of Delsborn and Björkman. In her brief conversations with Rimborn, Mrs. Palme had said nothing to indicate that they had met and spoken to the killer, but the policeman does not seem to have asked her this question directly. Christianson wrote in his report that Söderström had told him that the witness statements indicated that the Palmes had walked along with a third person, who had suddenly shot the prime minister. Christianson then quoted Mrs. Palme as saying that she and her husband had been to see the film *Amadeus* [sic] at the Grand cinema, that they had decided to walk home to the Old Town, and that they had not been accompanied by any other person. At the press conference, Holmér curtly declared that there had been no contact between the Palmes and the killer prior to the murder, and this has been accepted as the official truth ever since. During the first weeks after the murder, Sweden was in a state of collective shock, and Hans Holmér was widely regarded as the strong man who would deliver the country from its national trauma. It was considered close to treason to question the police-master's pontifications, and no journalist dared to ask awkward questions or to criticize his selection of which witnesses to believe.

At the press conference, Hans Holmér confidently described the killer as wearing a blue parka, dark trousers, and a flat cap. This agreed with Mrs. Palme's description of the killer as wearing a blue parka and also with Mårten Palme's description of a man he had seen following his parents from the cinema. Holmér also knew that a traffic warden had observed a man fitting this description walking down the Snickarbacken, a street parallel to David Bagares Gata, between 11:15 and 11:30; as the man passed the traffic warden, he seemed to hide his face with one hand. Holmér rather optimistically seems to have decided this was the killer continuing his escape. The description of the killer Holmér presented to the Swedish people during that press conference was thus largely based on testimony from witnesses who may not even have seen the killer. Mårten Palme's observation may well have a perfectly innocuous explanation, and with regard to the traffic warden, it was later discovered that she saw the man at 11:16, several minutes before the murder was committed.[7] This debacle, as well as the testimony of the murder scene witnesses, undermined the police-master's conviction about the killer's headgear: a meeting later that eventful day resulted in the conclusion that the murderer might have worn a cap, or he might not have.

But the damage was done, particularly since the early description mentioning the cap was not publicly withdrawn. It may well be that people who had observed a man near the murder scene never reported it to the police, since the man they saw was not wearing a cap. We will never know whether such witnesses exist. Furthermore, witnesses are easily influenced, particularly in an extraordinary case like this, and they have a subconscious wish to help the police solve the case. Many sad examples of this tendency can be found in the police investigation. Leif Ljungqvist, one of the main murder scene witnesses, had been "lost" by the police officers the night of the murder, but he himself reported to police headquarters on March 1, saying that the killer had been wearing a dark overcoat; he did not believe it was a parka. The next time he was questioned, on April 27, he had read the newspaper reports and changed his story accordingly, giving a much more detailed description of the killer's blue parka, his too-short trousers, and his ordinary walking shoes. Nor was the witness Jeppsson exactly a model of consistency: he had initially described the killer's attire simply as dark clothes and a cap, but in a later questioning, he was much more positive about the killer's blue parka and flat cap. Cab driver Hans Johansson had originally been confident the killer had been bare headed; he later said the killer might well have worn a cap of some kind. Charlotte Liljedahl, one of the passengers in Delsborn's cab, also at first denied she had seen the killer with any headgear, but later helpfully told the detectives that "he might still have worn a flat cap or something." In an even more questionable passage from the same police interrogation, the young woman clearly describes the killer's long dark overcoat, reaching below the knees; a detective then asks her, "What kind of coat would you estimate this to be? Was it a long parka?" This she clearly denies, however. Another young woman, Ulrika Rytterstål, vacillated when describing the killer's attire, although she had a clear memory of the coat fluttering between his legs. She admitted that she was not one to contradict the television and newspaper reports, which seemed to agree that the killer had worn a short parka; she finally settled for a three-quarter-length jacket. Christina Wallin, another young murder scene witness, also vacillated. In two early questionings, she said nothing about any cap. In a third questioning, she said she had a memory of the killer wearing some kind of headgear, but admitted she might have been influenced by the media. Many other, although less striking, examples exist of evidence being biased in the direction of what the witnesses perceived as the "correct" official version.[8] But what about the newspapers? On March 1, they gave a very fair summary of the early descriptions of the killer as wearing a long dark overcoat. But now, the journalists were eating out of Hans Holmér's hand and questioned nothing of what he said; the blue parka and the cap had become the official truth. A particularly ludicrous example is the following statement from a newspaper journalist: "The killer was wearing a short blue parka, which many witnesses have mistaken for a long dark overcoat."[9]

It is an important fact in witness psychology that the earliest testimony, the one made immediately after the observation, is the most reliable one. It is interesting to go back to the initial testimony of the murder scene witnesses, before they were influenced by one another and by the pressure from the police and media to say the "right" things.[10] It is recorded that apart from Mrs. Palme, at least thirty-six witnesses saw something of the murder. Of these, twenty-one claim to have seen the killer. Morelius and Björkman form a category of their own, since they actually saw the murder being committed. These two also had more time than the other witnesses to observe the killer. It is interesting that their descriptions tally in almost every respect: the gunman was tall, broad-shouldered, and agile, and wore a long dark overcoat and a close-fitting, dark blue, knitted cap. Björkman made a drawing of this knitted cap, which he could clearly recall in spite of his intoxicated state. Three people saw the killer on the run: Jeppsson, Nieminen, and her boyfriend Zahir. Jeppsson saw only that he was wearing dark clothes. Nieminen and Zahir both observed that he wore a knee-length black overcoat that fluttered as he ran. Nieminen added that he wore dark trousers and a dark sweater. At least sixteen people had a more or less clear view of the killer running off. Three of them saw only a person in dark clothes. Of the other thirteen witnesses, ten observed that the killer was wearing a dark overcoat. Many of them specified that this coat reached at least down to the knees, that it was probably black, and that it fluttered around the man's legs as he ran away. Some witnesses added that the killer was wearing dark trousers, while there is complete disagreement as to whether he was wearing a cap or not. Some witnesses thought he was either dark haired or wearing a close-fitting dark cap; others vehemently denied that the killer was wearing a cap at all. Of the three witnesses who denied that the killer was wearing a long dark overcoat, two described a man wearing a short blue or dark parka and a cap. This is a good description of the garments worn by the witness Björkman, who was not far from the Palmes when the shots were fired. Finally, one witness saw a man wearing a short, brown, leather jacket running off; it is not known who this might have been or if the observation is reliable.

Hans Holmér was by no means the obvious leader of the murder investigation. The chief of national police, Holger Romander, was nominally his superior. Also outranking Holmér was Tommy Lindström, the commander of the National Crime Squad, a maverick officer known for his cleverness and audacity. Another possible leader worked for the civilian secret police, the SÄPO. Its nominal leader was a certain Sven-Åke Hjälmroth, but the real strongman was commander Per-Gunnar Näss, another able and effective operator. Under normal circumstances, it would have been up to Romander and Lindström to select an experienced detective, like captain Otto Andersson of the National Crime Squad or captain Arne Ivrell of the Stockholm Murder Squad, to lead the murder inquiry. But to the Social Democrats, Holmér must have appeared the ideal leader of the investigation. His loyalty could be relied on, he had previously taken part in politically sensitive operations, and he gave an impression of great energy and determination. No mere detective could grasp the big picture in a complex case like this, they reasoned; but Holmér would be able to draw from the resources of the Stockholm police, the National Crime Squad, and the SÄPO, liaising with diplomatic and political skill. Another advantage for the Stockholm commissioner was that he was used to dealing with journalists; he skillfully managed to avoid accusations of police incompetence in the early part of the hunt for the murderer. In his press conferences, transmitted on live television, the charismatic Holmér presented himself as a tough, determined policeman who would hunt down the killer by any means necessary. He became extraordinarily popular, since the people wanted the reassurance of a strong man taking charge. The murder had shaken the nation to the core, and Holmér adroitly played on these feelings.[11] Olof Palme was as popular dead as he had been controversial alive, and the Dekorima corner was kept covered in flowers, with Social Democratic zealots standing vigil and politicians from all over the world coming to pay tribute to Sweden's great international statesman.

Hans Holmér was determined to be more than the nominal leader of the investigation. Every important decision had to go through him, and he recruited loyal officers to form a staff under his own leadership. The so-called Palme Room, chaired by Holmér and his second in command, Hans Wranghult, was staffed by the aforementioned Tommy Lindström and Per-Gunnar Näss, and also government observer Klas Bergenstrand, commander Stig Lennart Pettersson, and captains Nils Linder and Wincent Lange. Because of an old rivalry between the National Crime Squad and the detectives of the Stockholm police, many of the police administrators thought it beneficial that Holmér and the Palme Room were taking charge. The problem was that Holmér had never conducted a murder inquiry. Most of the other men in the Palme Room were also administrators, some of them completely lacking experience in detective work. The top-ranking Stockholm detectives, who were used to running their own investigations, were relegated to reading through the immense number of tips from the public.

With characteristic determination, Holmér built up the largest police task force ever seen in Sweden. Not fewer than three hundred detectives worked on the Palme inquiry, with further support from hundreds of uniformed officers. Right from the beginning, Holmér made it clear that he was the man in charge. Stig Lennart Pettersson later said that although many experienced policemen were sitting at the round table in the Palme Room, he had never seen so many silent people. The other officers' belief in authority and lack of moral courage prevented them from criticizing the police-master; they also feared that their careers would be jeopardized if they did so. These fears were by no means unfounded, since the police-master was easily offended and took drastic action if his underlings annoyed him. The experienced detective Otto Andersson, thought by some to be the obvious leader of the investigation, was summarily discharged to other duties after daring to criticize Holmér's dictatorial running of the murder inquiry.

One of the first duties for Holmér's Palme task force was to find out who could have known that the Palmes would go to the Grand cinema that evening. It turned out that Lisbet Palme had talked about going to see a movie to Mårten Palme's girlfriend and to some of her friends at work; she had mentioned only the Spegeln cinema, however. Olof had hinted to one of the people interviewing him in the afternoon that he might go to the movies, but mentioned no particulars. Lisbet said that it was a rare occurrence for the workaholic Olof to find time to go to the movies. Police experts found no evidence that the Palme apartment had been bugged or that the phone had been tapped. Nor was anything sinister noted at Olof's office in the government building or Lisbet's office at the social services. In 1986, high-quality bugging equipment was very hard to come by in Sweden, as was the expertise to install it; it is telling that when the Swedish police themselves planned to use covert surveillance in the murder investigation, they had to ask the CIA for help. Anyway, the decision to see *The Brothers Mozart* at the Grand cinema was made at a very late stage in the evening, and it is unlikely that any outsider would have been able to glean this information. The detectives also discovered that during the four weeks preceding the murder, Palme had walked to work unguarded at least thirteen times. In addition, he had taken Lisbet to a restaurant and gone on a skiing trip without his bodyguards.[12] Holmér speculated that Palme must either have had a fatalist approach to his own security, or an overreliance on the docile nature of the denizens of his utopian People's Home. At least, there was no indication that Palme had felt particularly threatened in mid-February.

Some mysteries also remain unexplained with regard to the murder site. The Tunnelgatan led to a tunnel under the Brunkeberg ridge, but this tunnel was closed late at night. The ridge could be ascended three ways: by elevator, escalator, and stairs. The police were surprised the killer had chosen the last option. He might have known the escalator worked only sometimes; he might have wanted full control of what was happening, which would have been impossible in an elevator or the housed-in escalator. He might have trusted his own agility and fitness, or he might have had a hideout nearby and thus no need to conserve his energy. The Tunnelgatan stairs were an excellent escape route, and Holmér thought this yet another indication that he was dealing with a criminal of superior intelligence and cunning. It was impossible to pursue the killer up the stairs in any other way than by foot, and he would have a good view of possible pursuers when looking over his shoulder at the top of the stairs. The streets near David Bagares Gata were dark and quite empty of pedestrians, and there was no obvious way for a police car to head off the killer's escape route.

Due to the sense of national outrage, the police were deluged with tips from the public.[13] Several drunks and madmen turned themselves in as the killer, but were angrily dismissed when it turned out that they had been nowhere near the murder site. Two girls claimed to have seen every detail of the murder, including the killer's long dark overcoat and flat cap with earflaps, but the police were able to prove that they had invented their story. The police also received a torrent of letters containing well-meaning advice. Concerned citizens asked whether the other Swedish political leaders had alibis for the murder night. Many people pointed fingers at a large protest march by disgruntled farmers that had taken place earlier on February 28: Had one of these men turned his tractor around, driven up to Stockholm, and shot Palme? Mystics believed that the shape of the bloodstain on the snow might form a guide to the killer's identity, and recommended that the opinion of Uri Geller be sought. Soothsayers, astrologers, and clairvoyants offered their services. It was suggested that in the search for the murder weapon, an army of people with divining rods should march through every field and park; a large force of gravediggers should exhume all recently dug graves; and the boy scouts should be mobilized to search the bins at every dog latrine in Stockholm. Another enthusiast suggested that every person who had seen the late showing of *The Brothers Mozart* on the night of the murder should reconvene in the cinema and seek out their seats from that night. The sole empty seat would be that of the killer, it was optimistically hoped, and the people sitting nearby could identify him. Another letter writer had the bright idea that the police should announce that they had a star witness who was capable of identifying the killer with certainty. As in an American B movie, Palme's killer would then come to "neutralize" the witness and could be easily caught by the police stakeout. The writer freely offered herself as the bait in this covert operation.

Another early lead came from a newspaper reporter who had found out that just fifteen minutes after the murder, someone had called an elderly couple living in a Stockholm suburb, saying, "Now Palme is dead!" The old man thought it was a hoax call and responded, "What the hell do I care?" The police initially thought this incident very important, since at 11:35, very few people knew that Palme was dead. Was it the killer or an accomplice announcing that the deed was done? Analyzing how the phone number might have been misdialed, mathematicians were set to work trying to figure out who could have been the intended recipient of this mysterious phone call: Was it a right-wing extremist, a leader of the World Anti-Communist League, or a telecom engineer who was supposed to destroy all evidence of a previous phone-tap operation at the Palme apartment? It turned out, however, that the phone call had actually been made at a much later time, by the old woman's brother.[14]

In spite of all Hans Holmér's bravado, the hunt for the murderer, which had begun as such a farce, continued in the same vein. As we know, the police had fenced in only a very small area around the pool of Olof Palme's blood that was still visible on the snow, and during the night, many people had barged through the police barriers to leave flowers and wreaths at the murder scene. Thus there was no point in looking for the murderer's footprints. Although the murderer had been seen to linger near the Dekorima display window, no one got the idea that it might be profitable to search for fingerprints on the window glass; there is no hard evidence that the murderer wore gloves.[15] The most important work at the crime scene was of course to search for the two bullets, but again almost incredible blunders occurred. The police technicians started out well, using impressive-looking metal detectors and then a large machine that vacuumed the ground and picked up any loose objects. Bag after bag of snow and ice was picked up, to be melted at police headquarters, but still no bullets were found. The police technicians declared themselves completely nonplussed.

Then, an Indian journalist who was strolling by found one of the bullets on the opposite sidewalk, which the police had not thought of examining. The day after, a woman who brought a bunch of roses in Palme's memory found the second bullet very near the site of the murder, on a mound of snow in an area that had already been searched by the police technicians. It is recorded that two murder scene witnesses noticed a ricochet mark from one of the bullets, but this does not appear to have been investigated by the technicians, and

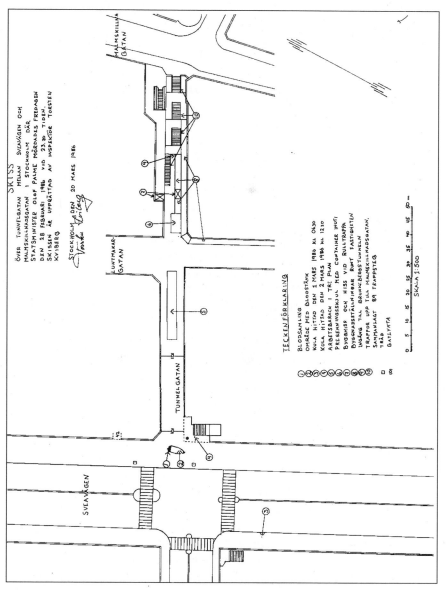

The murder site. The official police sketch, showing the Tunnelgatan stairs and the location of the two bullets. The legend reads: 1. the bloodstain, 2. area of blood spatter, 3. site where the "Lisbet bullet" was found, 4. site where the "Olof bullet" was found, 5. building site barracks in the Tunnelgatan, 6–8. further scaffolding and building works, 9. entrance to the Brunkeberg tunnel, 10. stairs up to the Malmskillnadsgatan. Reproduced by permission of the Swedish National Police Board.

valuable information was thus lost.[16] It seems most likely that it was the "Lisbet bullet" that ricocheted to the opposite sidewalk, a not illogical site according to later police test shootings. The site of the "Olof bullet" is more puzzling, since it should have traveled much further. Leading detective Ingemar Krusell did not agree, claiming that test shootings in Wiesbaden, Germany, indicated that a rotating bullet striking the sternum may lose a lot of its momentum and drop near the victim's body. Krusell even claimed to have seen a light reflection from the bullet near the mound of snow in a very early police photograph from the murder scene, indicating that it had been there all the time. But the "Olof bullet" showed marks indicative of considerable wear that discredited the theory that it had remained undisturbed at the place it had fallen. The bullet may have been surreptitiously kicked and walked on by police and onlookers or possibly passed through the vacuuming machine before being dropped near the site of the murder.[17] Nor can the possibility be ruled out that the bullet was taken as a souvenir by one of the many people walking around the murder scene during the night and then replaced after that same person had sobered up and realized its value as evidence.

According to the first police communiqué, the bullets were copper mantled and very uncommon, possibly specially made for the murder. But an enterprising journalist asked the opinion of an experienced arms dealer, who bluntly stated that they were in fact Winchester .357 magnum armor-piercing ammunition, available in most weapon stores. After studying the literature, the police shamefacedly had to agree.[18] The state ballistics laboratory added that its technicians would of course have recognized the bullets, had the police bothered to consult them. This evidence that the killer was using a .357 magnum revolver agrees with the testimony of Anders Delsborn, the only murder scene witness who clearly saw the killer's handgun: it was large, had a long barrel, and made a very loud noise. At one of his press conferences, Hans Holmér sat dangling two Smith and Wesson .357 magnum revolvers, asking for information from the public about owners of such handguns who had been behaving suspiciously. Some detectives thought it unwise to divulge important information like this to the general public, but the attention-loving Holmér did not agree. The result was another flood of tips, now about Smith and Wesson revolvers, from every corner of Sweden.

The autopsy showed that Olof Palme had been shot in the back, and that the shot had severed both the spinal column and the aorta.[19] As indicated by the extensive injuries and by the size of the bruise on his forehead, Palme died before his body hit the pavement. The autopsy also showed that Palme was otherwise healthy and fit; had his life not been cut short in such a dismal way, he may well have had many years yet to make his mark on European politics and then lived to a ripe old age. The two bullets found in the Sveavägen were

Hans Holmér at a press conference, brandishing two Smith and Wesson revolvers.

sent to the Swedish state criminology laboratory for further investigation. They were Winchester armor-piercing ammunition, probably fired from a .357 magnum Smith and Wesson revolver, although certain less common brands of revolvers, like Ruger, Taurus, and Kassnar, could not be ruled out. The revolver probably had a barrel length of at least six inches. Independent examinations of the bullets at laboratories of the German Bundeskriminalamt and the FBI agreed, although they added some uncommon foreign brands of revolvers to the list of possible murder weapons. The German laboratory hoped to prove that the two bullets were really those that had killed Olof Palme and injured Lisbet by examining tissue fragments that might remain on them, but this was not possible, since the Swedish laboratory had cleaned the bullets when routinely making casts of them.[20]

The German laboratory also received the clothes worn by the Palmes, which were closely investigated. It was determined that both the Palmes had been shot at very close range, Olof from just twenty centimeters and Lisbet from seventy centimeters, and that the killer was likely to have been taller than his victims. This corroborates the crucial witness statements from Morelius and Björkman about the tall, well-built killer being very close to his victims. One of many minor unsolved mysteries surrounding the murder of Olof

Palme is why so many of the murder scene witnesses compared the noise made by the gunshots to firecrackers or a popgun. In a phenomenon called "auditory exclusion," a person startled by a great and unexpected noise nearby has a tendency to underestimate its intensity. It may also be speculated that Lisbet Palme was protected from the noise by Olof's body, and Björkman by the body of the murderer. But the sound of a .357 magnum revolver fired nearby is enough to leave the ears ringing for several minutes. It is also peculiar that several people sitting in cars did not hear the shots at all. It is possible to fit a silencer to a .357 magnum, but this requires painstaking specialist work, and the silencing is still not as effective as with a pistol, in addition to which the weapon becomes even longer and more unwieldy.

It has also been speculated that the killer used homemade or defective ammunition, but this possibility has been ruled out by the ballistics investigation.[21] From an early stage, there have been rumors that the two bullets found at the Sveavägen were not those that killed Olof Palme and wounded his wife. These rumors were fuelled by one of the police technicians, who asserted that if these bullets had been in their respective locations after the murder, his team would have found them. It was speculated that the bullets were planted by someone as part of an elaborate conspiracy, to hide that Palme had been shot from a long range or by a small-caliber weapon. Holmér completely disregarded these speculations, since he was convinced the bullets were the right ones. It was not until June 1987 that a lead isotope investigation, comparing the bullets with the lead residue found on the garments worn by the Palmes, proved him right.[22]

An important task for the police was of course to question Mrs. Palme. Two detectives spoke to her at the Palme apartment at 3:00 p.m. the day after the murder. Mårten Palme and Ulf Dahlsten were also present. Mrs. Palme did not allow the detectives to tape the conversation. She said that after the movie, she and her husband had walked along the Sveavägen with their arms locked. She was walking to the right, Olof to the left. Just at the intersection with the Tunnelgatan, she heard two bangs resembling the sound of firecrackers. They did not sound like they came from very near. She turned to Olof to comment that the children's fireworks were frighteningly loud, but he had collapsed, bleeding profusely from the mouth and the chest. She was herself being dragged down with him because of their locked arms when she heard another bang and felt a sharp pain across her back. She could only just see a man run into the Tunnelgatan. He stopped for a moment to look back and then ran away. She described him as six feet tall, with dark brown hair and a short neck. He wore a short blue parka and dark gray trousers. She mentioned nothing about the man's face.

Mrs. Palme was shocked to find that the day after, she could read her own words in one of the evening newspapers. Her opinion of the Stockholm police had never been high, and the bungling of the early murder investigation and this uncalled-for leak to the tabloid press made her angry and resentful. Holmér responded by personally handling all further contact with the widow. As charismatic as ever, the police-master convinced her that she could rely on him and then carried out some very polite and superficial questionings. When the prosecutors suggested that Mrs. Palme should take part in the reconstructions that were staged at the crime scene, Holmér bluntly refused.[23]

In the weeks after Olof Palme's death, Holmér became increasingly convinced that the murder was the result of a conspiracy. The killers must have followed their victim from the Palme apartment to the cinema, he speculated, and then stood ready to target the various routes the prime minister might travel home after the film. Such a formidable gang of killers must have had a means of communicating with one another, and since cell phones were not used back in 1986, Holmér made an appeal for observations of people using walkie-talkies near the murder site or along the way the Palmes had traveled from the Old Town to the cinema. Holmér's appeal resulted in a multitude of observations of mysterious men with walkie-talkies all over Stockholm, all of doubtful value to the murder inquiry. Holmér was particularly interested in a sensational story told in an anonymous letter sent by a man claiming to be a traveling salesman of women's fashions; the letter had been posted in the small town of Skelleftehamn. Not far from the Dekorima corner, the salesman had seen a very tall, blond man speaking German into a walkie-talkie. He had called out, "Das Auto! Das Auto!" and this was believed to be a reference to the gang's getaway car. The "Skelleftehamn witness" wrote back with further details but never divulged his name, although Holmér promised that his testimony would be treated with absolute confidence, and that his wife would never know what escapades the provincial lingerie salesman had been up to in the Swedish capital.[24]

Another lead that caught Hans Holmér's interest was an observation made by a cab driver at the Snickarbacken, not far from where the killer had been last seen. The cab driver had just let off a passenger at a nearby restaurant, at about 11:35, when he saw a man walk up to a blue Volkswagen Passat. The man took off his overcoat and put it in the car and then put on another jacket before driving off. The cab driver described him as five feet ten inches tall, with a stocky build, and wearing a flat cap. Just after the man drove off, the witness saw two police officers come running down David Bagares Gata. Holmér decided this must have been the killer disguising himself before driving off, and announced the breakthrough at another grand press conference on March 3. The result was another deluge of tips, this time about blue Volkswagens observed in every corner of Sweden. In the meantime, the police painstakingly checked all two hundred blue Volkswagen Passats in Sweden, but without finding anything worthwhile.

Reading the newspapers, the police officers who had been pursuing the killer were amazed that they had come so close to capturing their prey. Some journalists worked out the timing of the story: Olof Palme had been shot at 11:21 and the cab driver had made his observations fifteen minutes later—but it took one of the newsmen less than three minutes to run this presumed escape route. Would the killer really have waited for his pursuers somewhere along his escape route? Anyway, the description of the man did not tally very well with what was known about the killer's description and attire, and Holmér's idea about the blue Volkswagen escape car slowly faded into obscurity. This debacle marked the end of Holmér's early honeymoon with the media, and the newspapers even dared to voice some criticism of the early police response to the murder and the police-master's own unconventional initiatives in the murder hunt.[25] At another press conference, Holmér admonished the journalists that they should not speculate and that it was wrong of them to criticize the authorities in the middle of a national crisis. In a large, painstaking murder investigation, there had to be some mistakes and false leads, he pointed out, just as misprints occur in newspapers.

Holmér's popularity showed no signs of abating. People from all over Sweden wrote to him saying that he had their support, and that the irresponsible newspaper criticism should not lower his spirits. His rugged looks made "the Clint Eastwood of the People's Home" a favorite among the ladies, particularly after the newspapers divulged that he was divorcing his wife. He received many love letters and even offers of marriage; he was to make a secret sign during his next television press conference if he accepted the hand of his unknown correspondent. Women of a certain age tried to entice their favorite policeman by sending him bags of freshly baked cakes and jars of homemade jam and pickled herrings.[26] A journalist visiting Holmér just before Easter was amazed at all the bunches of red roses and boxes of chocolates and marzipan eggs that were scattered around the Palme Room. When a timorous admirer alerted Holmér to the risk that the murderer might send a box of poisoned chocolates to get rid of Sweden's supersleuth, the ready-witted police-master replied that he always had one of the detectives taste his delicacies before he himself dared to tuck in.

Hans Holmér and his second in command, Hans Wranghult, shared a belief in unconventional high-tech methods of tracking the elusive criminal. To try to detect the murder weapon, they had central Stockholm photographed from the air by a low-flying fighter aircraft. This novel and raucous expedition, which made many people fearful that the Soviets were coming, had to be repeated, since the pilot had forgotten to load the camera with film. Even with film there were no results. Using a complicated machine for reconstructing faces, specially imported from Wiesbaden in Germany, Holmér then tried to develop an image of the killer. He was convinced that Lisbet Palme had never seen the murderer, and that the man she had described was actually the witness Björkman in his blue parka; this belief was shared by leading prosecuting attorney Karl-Gerhard Svensson. None of the other murder scene witnesses had seen the killer at close enough range to describe his face.

Instead, Holmér used a drawing made by a young woman who had seen a running man not far from the murder scene, between 11:30 and 11:40 the night of the murder. He had almost bumped into her and had looked startled and turned away, perhaps realizing he had been observed. She was a trained artist and made a sketch of him for the police. Some of the other men in the Palme Room objected that it was not certain that she had seen the killer, but Wranghult overruled them. On March 6, Hans Holmér held another of his spectacular press conferences to present a "phantom image" of the killer to the world press. "The Phantom," as he was dubbed by the press, was a sinister, foreign-looking character. Lean and grim, with a long nose and thin lips, he certainly looked like a murderer. The young woman herself objected that the image had little resemblance to the man she had seen, but nobody seems to have listened to her.

Every Swedish newspaper had the Phantom on its front page. Holmér receive much praise for this novel approach to detective work, and the press was again eating out of his hand. The journalists seem to have reasoned, "Now we at least know what the killer looks like." The Phantom was shown on CNN, ABC, and NBC, and the BBC showed his ugly face to thirty million Britons. He was on the front page of the *New York Times* and many other American newspapers. Newspapers in faraway countries like Chile, Mexico, and Hong Kong followed suit; the *South China Morning Post* adding the information that since this man had shown he could be extremely dangerous, he should not be approached without caution. The Stockholm police switchboard came close to breaking down as the detectives received another deluge of tips. The Phantom seemed to be sitting at every bar in every Swedish town. The majority of calls came from people who thought they knew the Phantom. Wives denounced their husbands, workmen their employers, psychiatrists their patients, and children their teachers. All over the country, nervous old women saw the Phantom lurking outside their houses. The Swedes had become a nation of police informants. The police made several arrests, but all these pseudo-Phantoms turned out to be honest, respectable people. One man who

The Phantom (left) and the Shadow. Reproduced by permission of the Swedish National Police Board.

closely resembled the Phantom was arrested twice, and the police gave him a card to show overzealous officers and vigilantes to prevent this from happening again. Another pseudo-Phantom, a French tourist on a skiing holiday in Sweden, had to wear his goggles all the time, to prevent people from calling the police.[27]

Under normal circumstances, the purpose of a phantom image is to make it known that a crime has taken place and to find witnesses and get valuable tips. But in this instance, everyone knew about the murder already, the vast majority of witnesses had been found, and the police had more tips than they could deal with. Most importantly, it should be nearly 100 percent certain that the image in question is that of the killer. In the Palme case, the observation on which the image was based was made at least nine minutes after the murder, suggesting that either the killer had lingered unnecessarily in an area that was now being actively searched by the police, or the woman had seen a completely irrelevant person. In June 1986, the police found a man who had several times been questioned because of his resemblance to the Phantom and who had been walking in the area in question, on perfectly legitimate business, the night of the murder.

It thus became clear that the observation was very likely not of the killer, but not before the construction of the Phantom had done serious harm to the murder inquiry. Some witnesses changed their descriptions of the killer to make them resemble the Phantom; other people may never have reported their observations to the police, because the man they had seen did not resemble the Phantom. There were also quite a few instances of people claiming to have seen the Phantom in suspicious circumstances in the days preceding the murder. The most glaring example is that of the subway ticket seller who had sold Palme his ticket; he first denied seeing anything suspicious, he then told the police he had a vague memory of seeing the Phantom enter the subway station, and he finally was portrayed in the newspapers claiming that he had seen the Phantom pursuing the Palmes the night of the murder.

A South American refugee provided the police with material for a second phantom image: a tall blond man who, he claimed, had followed Palme around the day before the murder. Another flood of tips came from people who thought they knew the Shadow, as the press named this suspect. The immigrant later confessed that he had made up the whole story, because he had feared that the publication of the first, foreign-looking image would give rise to racist feelings among the Swedes! The 1999 commission justly blasted the decision to release the two phantom images as the greatest single mistake in the murder investigation. As a result, the police received eight thousand tips, all of very dubious value; this huge load of worthless baggage would be weighing down the murder investigation for months to come.[28]

THE FIRST MAIN SUSPECT

THE ODDBALL SCHOOLMASTER

In the early stages of the murder investigation, a fifty-four-year-old detective sergeant named Börje Wingren took vigorous part in the hunt for the killer. He heard about the murder on the radio when he was sitting in his apartment late at night, working on a complicated bridge problem, and promptly ran down to the police headquarters nearby. Captain Nils Linder was taking charge of the detectives, and Wingren was first sent to the Royal Viking hotel, where a man had been talking confusedly about Palme being killed before the radio bulletin was transmitted. He turned out to be an old drunk who had passed by the murder scene, where someone had told him what had happened. Wingren knew that just a few days before the murder, an insane Austrian man had made threats against both Hans Holmér and Olof Palme, but the police had not taken him seriously. Wingren was getting worried that this man was a more serious criminal that had previously been suspected, and that he had made good his threat to shoot the prime minister. The police were out looking for him, but as yet with no success.

In the early hours of March 1, Mårten Palme himself contacted the police, since he thought he had important information to divulge. When Börje Wingren picked him up outside the prime minister's apartment at 5:00 a.m., he said that his distraught mother had finally been able to go to sleep just before he left. Young Palme told the detectives that he had seen a scruffy-looking man in a blue parka standing outside the Grand cinema, and suspected this might have been the killer waiting to follow the Palmes toward the Dekorima corner.[1] Wingren immediately showed him a photograph of the "Mad Austrian," a wild-looking character with staring eyes, thick lips, and a huge beard. Young Palme was doubtful, but Wingren told him that the photograph was ten years old and that a man's face can change a lot with time; he then started making grimaces to illustrate this. Taken aback by the detective's strange behavior, Mårten Palme reluctantly admitted that if his face had changed dramatically, the Austrian might have been the man he saw. In the police report, Wingren wrote that far from being doubtful, young Palme had at once identified the Mad Austrian as the man he had seen outside the cinema. In the morning, the Austrian was finally located: he had spent the night with a prostitute, and was unceremoniously dragged out of her bed by the uniformed police. But he was a very lucky man: one minute before Palme was killed, he had been stopped for drunkenness by a police patrol in another part of Stockholm, and clearly had had nothing to do with the murder.[2]

The above anecdote about his hunt for the Mad Austrian suggests that Börje Wingren was something of a maverick, with an unconventional approach to detective work. He had recently joined the Stockholm police, transferring from a precinct in southern Sweden, where some of his superiors had formed a low opinion of his professional integrity. When Wingren wanted to move to Stockholm, they warned some senior officers there that he entirely lacked judgment and several times had been in trouble for various indiscretions. Captain Nils Linder thought Wingren a good, ambitious cop, however, and the maverick detective was able to start a new career in the Swedish capital.[3]

In spite of Wingren's lowly rank within the police hierarchy, his dynamic and forceful personality made him one of the key players in the early phase of the investigation of the murder of Olof Palme. Soon, he found another lead. That same eventful night, two young women had contacted him to say that when they were at the Saga cinema in central Stockholm, a strange man had clandestinely sneaked in about forty-five minutes after the film had started. This was about twenty-five minutes after the murder, and Wingren suspected that they had seen the killer seeking refuge from the police. He had read a book about the Kennedy assassination and knew that Lee Harvey Oswald had been arrested in a movie theater. Wingren detective's intuition therefore told him that a movie theater was a typical place to hide if you had just killed a president or a prime minister. A week later, another detective brought in a thirty-three-year-old man named Viktor Gunnarsson for questioning, since he had made unbalanced and threatening remarks about Palme before the murder. Wingren's intuition was again set to work, and he suspected that Gunnarsson might well have been the man trying to hide in the Saga cinema.

There is no question that Viktor Gunnarsson was an odd character. He had traveled extensively and spoke fluent English, French, and Spanish, among other languages. By no means a workaholic, he lived on the country's generous social benefits in between doing odd jobs for a few months at a time. He had once been a security guard, but was dismissed after being suspected of stealing from his employer. On and off, he worked as a translator, a newspaper boy, and a baby-sitter. Gunnarsson then tried his hand at teaching, but was fired from schools with clockwork regularity, once for striking a boy who had annoyed him, at other times for setting his pupils a very bad example with regard to punctuality and behavior. Gunnarsson had lived in the United States for a few years before returning to Sweden, and his political views were extremely right wing. He made it no secret that he thought Palme a dangerous communist who was selling out Sweden to the Eastern bloc. One school had fired him for teaching his pupils the "truth" about the Vietnam War, from a pro-American standpoint. The female sex was Gunnarsson's prime interest in life, as one of his teacher colleagues put it. At the time of his arrest, he had finally found a job that he liked wholeheartedly: he was teaching an all-female class of would-be holiday tour guides.

The evening of the murder, Viktor Gunnarsson had gone to a café called Mon Chéri, situated in the Kungsgatan not far from the murder site. He often used to hang out in this café, talking to strangers and trying to pick up women. This evening, he met three young women and joined them at their table. Introducing himself as the American Vic Gunnison, and speaking Swedish with an American accent, he started talking politics, boasting that he had three times debated against Olof Palme in various open-air meetings. Each time, Palme had retreated in confusion, hammered by Vic's clever arguments. Another time, he had debated against Communist leader Lars Werner, and the latter had been so annoyed by the American's ready repartee that he had wanted to resort to fisticuffs to settle their dispute. Vic said that he himself should have a seat in the government, to combat Palme's bullshit attitude and save Sweden from communism and atheism. One of his remarks was "If you say what you think in Sweden today, you will get shot in the back!" Annoyed by Vic's endless harangues and half-baked political claptrap, one of the women finally told him to shut up. Olof Palme was her uncle, she lied, and she did not want to hear any more insulting remarks about him. The morning after, all three women remembered this bizarre conversation with a frisson of horror when they saw the newspaper headlines: was it the killer they had met, on his way to shoot Olof Palme in the back?

The young women, all of them alert, clear-headed witnesses, told the police that Vic had been wearing a green jacket and blue jeans. Although they agreed that his behavior had been both uncouth and unbalanced, none of them had thought him obviously insane. When they had left the café at 10:40, their talkative admirer had been sorry to see them leave, and he had given them all his telephone number. Thus it was easy for the police to track him down, and he was brought in for questioning on March 8. When questioned by Wingren and another detective, Gunnarsson seemed incapable of giving a straight answer to a straight question. When asked why he gave people a false name and pretended to be an American, he airily said that this was just a bit of fun, and Vic Gunnison was in fact his artist's name. He admitted that he had met the three women at Mon Chéri, but was evasive with regard to what he had done later that fateful evening. Finally, the two detectives managed to elicit that after leaving Mon Chéri, he had gone to the Rigoletto cinema to watch *Rocky IV*. After enjoying the antics of the grunting, muscle-bound pugilist, Vic felt hungry and went to have a late-night snack at the local McDonald's. Sure enough, some boys reported to the police that an odd, talkative man had come barging into the hamburger restaurant at 1:10 a.m. Speaking English with an American accent, he had made it clear that he disliked Palme intensely, and this of course struck the boys as remarkable when they later learned about the murder. Thus the police knew that Gunnarsson had been in close proximity to the murder site both before and after the killing of Olof Palme.

On the evening of March 8, after Gunnarsson had been questioned all day, Börje Wingren arranged an identification lineup with the two witnesses from the Saga cinema. One of them vacillated between Gunnarsson and another man before finally picking out the suspect. The other witness did not pick out anyone from the lineup. Gunnarsson, who was completely unfazed by the situation, decided to pull a prank: as he approached the one-way mirror behind which the second witness was sitting, he made a threatening gesture as if he was going to strike her through the mirror. Believing that he could really see her, the poor woman broke down sobbing, and the detectives angrily called the weird suspect to order.[4] One of the detectives then showed both witnesses photographs of Gunnarsson. In the police protocol, Wingren wrote that after picking out Gunnarsson's photograph, they both felt certain he was the man they had seen at the movie theater. But when Wingren presented the case against Gunnarsson to Hans Holmér and the Palme Room, their reaction was not what he had wanted. Holmér said that the suspect seemed just plain crazy, a case for psychiatric care rather than criminal prosecution. To Wingren's great chagrin, Gunnarsson was released. As cheerful and arrogant as ever, he went back to the school, boasting to his amazed girl pupils that the police had questioned him for eleven hours, suspecting him of having murdered Olof Palme. With his intellectual superiority, he said, he had simply been making fun of them.

But Börje Wingren was by no means giving up: with admirable doggedness, he kept on accumulating evidence against the oddball schoolmaster. It turned out that Gunnarsson had retrieved his green parka from a friend's basement on February 27, the day before the murder, and the Mon Chéri witnesses verified that he had worn this garment the night of the murder. They added that he had carried a small bag, resembling somewhat the one the witness Nieminen had seen the killer trying to open or close during his mad dash down David Bagares Gata. Wingren had a problem with regard to the two Saga witnesses, however, since the movie theater staff were unanimous that no ticket had been sold to any latecomer that evening, and that it was impossible to sneak in unobserved. The dynamic detective was convinced that his two witnesses were telling the truth, however. After a thorough investigation, Wingren and his colleagues suspected that the janitors were in the habit of drinking wine in the basement while the films were played, and that they were lying to cover up this fact. The stalemate was broken when one of the janitors, relishing his few minutes of fame as a star witness, later told a newspaper journalist that a strange man had indeed bought a ticket very late that evening, although he and the ticket seller could (or would) not describe this individual. Thus, it remains unknown whether these unreliable witnesses had lied to prevent their indiscretions being known, or if they were now lying to the journalist (and the police) about the latecomer they could not describe.

At a dawn raid on March 12, the police brought Gunnarsson in for further questioning. Wingren had worried that the schoolmaster would have used his four-day respite to destroy evidence, but when his tiny apartment was searched, a quantity of right-wing pamphlets were found, some of them with handwritten notes that left it no secret that Gunnarsson detested Palme and his politics. The police also found the green parka, which was sent for forensic examination. Gunnarsson's phone book contained no fewer than 2,293 names! In his calendar, the page covering the week before the murder had been torn out. On an American newspaper found in his apartment was a crude drawing resembling a tombstone marked with the letter *P*!

Börje Wingren was a tough cop, and he did his best to give Gunnarsson a hard time during the lengthy questionings. It annoyed him greatly that the weird suspect was not at all impressed with his interrogation techniques. Completely unfazed by the seriousness of his situation, Gunnarsson just laughed when Wingren told him, later on March 12, that he was now formally under arrest, suspected of having murdered the prime minister of Sweden. For several days, Wingren directed a fusillade of questions at the suspect. He tried to bluff Gunnarsson by saying that the two Saga witnesses were people who knew him well, but the suspect kept denying he had set foot in that cinema. Gunnarsson still vacillated when asked to describe his movements between 10:30 p.m. and 1:00 a.m. the night of the murder; however, he finally volunteered that he had spoken to two boys, one of whom was of Pol-

ish descent, before leaving Mon Chéri to eat a hamburger at McDonald's before *Rocky IV*. Wingren did nothing to try to find these two boys, since he was
convinced Gunnarsson was lying.

As for Gunnarsson's alleged later visit to the Rigoletto cinema, Wingren
shouted, "You lie! You never went to the Rigoletto! None of the staff there
ever saw you!" He then forced Gunnarsson to give a blow-by-blow account of
Rocky IV, something the oddball schoolmaster accomplished with enthusiasm. "You could have seen that film any day," Wingren muttered. When the
suspect confidently stated that very many people had been in the theater for
Rocky IV, his tormentor exulted, "Now I have taken you in a lie! In fact, just
103 people saw the movie, in a cinema with the capacity to seat 1,201." Undeterred by this setback, the teacher took a perverse delight in teasing and annoying his opponent and imitating his country dialect. Gunnarsson alternated
between Swedish and English and replied "Bullshit!" to the frantic detective's
accusations; he even imitated his favorite actor, Eddie Murphy, in "Beverly
Hills Cop." Furious, Wingren roared, "Admit that you did it, you bastard, we
know everything about you!" and shook his fist in Gunnarsson's face, but to
no avail.[5] When he was locked up in a cell after each day's questioning, many
policemen came to see Gunnarsson as a curiosity. As lighthearted as ever, he
willingly entertained them, cracking jokes and imitating various actors until
the cops were laughing uproariously.

At this stage of the investigation, Hans Holmér was becoming convinced
that Gunnarsson was one of the people involved in the murder conspiracy, if
not the actual killer. He was impressed by the energy demonstrated by
Wingren and his detective colleagues and the steady flow of damaging evidence against the schoolmaster. The arrest was front-page news all over the
world, and the Swedish newspaper press became a willing ally of the police,
uncritically repeating every damning circumstance linked to Gunnarsson.
Under Swedish law, it is not permitted to divulge the name of a murder suspect, but "the thirty-three-year-old," as he was called, was made into a mur-
derous monster. There was talk that he belonged to a right-wing extremist
movement, and the papers speculated that he held Nazi meetings in his apartment, since suspicious-looking foreigners had been seen to enter it. Gunnarsson retorted that his foreign friends were in fact refugees from Chile and Ar-
gentina, and thus very unlikely to have any fascist leanings.

Few of Viktor Gunnarsson's acquaintances had much good to say about his
character, and the police and newspapers latched on to their damning testimony with gusto.[6] Gunnarsson lied and cheated, tried to impress people by
pretending to be an American playboy, and seduced women by telling them
that he was a famous film director who would make them movie stars. Another of his untrue stories was that he had once served in the U.S. Army and

fought in the Vietnam War. He sometimes added that he had killed several "gooks," some with his bare hands, others with an M-16 machine gun. Not fewer than seventy former girlfriends of his contacted the police, some of them with spicy tales to tell. One said that Vic used to say that he had been trained by the FBI and CIA and had access to a powerful handgun; another, that he had once said that Palme was on a death list and that blood would flow on the streets of Stockholm. Wingren was amazed when Gunnarsson admitted to knowing some people in the CIA, but the suspect then ruined this sinister effect by claiming that he had just been carrying a fake FBI badge in his wallet to impress the ladies! A headmaster told the police that he thought Gunnarsson was very unsuitable as a teacher: he was irresponsible, silly, and easily led, and lived in a world of his own. A restaurant waiter added that he had banned Gunnarsson from the premises, since he always went up to people, even complete strangers, and tried to impress them with his ridiculous stories. In marked contrast to his lecherous tendencies and compulsive lying, Gunnarsson claimed to be a born-again Christian. He did belong to a Free Church congregation, although the parsons joined the chorus of damaging character witnesses, saying that Gunnarsson was sometimes disposed to be deceitful, and that he had illicitly been using the church premises to teach Swedish to various immigrants.

On Hans Holmér's initiative, much police work was devoted to finding out more about Gunnarsson and to investigating whether he was part of a larger conspiracy. As we know, Holmér was convinced the murder was the work of an accomplished team of assassins, and he doubted that anyone as unbalanced as Gunnarsson could have pulled off such a skillful murder single-handedly. He also had to admit that the schoolmaster's actions the evening of the murder—boasting to everyone how much he detested Olof Palme and freely giving people his telephone number—were hardly those of an ice-cold professional killer. Both Lisbet and Mårten Palme failed to pick Gunnarsson out in lineups.

Still, Holmér was pleased to have a suspect in custody, particularly during the funeral of Olof Palme on March 15, attended by leading politicians from all over the world. Some of the Social Democrats were frightened that the killers of Olof Palme would come back with a vengeance during this ceremony and wipe out the rest of the world's socialist leaders in one blow. The policemaster did not agree, although he made sure the security arrangements were rigorous, involving a force of two thousand cops. The only drama came when Israeli premier Shimon Peres refused to go by car in the funeral cortege, since, as a Jew, he could not travel in a motor vehicle during the Sabbath. Holmér gruffly replied that he could either go by car or remain in his hotel room. Peres

The first police lineup seen by Lisbet Palme. A jolly-looking Viktor Gunnarsson is number 5. Reproduced by permission of the Swedish National Police Board.

ignored him, however, and walked the whole way, surrounded by bodyguards armed to the teeth. In the end, Holmér was pleased when the funeral was carried out without a hitch, himself regaining some much-needed prestige.

The police received tips that Gunnarsson had once delivered newspapers in the Old Town, and that he might have made a note of the code to open the door to the Palme house for surveillance use. It turned out that he had indeed delivered newspapers in the area, but not for very long, and nowhere near Palme's apartment. Other people told the police that Gunnarsson had a tall blond German friend, and the police speculated that this might be the elusive Shadow. The German was arrested, but Lisbet and Mårten Palme failed to pick him out from the police lineup, along with sixteen other witnesses, and it was soon apparent that he was perfectly innocent. Gunnarsson's green parka was sent to Wiesbaden in Germany for forensic testing, and police hopes rose when the jacket was found to contain some particles suspected to be gunpowder residue. In another of the endless questionings, Wingren asked the suspect to admit he had handled firearms before. When Gunnarsson denied it, the detective screamed, "Now I have taken you in another lie! The world's foremost experts have just found gunpowder residue on your jacket! Can you explain that?" Smiling superciliously, Gunnarsson replied, "The police must have planted it!" Wingren looked as if he might explode.[7]

It then appeared as if the police had finally struck lucky. An African man working as an unlicensed cab driver told them that the night of the murder, a strange man had tried to board his vehicle not far from the scene of the murder. Screaming, "Drive me anywhere—I will pay you anything you want!" he had pulled out a wallet to show that he had money. The African had been reluctant to pick him up, however, since the man was a desperate-looking character and appeared to be on the run. The mystery man had finally run off into the night, yelling, "You will suffer for this you damned nigger!" At a police lineup, the African appeared to pick out Gunnarsson. Wingren and Holmér were overjoyed, and "the Negro," as the racist policemen called their star witness, was the hero of the day. Holmér even recorded that the jubilant detectives joked that to reduce the frequency of serious crime, more Negroes should be imported and posted on every street corner of the Swedish capital![8]

The long and grueling questionings, and Wingren's gruff hostility, had finally taken their toll on the once cocky Viktor Gunnarsson. Going to bed that night, he realized the full horror of his situation. He was surrounded by people who wanted to frame him for a crime he had not committed. The newspapers had made him into a monster, and every person wanting to malign the hated "thirty-three-year-old" was greeted with open arms. Even his former wife, who lived in the United States, had denigrated him on national television. Several Swedish newspapers had broken the law and published his name and photograph, with the excuse that the murder of Olof Palme was a national emergency, and that the identity of the killer must be made known. The frightened Gunnarsson realized that if he died in his sleep, he would be known forever as the murderer of Olof Palme, and Hans Holmér would become Sweden's national hero.

Viktor Gunnarsson was put in an isolation cell and guarded rigorously around the clock to prevent some Swedish Jack Ruby from ending his life before he was put on trial. As prosecutor Karl-Gerhard Svensson was preparing to formally charge Gunnarsson with the murder, he and his assistant had occasion to read through some of the police files. To their horror and astonishment, they found evidence that Wingren had coached "the Negro" before the lineup.[9] Completely disregarding standard police procedure, the maverick detective had ordered his colleagues to show the witness a number of photographs, including one of Gunnarsson, but the African had picked out two other men (numbers 4 and 8). At the actual lineup, the confused witness, who spoke very little Swedish, asked to see "number 4 and 8, the ones I showed them yesterday," clearly referring to the two men whose photographs he had picked out the day before. No interpreter was present. As the men in the lineup approached him one by one, the African again asked to see "number 8 and the second one." Gunnarsson's defense lawyer, who knew nothing about the photo lineup the day before, was nonplussed. Wingren then cleverly turned the situation around, asking the African if by "the second one" he meant number 2 in the current lineup (Gunnarsson), and the obedient witness readily complied.

Furious, Svensson ordered a direct confrontation between Gunnarsson and the African on March 19, during which the latter faltered considerably, admitting that he had not seen much of the face of the man who had tried to enter his car the night of the murder. The man had screamed at him in Swedish and English, he said. Gunnarsson then started to speak French, the African's own language; he came from the small French-speaking country Benin. The African was amazed, saying that if Gunnarsson was able to speak such good French, he could not be the man who had frightened him. During these bizarre proceedings, Svensson formed a very low opinion of the African, and even doubted whether the incident with the man demanding transportation had taken place at all.

He ordered that Gunnarsson be immediately released. At just about this time, the padded Hans Holmér was preparing another of his grandiose press conferences, expecting to announce that Gunnarsson had been formally charged with the murder. At the last minute, Wranghult came running to tell him the disastrous news. The police-master had to change his speech completely, but it must be admitted he handled the situation brilliantly. The integrity of Sweden's justice system was a pinnacle for the rest of the world to emulate, he boasted, and then went on to criticize the newspapers that had published Gunnarsson's name and picture. The stage was thus set for him to announce that since an important link in the chain of evidence against the suspect had been found wanting, the thirty-three-year-old had been released.

Hans Holmér's unctuous speech was just for the gallery. Furious with Svensson, the police-master went to the prosecutor's superior, Claes Zeime, demanding that he immediately be replaced. When Zeime refused, Holmér went to his friends in the government. Svensson and his subordinates realized that their days working on the Palme inquiry were numbered. They even suspected, perhaps not entirely without reason, that Holmér was bugging the office he had kindly offered them at police headquarters. Svensson tried to reach a compromise with the police-master, demanding that at least the maverick Wingren be removed from the investigation, but Holmér curtly refused, feeling he had the upper hand in the conflict.

Nevertheless, Svensson had found a vital lead. Acting more as Gunnarsson's defense lawyer than as a prosecutor, he tried to get the police to find the two boys Gunnarsson claimed to have spoken to at Mon Chéri after the three women had left, but Holmér and his men did very little. They instead demanded that Gunnarsson be confronted with seventy-four witnesses, to investigate whether he had been anywhere near the site of the murder. Svensson refused, claiming that such a marathon series of lineups would be completely unnecessary, but Gunnarsson and his defense lawyer had no objections. A total of fifty-five lineups were eventually performed, some of them in late April, others in mid-May, without any murder scene witness picking Gunnarsson out. A woman identified him as a man she had seen behaving mysteriously at a Kentucky Fried Chicken restaurant opposite the Grand cinema at 9:00 p.m. the night of the murder, but it turned out that she, too, had previously been shown Gunnarsson's photograph by the police. The police later found a man who had been waiting for his girlfriend at the restaurant about this time and who fitted the witness's original description very well.[10]

From this time onward, the case against Gunnarsson was rapidly undermined. On May 12, Svensson finally managed to persuade the police to make a formal media appeal to find the boys at Mon Chéri. Two boys promptly responded, one of whom was of Polish descent, just as Gunnarsson had said; they claimed to have spoken with the schoolmaster until after 11:00 p.m. Thus Gunnarsson's own statement that he had remained at Mon Chéri could be confirmed by two alert witnesses, meaning he could not have been waiting for the Palmes outside the movie theater.[11] Svensson also investigated some of the other "evidence" against Gunnarsson, and found that the damning statements about "blood on the streets of Stockholm" had been deliberately taken out of context: what Gunnarsson had actually said was that when the Russians invaded Sweden, they would kill Palme and his hangers-on in a bloodbath. The long-awaited verdict from the German experts scrutinizing the green parka was that one of the two particles of gunpowder residue was definitely not from Winchester .357 armor-piercing ammunition; the second one could be excluded with 95 percent certainty. As for the African and his testimony, it is notable that a few weeks later, he again contacted the police, this time claiming to have seen the elusive Phantom walking down the Sveavägen shortly before the murder. It is very likely that he was one of the many unbalanced characters interfering with the murder investigation by telling untrue stories, or a scoundrel hoping to get his hands on part of the reward.

The prosecutor Svensson formally wrote Gunnarsson off as a suspect on May 16. The police kept investigating him for quite some time, however, and in early 1987, some further incriminating circumstances were brought to light. Gunnarsson's phone book contained the name of a notorious violent criminal, and also those of some Bulgarian gangsters. A key found in his apartment fitted the lock of a shop owned by one of the Bulgarians. A former girlfriend of Gunnarsson's claimed to have seen a large revolver in his apartment. Rumors also spread that Gunnarsson had been trying to change his identity and leave Sweden. The result was that the prosecutors reopened the case against him. The police arranged two lengthy phone-tap operations, but without anything incriminating coming to light; in particular, they found no link between Gunnarsson and organized crime. The schoolmaster was again questioned by the police in January 1988, but under much more relaxed conditions than back in 1986. Detective lieutenant Åke Röst, who led the questionings, found Gunnarsson an odd character who was not always disposed to tell the truth about his activities, but the case against him was very weak indeed. Had it not been for his own habitual bragging and untruthfulness, and Wingren's bungling of the early police investigation, he would have been cleared at a much earlier stage.[12]

Börje Wingren wrote a book directly accusing Viktor Gunnarsson of murdering Palme.[13] His strongest arguments are that Gunnarsson hated Palme and his politics, that he was definitely close to the murder scene on the night in question, and that he was not frank with the police regarding his whereabouts. Most people would have stuck to the truth when accused of murder, but the oddball schoolmaster changed his story, lied and played games with the police. With his megalomaniac attitude, Gunnarsson saw himself as being sent by God to free Sweden from communism and atheism, Wingren suggested, and he was definitely crazy and fanatical enough to kill Olof Palme. The detective goes on to argue that Gunnarsson's clothes were not unlike those worn by the murderer. When shown a series of photographs of coats and jackets, Anna Hage and some other witnesses picked out his green parka as the garment most resembling that of the killer. Still, the difference between Gunnarsson's green parka and the long black overcoat that the best murder scene witnesses were certain the killer was wearing is a notable one.

In his book, Wingren also points out that a witness tentatively identified Gunnarsson as a man who was running on the Regeringsgatan, not far from the murder scene, a few minutes after the murder, but this witness himself admitted he could see hardly anything of the running man's face. Wingren stubbornly upholds the credibility of the African and accuses Svensson of incompetence for releasing the suspect. The three women at Mon Chéri said that the bugbear "Vic" had smelt strongly of garlic: was it just a coincidence that the African said exactly the same thing about the man who had tried to get into his car? The African also observed that the man had been wearing only one glove; had the man discarded the other one because it was stained by gunpowder residue? A left-hand leather glove had been found in Gunnarsson's apartment, without the right-hand one; when confronted with this anomaly, the schoolteacher said simply, "One glove is better than none!"

Wingren's book recounts that some witnesses had seen Gunnarsson without his bushy dark mustache in the days before the murder: Had he shaved it off and later regrown it to disguise his appearance? This is a question the police could easily have resolved had they made a systematic inquiry among the suspect's friends, colleagues, and pupils, but no evidence proves this was ever done. One of the alibi witnesses from Mon Chéri resolutely stated that Gunnarsson had his mustache the night in question. And if Gunnarsson had shaved his mustache, this would serve to further undermine the credibility of the African, who confidently stated that the man who had approached his car had had a mustache. Wingren also tells his readers that someone wrote a series of anonymous letters to various dignitaries, claiming to have knowledge of who murdered Olof Palme. Since the letters contained American slang, and since the writer emphasized that the thirty-three-year-old was innocent, Wingren proposes that they were written by Gunnarsson himself. This is possible but far from certain; in either case, the letters prove very little.[14]

In his book, Wingren wisely refrains from commenting on whether Gunnarsson was part of a larger conspiracy to murder Olof Palme. Later authors have been less prudent, boldly suggesting that the oddball schoolmaster was a hitman in the employ of the CIA, just as he himself bragged to his girlfriends.[15] These authors have a point, in that it would have been nearly impossible for Gunnarsson to murder Palme on his own. When the three women walked into Mon Chéri between 9:00 and 9:15, Gunnarsson was there. Some other witnesses, including a restaurant waiter, hinted that he had already been at Mon Chéri for quite some time, having arrived perhaps as early as 7:00 p.m. No one saw him sneak out of the café during this time. Thus Gunnarsson would have been unable to stake out the Palmes at the Grand cinema. The three girls agreed that the teacher had been talking to them until they left at 10:30 or 10:40. He then remained at Mon Chéri chatting with other people, the two boys among them, for at least thirty or forty minutes more, perhaps as long as an hour. One of the boys was certain that he had consulted his watch when Gunnarsson talked about catching a movie, and that it had been well after 11:00 p.m.

Had Gunnarsson been on his own, he would have needed superhuman powers of speed to catch the Palmes outside Dekorima, as well as remarkable talents of telepathy to know exactly where they were and which way they were going home. It is not a likely scenario that the schoolmaster would one minute be chatting to various strangers at a café and then suddenly dash off to shoot the prime minister, whom he bumped into by complete accident. And where would he get the .357 magnum revolver? It seems unlikely that he carried a large handgun with him routinely. Wingren has suggested that he might have kept it in his camera bag, but it is questionable whether a long-barreled revolver would fit into such a small bag.

If it is presumed that Gunnarsson was part of a larger conspiracy, many of these difficulties disappear. He could have left Mon Chéri at 11:10 or so and then met the coconspirators to find out where the Palmes were and get the revolver. It would not have been technically impossible for him to run to the Dekorima corner to await the Palmes there, perhaps as a part of a larger gang of murderers staking out various possible routes home for the prime minister. The main drawback of this theory is that no sane person would involve such a man as Gunnarsson in a life-or-death conspiracy. We know about his scatter-brained, impetuous nature and his habit of bragging even to complete strangers about his exploits. If the CIA really had a reason to assassinate Palme, plenty of tough, experienced operatives could have served as the hit man. Even if the CIA wanted an assassin with local knowledge, they would not have hired a clearly unbalanced individual who had no experience with firearms and whose coolness under pressure could by no means by relied on. Nor can it be considered rational of Gunnarsson, had he been part of a murder conspiracy, to sit chatting to people most of the evening, making it clear to everyone that he disliked Palme and freely handing out his telephone number.

No technical evidence against Gunnarsson exists, and no evidence he ever possessed a firearm, apart from gossip from imaginative people doing their best to help the police solve the murder. Not a single murder scene witness was able to pick him out: one of them even emphatically denied he was the killer. The scandalously incompetent police work renders it very questionable that Gunnarsson was the man who entered the Saga cinema, nor can the confused testimony of the African be given any credence. The emergence of the two alibi witnesses from Mon Chéri meant that the police had no conclusive evidence that Gunnarsson had lied about his whereabouts the night Palme was killed. Importantly, Gunnarsson had no history of violent crime. Once, a headmaster had sacked him abruptly and told him he was completely useless as a teacher, adding that he should see a psychiatrist since he was clearly not right in the head. Many people would feel a strong urge to resort to physical violence if insulted in such a way, but Gunnarsson just skulked off. In a bizarre, ghostwritten autobiography that he published to try to get some money out of his unwelcome notoriety, Gunnarsson asserted that he was not a violent man and always avoided a fight.[16] Nothing indicates that he possessed either the audacity or the strength of character needed to plan and carry out an assassination. And as for the allegations that he possessed a superior intelligence, based mostly on his linguistic aptitude, it must be said that his adult life story was a record of one failure after another. He could not even find a permanent job, and most people regarded him as a buffoon who could not be taken seriously.

In a discussion of Viktor Gunnarsson's guilt, it is important also to scrutinize the activities of his main accuser, Börje Wingren. The two prosecutors, Claes Zeime and Karl-Gerhard Svensson, blasted the police work as completely incompetent, stressing that Wingren had had a bad reputation even before he came to Stockholm; among other things, he had been accused of falsifying evidence in another murder case. Leading detective Ingemar Krusell added that in spite of Wingren's many years of police experience, his questionings were parodies that could be used in the police academy as examples of what not to do; they showed how a verbally gifted suspect could turn the tables on a slow-witted detective.

The 1987 commission bluntly accused Wingren of deliberately coaching the African to frame Gunnarsson. The National Audit Office experts added that Wingren had falsified his questioning of one of Lisbet Palme's colleagues to indicate that she had seen the Shadow. In agreement with the 1999 commission, they found it amazing and culpable that a man with Wingren's background and methods was employed in the investigation of the murder of the prime minister. Other authors have suggested that Wingren even tried to bribe a Swedish gangster to testify that he had sold Gunnarsson a revolver prior to the murder.[17] Wingren himself has retorted that none of the earlier accusations against him for various indiscretions had resulted in a conviction. Both before and after the murder of Olof Palme, he took part in successful murder investigations. Yet his desire to be the man who solved the murder of the prime minister and his dislike of the irritating Viktor Gunnarsson seem to have overcome whatever sound judgment he possessed, and he must take a large amount of the blame for the disastrous police mistakes in the case.

In 1989, Gunnarsson was formally written off as a suspect for the second time. The prosecutors and police were in perfect agreement that he was innocent, but some members of the Swedish public were reluctant to agree. Rumors that the hated thirty-three-year-old had murdered Olof Palme still circulated. Several daily newspapers had published Gunnarsson's photograph, and his situation soon became impossible. People screamed "Murderer!" at him in the streets and threatened him with violence, and it was impossible for him to get a job. Viktor Gunnarsson was finally hounded out of Sweden by the universal hostility he encountered. He emigrated to his beloved United States, where he settled in Salisbury, North Carolina. Local people soon began to gossip about this mysterious Swede, who was quite a ladies' man and who seemed to have ample funds, although he never did any work. In early 1994, Gunnarsson's naked body was found in a ditch outside Salisbury; the investigation concluded that he had been murdered by a former policeman whose girlfriend he had seduced.[18] Viktor Gunnarsson was clearly a weird character, but he was not the murderer of Olof Palme, rather a second victim.

RED HERRINGS

It is a curious circumstance that three people independently warned the authorities about an impending assassination attempt on Olof Palme.[1] On February 8, 1986, Yugoslav former soldier of fortune Ivan von Birchan approached the office of one of the Stockholm civic councilors, claiming that a CIA agent named Charles Morgan had tried to hire him to kill Palme. Although he would have been paid $2.8 million for the assassination, von Birchan declined. The reason the CIA was trying to kill Palme was that a secret organization headed by Henry Kissinger and Caspar Weinberger wanted to prevent him from being elected secretary-general of the United Nations. The police were initially quite interested in this lead, particularly since the Yugoslav had more than once met Viktor Gunnarsson. Von Birchan knew that Gunnarsson himself used to pretend he was a CIA agent but had not believed him. Other people described the Yugoslav as a swindler and habitual liar, however, and the elusive Charles Morgan was never tracked down.

On February 20, 1986, right-wing extremist Anders Larsson sent Palme a letter containing a newspaper cutting with the words "Olof Palme dead." When asked by the newspaper press, Larsson first said that this had just been a sick joke, and that he had been amazed and appalled when someone had shot Palme. He then hinted that he had gotten the advance word of Palme's death from a right-wing friend of his who had a small antiquarian bookshop; this friend had heard from secret service sources that the SÄPO were planning to kill Palme. But Larsson, too, was known as an unreliable character who told bogus stories to make himself seem interesting, and he was a copious writer of confused letters to various authorities. His right-wing activities had caused the SÄPO to put him under surveillance, and his accusation that they were involved in the murder could have been an attempt at revenge. Again, the only good explanation for his warning Palme just eight days before the murder is plain coincidence.

On February 27, a crazy immigrant living in southern Sweden actually phoned Palme's secretary, saying that a man from Gothenburg had threatened to kill both himself and the prime minister. The caller objected to the special tax that Palme had put on camels (he himself owned some of these animals), but the secretary politely responded that the tax was on stock certificates, and the immigrant seemed much relieved.

Another obvious lead for the early police investigation was to investigate the many people who had shown an obsession with or a pronounced dislike of Palme, manifested in their personally contacting him or his family. Many of them were lunatics or fanatics and could quickly be written off. The only interesting lead was a young man who had corresponded with Olof Palme since 1979. He claimed to be a university student but was really a construction worker, and had made confused and bombastic boasts about being Palme's chosen successor. His sole claim to fame was that he had once received a scholarship from the Social Democrats to visit the United Nations headquarters in New York. The lure of the Big Apple had been too much for him, however, and he had behaved badly, drinking to excess and interviewing various dignitaries, pretending to be a newspaper journalist. This man had sometimes spoken of Palme with envy and hatred, and one of Palme's sons knew him as an objectionable person. He had a license to own a revolver, although not a .357 magnum. He claimed to have been active at a Norwegian construction site at the time of the murder, but the foreman noted that he had actually absented himself shortly before the murder and bribed a workmate to collect his salary and sign his paperwork. The police went to the building site and started questioning people, with high hopes of a vital breakthrough, but the result was yet another farcical ending. The construction worker confessed that the reason he had abandoned his tools was that he had drunk so heavily that he felt incapable of locomotion on the morning of February 28. The workmates, who helped cover up his absence, later verified his story to the police.[2]

An additional line of inquiry was to investigate the many people who had made threats against Palme. In 1985 and early 1986, the prime minister had received ninety-five hundred letters. Of these, two hundred were threatening, abusive, or just plain weird. Some particularly vehement letters of abuse had come from an anonymous society that worked for the abolishment of road salt. A mad fisherman had written angry letters to the government claiming that amateur fishermen were threatening his livelihood. The man later wrote a threatening letter to the minister of agriculture, saying that if he did not prohibit amateur fishing by May 1, he would join the other parasite (Palme) in hell. But after months of painstaking police work, it was found that none of the identified writers of hate mail to Palme could be seriously suspected of having anything to do with the murder.[3]

One hot tip concerned some jolly Swedes on a vacation abroad, who had shouted, "Now let's see if anybody has shot that damned Palme!" when buying the newspapers from back home. The men were identified and admitted their words had been a sick joke. Suspicions were also aroused by the mysterious "Mönsterås Man," who had been traveling on a bus in the Swedish outback on February 27. He had been behaving uncouthly even by provincial Swedish standards, groping the female passengers and swigging liberally from a vodka bottle, before exiting with the words "Tomorrow I will go to Stockholm and shoot that bastard Palme!" But the local police force identified the Mönsterås Man as a patient just released from the local asylum; he had a solid alibi for the night of the murder.[4]

Aided by some leading Social Democratic politicians, the police also did their best to investigate whether recent political events might hold a clue to the killer's identity. Shortly before the murder, Palme had without warning increased the taxation on gains from the stock market, leading to a sharp market decline. Had a ruined market trader killed the Prime Minister as revenge? One of the darkest episodes in modern Swedish history had taken place in February 1946, when the Social Democratic government had cravenly agreed to extradite a large troop of Baltic freedom fighters to torture and death in the Soviet prison camps. Might some Baltic refugee have decided to kill Palme on the fortieth anniversary of this dismal event? Another hotly debated issue concerned the submarines infesting the Swedish archipelago. Not long before the murder, a group of naval officers had spoken up in the press to declare that they did not trust Olof Palme and his ability to make sure Swedish territory was defended. Palme's decision to visit Russia later in 1986 had also given rise to discontent among the military and police. Had one of these men snapped and decided to murder Palme, who was regarded as a Soviet collaborator by some right-wing elements? The police could find little or no solid evidence supporting any of these theories.

Nor had the relations between the Social Democratic ruling class and the Swedish secret police been particularly warm. The SÄPO showed little loyalty to the Social Democrats, whom they distrusted as dangerous left-wingers. The Social Democrats returned the SÄPO's distrust in full. In his youth, Palme had himself dabbled in secret service work, and he could thus well appreciate the need to have a loyal secret police organization. When, in the late 1960s, the communists were threatening to take over the trade unions, the Social Democrats went to the length of creating a secret organization of their own, the IB, that spied on communist elements at universities and workplaces. In 1972, left-wing journalists Jan Guillou and Peter Bratt exposed this covert organization in the media. Palme had trouble explaining the need for this loyalist secret police, the aims of which were certainly at variance with his own left-wing rhetoric. He took his frustration out on Guillou and Bratt, who were rewarded with lengthy jail terms for their great scoop.

At an early stage of the murder investigation, it was decided that Olof Palme's personal life was to come under scrutiny. Hans Holmér decided to take care of this in person, together with a friend of his named Ebbe Carlsson who had known Palme well. Nothing much is known about the outcome, except that Holmér quickly ruled out a motive related to Palme's private sphere. It is well known that Palme was financially very prudent: although he was a wealthy man, he lived frugally and had no extravagant tastes or addictions. Palme's family life appeared to be happy: his marriage was long lasting and his three sons, to whom he was devoted, were promising youths. The utmost secrecy was maintained concerning this part of the investigation. According to the archives of the 1999 commission, a certain detective, lieutenant Gunnar Hierner, was given the task to liaise with the Palme family. Although Lisbet Palme had a low opinion of the police, she agreed to speak to Hierner. After several conversations with her, he reported to Holmér that there was no chance the murder concerned a family drama or was a crime of passion.[5] The Palme apartment was not searched by the police until two weeks after the murder, nor were the neighbors questioned. Karl-Gerhard Svensson learned from Palme's brother that the prime minister had made daily annotations in a diary, and made concerted efforts to see them, since he believed that Holmér had been overhasty in writing off a murder motive related to Palme's personal life. Although Svensson tried for months, Lisbet Palme refused to hand over Olof's diaries, and Holmér made no effort to persuade her otherwise.[6]

Some commentators have not agreed with Holmér's benign picture of the prime minister's private life. Firstly, there were (unfounded) rumors that Palme had seduced the wife of another Social Democratic politician, or even that the furious husband had killed him as revenge.[7] Later in 1986, Swedish and British newspapers printed stories that Palme had had an affair with Emma Rothschild, the daughter of the immensely wealthy Lord Rothschild. It was speculated that he had phoned her just before leaving for the cinema; this, it was darkly hinted, was how the murderer knew he was going to the Grand cinema. Again, there does not appear to be much to these allegations, except the fact that Emma Rothschild was a close friend to not only Olof, but the entire Palme family.[8] According to persistent rumors, Olof Palme had an affair with Shirley MacLaine. These have lately been confirmed by Ms. MacLaine herself, but her additional claim that she was attracted to Palme because he was a reincarnation of Charlemagne does not aid her credibility. Once when Palme was in New York, he showed his friend Harry Schein a letter or telegram from Shirley MacLaine, inviting him to come and see her. Palme preferred to have dinner with his friend the bureaucrat, however, an unlikely choice if he had been enjoying an affair with the vivacious actress.[9] The archives of the 1999 commission mention nothing about any of these alleged affairs, but instead contain a brief and cryptic note from Lieutenant Hierner that the clandestine police investigation of the husband of Palme's private secretary, Anne-Marie Willsson, was long kept a secret even from the detectives investigating the murder. Thus, if Palme really had a skeleton in his closet, it would appear to have been closer to home.

Olof Palme was a very honest man, and there is no question of him taking bribes or engaging in dubious business ventures. It was quite a blow to him when, in 1985, he was accused of tax evasion in an unsavory scandal, the so-called Harvard case.[10] Palme had given a guest lecture at Harvard University without accepting any fee, instead arranging that one of his sons would get a scholarship to this famous university. His enemy Jan Guillou found out about this and asked the Prime Minister on live radio whether he had ever done any work under the table to evade taxation. When the startled Palme said no, Guillou sprang the news of the Harvard case: surely, Palme should have paid tax on this underhanded lecture fee. Palme's political opponents were jubilant, and even some of his own supporters crowed that the honest Palme had finally been exposed as a greedy tax evader.

The prime minister at first seemed almost floored by the Harvard case. It highlighted both the hatred and vindictiveness of his political enemies, and the malicious *Schadenfreude* that motivated so many people in his own party; in particular, Palme was outraged that his family had been attacked. To argue that as an international statesman, he would have been entitled to charge a much higher speaker's fee at Harvard would do little to impede the slowly grinding machinery of the Swedish taxation bureaucracy. But with his usual toughness, Palme shook off these blues: he firmly spoke out in the media and prepared an appeal against the decision to charge him extra tax. It is remarkable that on February 28, when Palme had just hours left to live, someone stole his appeal from the taxation office and deleted the computer files regarding this matter. From 1986 until 1997, the police investigated this mysterious business, but without much success. Could it be that a blackmailer or personal enemy deleted the files, and might this have been related to the murder? The police found no evidence of such a scenario. Instead, they strongly suspected two young clerks who had a reputation as hackers, although these men never confessed. Anyway, Palme knew the taxation laws very well, and he clearly believed that he had a good case against the deci-

Caricature of Olof Palme. Palme is depicted as a madman; on the lapel of his jacket is a hammer and sickle, along with a badge that says, "Don't touch my Harvard scholarship."

sion to charge him extra tax. He was posthumously proven right, since he won his case.

Another obvious line of inquiry was to investigate the various right-wing or pseudoreligious extremists who had been hostile to Palme and his politics. An ambitious trawling of Sweden's many small fascist and racist organizations showed only that these people were mostly sad losers, with no political and social influence and insufficient organizational skills to kill a cat, to say nothing of a prime minister. The same could be said for most of the religious bigots, although the Church of Scientology, a more sinister and accomplished sect of fanatics, was investigated for quite some time.[11] The Palme government had declared that this "church" should be counted as a corporation rather than a religious organization; the obvious taxation consequences of this, it was vainly speculated, could have prompted one of the Scientologists to pull the trigger.

The European Worker's Party, a right-wing sect run by the American Lyndon LaRouche, was another set of ominous players on the outskirts of Swedish politics.[12] Although almost nobody voted for them, and most Swedes regarded them as a joke, they had no shortage of funds, which they used to spread distasteful propaganda about Palme. The police received several tips regarding the European Worker's Party, the most promising one involving one of the sect's female leaders, who had been spotted by a witness at the Grand cinema the night of the murder. Her husband, another member, was reported to resemble the Phantom. It turned out, however, that the woman had an alibi. The police also made much of the fact that Viktor Gunnarsson had some pamphlets from the European Worker's Party in his apartment, and that he had once signed a document purported to be an application for membership in this organization. But it turned out that the European Worker's Party had been using a clever trick to recruit unwitting members. They would make a street appeal dealing with drug abuse or some other subject that people sympathized with, and a lot of pedestrians would sign their petitions. They then would change the letterhead so that the people who had signed unwittingly became applicants for party membership. Gunnarsson himself denied being a member of the European Worker's Party, although, significantly, he remembered once signing one of their street petitions that Sweden should join NATO. A European Worker's Party spokesman told yet another story: Gunnarsson had once been a member but had been excluded from the party for having crazy ideas.

An even more virulent enemy of Palme's was a strange doctor named Alf Enerström.[13] He had once been a member of the Social Democrats, but was excluded for differences in the abortion question in 1974. The year after, he

Gillar du Kissinger, Hitler, Palme och Djingis Khan?

— Om inte, då kommer du att gilla EAP!

Prenumerera på Ny Solidaritet!

Helår 130:- (stöd 250:-) ● halvår 65:- ● introduktion (3 mån.) 25:- ● pg. 57 50 45-0

DJÄVULENS DJÄVUL

UROPEISKA ARBETAR

DEN FOLKLIGE DIKTATORN

ETT FOLK
EN FOND
EN FÜHRER

Anti-Palme propaganda posters, depicting him variously as a devil and as a modern Hitler.

was fired from his job as company doctor in the Ko-Op supermarket chain, run by the Social Democrats. In 1976, Enerström beat up his fifteen-year-old son, whom he suspected of having cheated in school. This was a dangerous thing to do in Sweden at this time: the son called the police and social authorities, and was promptly removed into foster care! Enerström blamed Palme for this triple whammy, which had ruined, in quick succession, his political hopes, his professional career and his family life. He devoted the remainder of his life to bringing about Palme's downfall. Together with his wife, he formed an organization called the Social Democrat Opposition. He wrote many pamphlets and articles containing the most absurd and exaggerated accusations against Palme. After a while, no newspaper would touch his scurrilous missives, but then he purchased advertisement space to publish them anyway. Not many people took Enerström seriously, but just like the European Worker's Party, he was never short of money to continue his monomaniacal struggle.

After the murder, the police received many tips about Enerström. He had made unbalanced and threatening remarks about Palme, he had been seen in Stockholm the day after the murder, and he had later been observed bringing a suitcase full of cash with him on an airplane. Many people, including Enerström himself, hinted that quite a few wealthy Swedes were supporting him financially. After the murder, the sinister doctor openly exulted that his old enemy was dead, remarking that with the well-timed "intervention" on February 28, the haughty Palme had finally become a "down-to-earth politician." The police rightly doubted that Enerström had the mental and bodily strength to plan and carry out the murder, but this did not exclude the possibility that he was part of a larger conspiracy. From 1986 until 1996, the police kept investigating his activities, but without finding anything incriminating. They seem to have questioned his violent tendencies, but in that respect, the crazy doctor would have a surprise ready for them in late 2003. When some bailiffs and police came to evict Enerström from his apartment, he opened fire with a small-caliber pistol and wounded a policewoman. Since he appeared quite insane, he was sent to a mental institution.

One of the more obscure early clues to the Palme murder, and one that appears to have been insufficiently looked into by the police, is the "Skandia connection."[14] Next to the murder scene was (and still is) a large office block, headquarters of the Skandia insurance and financial corporation. A few days after the murder, Skandia graphic designer Stig Engström made a dramatic announcement in the newspapers: he had been one of the first witnesses at the scene and had helped in trying to resuscitate Palme; still the police had not wanted to hear his story. The "Skandia Man," as he was dubbed by the press, said that as he had been walking home after working late making a pamphlet about insurance for tractors, he had suddenly heard a bang like a firecracker. About ten yards ahead of him, a man was lying on the ground, and "a little old lady" was standing next to him. The Skandia Man sprang into action, he claimed, and was the first person to reach the victim. With his knowledge of emergency medicine, he promptly started the appropriate resuscitation maneuvers, later being joined by two young people. The victim's wife was running back and forth, but appeared calm and collected (no other witness agreed); she told him that the assassin had been wearing a blue parka. When she added, "By the way, they have shot me too," he thought her injury could not be very serious, considering the way she was running around. It took five or six minutes from when the shots were fired until the police arrived, according to the Skandia Man, and the elderly policeman who arrived first (Gösta Söderström) just stood uselessly around in front of his police car, without even approaching the crime scene. When the victim's wife ran up to him, pleading with him to help her husband, the placid cop said, "The ambulance is on its way, little lady!"

When the young police officers arrived in their van, the Skandia Man again took decisive action, he claimed. He promptly showed them the killer's escape route up the Tunnelgatan steps, and they ran off whooping like school-boys. He then realized that he had forgotten to tell them about the blue parka, and himself raced up the steps to try to catch them, but without success. Rounding the building site barracks, he returned to the murder scene and was shocked to hear a witness describe the killer: a middle-aged man wearing a long, dark blue overcoat and a flat cap—this was a very good description of himself! Suspecting that his own run up the stairs might have led people to mistake him for the murderer, he tried to point this out to another police officer, but was fobbed off with the words "Get lost, we already have a witness!" The Skandia Man then approached a young woman, who asked him whether he knew that the victim was Olof Palme. He told her she must be joking, and she angrily snapped back that she was certainly not in the habit of making such tasteless jokes. Since the police showed no interest in him, the shaken Skandia Man retreated to his company's lobby, where the security guards gave him a cup of coffee to steady his nerves.

When the police made inquiries, no other witness at the murder scene could recall the Skandia Man and his conspicuous actions. In particular, Anna Hage and the young man trying to resuscitate Palme, whom the Skandia Man claimed to have assisted, firmly said that there had been no such man. Nor was the Skandia Man observed by Leif Ljungqvist or Gösta Söderström, both of whom had been well placed to see him. Indeed, the thorough police investigation of the witnesses and what they had seen has made it clear that no such individual as the Skandia Man had been active at the murder scene, except possibly as a spectator.[15] His story about being mistaken for the killer is a ludicrous one: if he ran up the stairs after the policemen, this was at least four minutes after Palme had been shot, and no witness would have mistaken him for the killer, whom several people had seen running away just after the shots had been fired. Although Holmér strongly suspected that the Skandia Man was yet another unreliable witness making up bogus stories for the press, he ordered a detective to liaise with Skandia security to investigate him.

What they found was nothing short of sensational. The Skandia security guards could verify that Engström had been working late that night, all alone in his tiny office in the huge dark office block. The security guards also knew that he had left the building at 11:19. His exit would thus have been perfectly timed to see the murder—or to commit it. His clothes—a dark blue overcoat and a flat cap—were not incompatible with those described in the witness testimonies. It also turned out that it had been possible to enter the Skandia building through a rear entrance from the Luntmakargatan without being seen on closed-circuit television, and that this rear entrance had been left open and unalarmed from 10:35 until 11:22—just half a minute after the murder! Had the killer dodged his pursuers and doubled back into the Skandia building? The police also found out that one of the Skandia security guards had left the building by car at 11:35—had the killer been with her in the vehicle? In that case, the killer could not have been the Skandia Man, since he was definitely still on the premises at 11:45, speaking to the other security guards about the murder. The police still suspected him, however, and in late April 1986, they planned to enter his room clandestinely to look for compromising evidence.

Prior to this being done, however, the almighty Hans Holmér ordered a halt to the Skandia investigation, and the questions raised here have never been answered. The reason for this may well have been that Engström was a staid, middle-aged man without a criminal record or access to firearms. Rumors spread that he was a supporter of the European Worker's Party, involved in the printing and design of their propaganda material, but the Skandia Man denied this vehemently, and no person has found conclusive evidence to the contrary. According to another curious rumor, he was once involved in a court case in which Lisbet Palme was an expert witness, but this would hardly have given him a motive to shoot her husband. And if the Skandia Man had really shot Palme, why then approach the police afterward, when they might detect the gunpowder residue on his tidy blue overcoat? Furthermore, the witness observations of Jeppsson, Nieminen, and Zahir indicate that the murderer did not enter the Skandia building, but ran straight up the Tunnelgatan steps. In the only alternative scenario involving the Skandia escape route an accomplice would have been waiting for the killer by the crossing of Tunnelgatan and Luntmakargatan to take the murder weapon, and one of them would have hiden in the Skandia building. This is hardly logical, since the gun would have been an asset to the man running up the eighty-nine steps, had anyone attempted to impede his escape. Nor has any witness (Jeppsson was well placed) seen two people meeting or exchanging a revolver. Still, the sheer number of coincidences and unanswered questions around the Skandia connection should have attracted the curiosity of the police. But this was the time when Holmér was using his police force to harass the Kurdish separatist movement, with the effect that many other leads were left untouched.

THE KURDISH CONSPIRACY

From the 1960s onward, there was a considerable immigration of foreigners into Sweden. One reason for this was that booming industries needed workers, another, that the Social Democrats showed praiseworthy zeal in making Sweden a safe haven for refugees fleeing terror and persecution in their home countries. The vast majority of these immigrants were decent, hardworking people, and they did much to inject a cosmopolitan flavor into the somewhat narrow-minded Swedish culture. But this unrestricted immigration had its drawbacks, mainly that the country's generous social benefits, lax policing, and short prison sentences attracted criminal elements from abroad. Tougher and better organized that the homegrown villains, these foreign gangs established themselves in Stockholm and other major Swedish cities, working in prostitution, racketeering, and drug dealing. There was an established Yugoslav mafia in Stockholm, although they admitted other foreign criminals, and even like-minded Swedes, into their ranks. Their main activity was of course to bring illicit drugs into the country, and by the 1980s, these foreign gangsters were responsible for a major part of the smuggling of narcotics into Sweden.

Hans Holmér was well aware of this state of affairs and did much to alert Palme and other politicians to the negative consequences of unrestricted immigration. He had his eyes on the Kurdish separatist movement Partiya Karkeren Kurdistan (PKK): its members were tough, ruthless freedom fighters, hardened by years of brutal persecution from the Turkish authorities.[1] The PKK Kurds had a strong presence in West Germany, and used the lax Swedish immigration policy to establish a second headquarters in Stockholm. This was bad news for the Swedes, since some hard-core PKK members augmented the party funds through theft, robbery, and drug trafficking. They had an ample supply of firearms, which they used in a trigger-happy manner. In 1984 and 1985, two Kurdish dissenters living in Sweden were shot dead by PKK hit men who approached them from behind with powerful handguns. In both cases, the killers were caught and convicted. They had come to Sweden as visitors, with the express purpose of carrying out the death sentences on these two men, who had been branded as traitors by the PKK leadership. Afterward, the killers were proud of what they had accomplished, showing no remorse and no particular concern for their own fate.

The Swedish government was appalled by these ruthless assassinations, and the PKK was formally declared a terrorist organization. Hard-core PKK members presented quite a problem for Palme, however. Normally, such villains would have been deported, but it was considered inhuman to send them to Turkey, where they would face torture and persecution; no other country was likely to accept them. Instead, nine of the PKK hard core were forbidden to travel freely by a court order and were kept under secret surveillance. The PKK leadership was furious at this unexpected development. Sweden and Turkey were the only countries branding them as terrorists, and there was a risk that West Germany, where the PKK had a strong presence and had also murdered several people, would follow suit. Perhaps not entirely without reason, the PKK men connected the recent harsh treatment of their organization with the improved relations between Sweden and Turkey, including the contracting of a Swedish company to build the Istanbul subway. They also suspected that the Swedish secret police was trading information about them with the dreaded Turkish secret service MIT, and again they may well have been right. Led by the lawyer Hüseyin Yilderim, the Swedish PKK sympathizers began a campaign against the Palme government, demanding that they no longer be regarded as terrorists. To the detriment of their own argument, they made several threatening and bombastic remarks, saying that Sweden would be declared an enemy of the PKK if Palme did not relent.

Hans Holmér claimed that from an early stage, he had suspected that PKK had murdered Olof Palme as an act of revenge. After all, they were tough and organized enough to pull off such an assassination and disciplined enough to keep their mouths shut about it afterward. They had access to firearms, as well as fanatical adherents who did not hesitate to kill in the service of the PKK. Just like the two Kurds murdered in 1984 and 1985, Palme had been shot in the back. Some of the leading PKK members had had their phones tapped by the secret police, and Holmér learned that not long before the murder, they had spoken about "holding a wedding in the street." This was thought to be PKK code for a planned assassination. Holmér suspected that their saying the "poets" needed to attend this wedding was a reference to the assassins. He also knew that on March 1, a person professing to represent the PKK had phoned the evening newspaper *Expressen*, taking credit for the murder of Olof Palme. On March 3, however, the German branch of the PKK started circulating a leaflet claiming that the murder was the result of a conspiracy involving the CIA; the Israeli intelligence service, MOSSAD; and their Turkish colleagues, MIT. Later, the PKK repeated this accusation in its journal, *Kurdistan Report*, adding that the murderers' original plan had been to frame the PKK, but this attempt had been thwarted when Lisbet Palme described the killer as a blue-eyed Swede. Their attempt to depict the PKK as an organization striving for peace and human understanding was rather spoilt by the threatening and bombastic ending of the article, reminding Kurdish dissidents that if they did not mend their ways, they would suffer the same fate as Olof Palme.

As Wranghult later admitted, the main reason the police investigated Viktor Gunnarsson for so long was his dealings with various shady foreigners.[2] In particular, they were interested in anything linking him with the PKK Kurds. After Gunnarsson's release, the police learned he had once rented an apartment that had later been taken over by a Kurdish organization. The police raided the apartment, questioned all those present, and confiscated a list of members, but it turned out that this organization had nothing to do with the PKK. The police also knew that Gunnarsson had been teaching Swedish to various immigrants; fortunately for him, none of them had been Kurds. The obvious difficulties in finding a link between the right-wing Gunnarsson and the left-wing PKK led to this lead being dropped altogether.

The PKK conspiracy had been one of several major leads from day one of the murder investigation, and covert bugging operations against some leading members had been arranged in early March. After the case against Gunnarsson was dropped, Holmér and his men gradually concentrated their efforts on the PKK. In early May, Holmér received what he thought was another vital lead. A Finnish alcoholic named Seppo Ahlström told the police a remarkable tale: he had been in prison together with the Ustasja terrorist Miro Baresic and a notorious PKK gangster, and had been ordered to provide them with two Smith and Wesson .357 magnum revolvers two weeks before the murder. The boozy Finn, who had been hitting the bottle hard after being released from prison, was trembling like a leaf and almost delirious. Under normal circumstances, such a wreck of a man would have been given very little credibility by the police, but his story was exactly what Hans Holmér wanted to hear.[3]

Miro Baresic had quite a fearsome reputation.[4] In 1971, he and another Ustasja hit man had broken into the Yugoslav Embassy in Stockholm, murdered the ambassador, and urinated on the corpse. They were arrested by the police and sentenced to life imprisonment. The year after, three other Ustasja terrorists hijacked a Swedish airliner, demanding that Baresic and several other Ustasja men in Swedish prisons be released and brought on board the plane. The Swedish government acceded, and Baresic and his friends flew to Spain, where they turned themselves over to the authorities. Baresic found many friends in Franco's Spain and was not harshly treated. He later went to Paraguay, where he joined the dictator Alfredo Stroessner's secret police. In 1979, he accompanied a Paraguayan minister to the United States as a bodyguard. He was proud of his martial arts skills, and careless enough to enter an American karate contest under his own name. As a result, he was arrested by the federal police and brought back to Sweden, where he served five years in a high-security prison before being transferred to a regular prison ward.

Here, he met the PKK Kurd Naif Durak, who had been convicted of large-scale drug trafficking. Baresic's political opinions were right-wing extremist, and the PKK was formally a Marxist-Leninist organization, yet these two villains had so much in common that they soon became good friends. As the toughest criminals in the prison, they ruled the place, ordering the other convicts around at will. The feeble alcoholic Ahlström, who was in prison for receiving stolen goods, acted as their personal servant. Sometimes, the two kingpins allowed him to join their table, where they sat drinking brandy and playing poker.

Baresic and Durak had one problem in common—Olof Palme. Baresic had hoped to be freed soon, but the Palme government had decided that his sentence should last for eighteen years, meaning that he could look forward to several more years in prison. As for the Kurdish drug smuggler, he greatly feared being extradited to Turkey at the end of his prison sentence. Alm many times heard them cursing Palme, and Baresic once said, "That man can die!" when the prime minister was on the television. On February 15, Ahlström was allowed three days' leave from prison. Durak ordered him to get hold of two heavy handguns, allegedly for use in a bank robbery his countrymen were arranging. The Finn contacted a dealer in illegal firearms, who sold him two Smith and Wesson .357 magnum revolvers, which Ahlström duly delivered to Durak's apartment. The day of the murder, Baresic and Durak seemed quite nervous, and the former said, "Now we will see how Olof Palme will fare!" The day after, Durak seemed very jolly, hinting that his own son had shot the prime minister.

As the police began to check Ahlström's story about the two revolvers, things were not looking particularly promising. Not only was Ahlström suffering the consequences of many years of hard drinking, but he also had a reputation as a conniving liar. The boozy Finn's wife, who, he claimed, had accompanied him to Durak's apartment, at first refused to corroborate his story. Ahlström named first one man and then another as the arms dealer who had sold him the guns. But the police managed to track down a cab driver who could remember giving the drunken Finn a ride on February 15, to the address of one of the arms dealers. This convinced Holmér that Ahlström was telling the truth, and the police-master ordered that both Baresic and Durak be put under clandestine surveillance.

Some additional observations tended to strengthen Holmér's hypothesis that the PKK had been purchasing "hardware" for an impending assassination. Two Turks came to the police saying that a PKK Kurd named Aktas had been trying to purchase a handgun in early 1986. A Swedish robber testified that a Kurdish drug smuggler and friend of Naif Durak had approached him to purchase a revolver just three or four weeks before the murder. Another Swedish criminal, serving time in a prison outside Stockholm, had met a PKK tough named Bekir, who had been convicted for murder, arson, and drug trafficking. When the two convicts discussed politics and the Swede mentioned Olof Palme, the Kurd screamed furious threats that he wanted to kill Palme, and that there were others, in the PKK bookshop, who could carry out the assassination. When the Swede asked whether they planned to put a bomb in Palme's car, Bekir replied that Palme did not have any bodyguards and all one had to do was to shoot him in the back and run. He added that when the deed was done, the killer could go to the bookshop, where the lawyer (Yilderim) would take care of the rest. This PKK bookshop was situated on David Bagares Gata, not far from the murder scene, and the police of course suspected that it had been used as a hideout for the killer.[5]

By mid-1986, Hans Holmér had made up his mind that the PKK terrorists were responsible for the murder. To him, they were ideal suspects, since even if it was impossible to make a case against one particular member, it might well be possible to extradite most of the PKK hard core. This would rid the country of a gang of dangerous criminals and give the impression that even though there was not enough evidence to convict a killer, the people responsible for the murder of Olof Palme had been brought to justice. The PKK men were not particularly popular in Sweden, and most people would be pleased to see the last of them, Holmér hoped. By this time, the police-master was becoming desperate: he knew that for each month that went by, the chance of finding the real killer was diminishing. As is evident from his harsh treatment of Viktor Gunnarsson, Holmér was at this stage no longer looking for *the* murderer, but *any* murderer: any suspect falling into the hands of the police, against whom a reasonably good case could be brought, would do. By this time, Holmér had entrenched himself in a suite of armor-plated rooms in the penthouse of the police headquarters. Surrounded by his court of sycophants, he was pondering where to strike next against the Kurds. He was desperately grasping at straws, using his media contacts to make optimistic progress reports at any minor success.

Holmér was obsessed with the thought that Palme's killers were planning to assassinate him, the good cop who was closing in on his prey, like in an American B movie. He was never seen without his squad of muscular bodyguards, armed to the teeth with pistols and machine guns. Significantly, these bodyguards had been selected from the Baseball Gang. Holmér himself carried a pistol in a shoulder holster at all times, and also a miniature radio transmitter disguised as a tie pin, so that the bodyguards could track him down if the PKK gangsters kidnapped him. He also ordered a briefcase with a hidden machine gun, which his bodyguards were to use against any swarthy terrorist who dared to threaten him.[6] Much money was spent on armor plating Holmér's private lavatory and rendering it impossible for anyone to plant a bomb there. At the press conferences, security was rigorous in the extreme, since Holmér and his bodyguards saw disguised PKK terrorists everywhere. Sniffer dogs were on the prowl, and the journalists were frisked and examined with metal detectors to expose hidden weapons.

Holmér had informed the acting head of the secret police, Per-Gunnar Näss, that the PKK were his prime target. Näss, an active and unscrupulous character, loyally joined in, arranging phone taps for several of the Kurds involved. Others had bugging equipment clandestinely put into their apartments. The strict Swedish laws against secret surveillance were broken more than once during these extensive bugging operations. Holmér and Näss believed that they could later justify the bugging operations by claiming that a state of national emergency had been in effect.[7] An even more questionable tactic was to harass the PKK men, hoping that they would break under the pressure. One of the PKK men owned a grocery store, and he gave a vivid description of how the police scared his customers away by repeatedly approaching them and asking for their identification documents.[8] The PKK bookshop near the murder site, and other known meeting places, were regularly searched. On other occasions, police agents tried to infiltrate the bookshop by asking to use the phone or pretending to be drunk, but the PKK men were not fooled by such simple tactics. A secret police agent named Jan-Henrik Barrling, recognized as a leading Swedish expert on the PKK, was employed by Holmér as one of his foremost lieutenants in his campaign against the Kurds. This may have been beneficial had this man been a clearheaded officer, but it was an official secret that Barrling was biased against the PKK, which he suspected of being responsible for a veritable crime wave, both in Sweden and abroad.

At a meeting with the prosecutors in August 1986, Holmér outlined his grand plan. The surveillance of the PKK men was progressing satisfactorily, he pontificated, and now the time had come to strike. In what he called "Operation Alpha," more than fifty Kurds were to be arrested and interrogated by the police. Holmér felt certain that the killer would be among them. The plan would then be to file criminal charges against as many as possible of the PKK men, including the charge of conspiracy to murder Olof Palme. Claes Zeime and his subordinates Solveig Riberdahl and Anders Helin were awed by the scope of the police-master's imagination, and they likened the coming raid to the D day invasion of Normandy. Yes, Holmér bragged, this would be the greatest terrorist trial the world had ever seen.[9] The prosecutors believed that Holmér must have a very strong case against the PKK to be planning such a crusade. They presumed that the reason he did not present his evidence in detail was his usual fondness for secrecy. Zeime and Helin made no objections to Operation Alpha, but Riberdahl asked whether the police were not distancing themselves from the crime scene in their single-minded pursuit of the PKK. She particularly wanted the police-master to allow some police detectives to investigate reports that a man might have been keeping Palme under surveillance outside the cinema, but Holmér refused. No fewer than 150 policemen were preparing for Operation Alpha, but he was unwilling to allow even three or four detectives to investigate this other lead. Knowing Holmér's great influence with the government, Riberdahl had to give way.[10]

Holmér knew that in late 1985, the PKK had murdered a Kurdish dissident in Denmark. In the investigation of this murder, the Danish police had been assisted by a mysterious Kurd who worked for the Turkish secret service, MIT. This same man also offered his services to the Swedes. He was certain that the PKK had shot Olof Palme, he said, and for the sum of one hundred thousand German marks, he offered to find out the name of the killer. Holmér provided the money, and the Kurd reported back that at a meeting in Damascus, the PKK leadership had decided that Olof Palme had to die. The PKK leader Hasan Güler had been chosen as the killer. Two other PKK men had accompanied Güler to Stockholm, provided him with the revolver, and posted him by the Tunnelgatan steps. Holmér knew that Güler was being held in prison in Germany for various other crimes.

With high hopes for a vital breakthrough, Holmér sent police detectives to Germany to interview him. Ingemar Krusell, who up to then had been a loyal adherent of Holmér and his colleagues in the Palme Room, later described his surprise and dismay when he saw that the suspect was just five feet four inches tall. Although definitely a serious criminal, Güler was a very unlikely candidate for the tall, well-built man running up the Tunnelgatan steps. Krusell also knew that the PKK usually chose very junior members as assassins, whereas Güler was a member of the PKK Central Committee. Krusell began to suspect that as the men in the Palme Room built their castles in the sand about the PKK conspiracy, they were progressively distancing themselves from what had really happened the evening Palme was killed. Krusell was also amazed by the lack of professionalism shown by Barrling during their visit to Germany: Was this man really one of Holmér's chief advisers?[11] It later appeared likely that the police informant had had little or no inside knowledge, since the rumor about Güler's involvement had been discussed in the Turkish newspapers. When the hapless Swedes belatedly tried to raise the matter of their one hundred thousand marks, the Kurd had wisely made himself scarce.

In December 1986, Hans Holmér finally appeared to get lucky. Naif Durak, who had been released on parole by this time, went to a nightclub called Stampen, situated in the Old Town. As the PKK tough was swigging his beer, he started talking politics with some other Kurds at an adjoining table, but these men turned out to be very much against the PKK. Being severely outnumbered, Durak did not start a fight, but quietly crept out to phone his son for reinforcements. Together with two other PKK men, young Durak hastened to his father's aid, and the short-tempered Kurds started a fight that could have graced an old-fashioned western film.[12] Fists were flying, knives drawn, and chairs smashed.

When the police arrived, the two Duraks had been knocked down in the fight and were not going anywhere. The other two PKK men dashed off, but one of them was grabbed by the police and found to carry a formidable-looking switchblade. The other man was pursued by the police through the narrow streets of the Old Town; he pulled a gun and fired several rounds at the police cars before being arrested. Holmér immediately took this opportunity to obtain search warrants for the apartments of all the PKK men involved, and also the PKK bookshop at David Bagares Gata. The overzealous policemen confiscated large amounts of material, but the only interesting find was a small bag filled with a white powder: heroin, the police hoped, but it turned out to be a Turkish preparation for the removal of unwanted body hair. The gunman, who had an earlier warrant against him for drug trafficking, was the only person charged with any crime.

Most people would have been reluctant to take matters further after such a setback, but not Hans Holmér. He had made his plan of action and he was sticking to it. After prolonged wrangling with the prosecutors, who were rapidly losing their enthusiasm for the PKK lead, Holmér finally managed to obtain search warrants and arrest orders for twenty-six people. This was fewer than he had originally planned, but at least Operation Alpha could go ahead. In a series of dawn raids on January 20, men, women, and children were rounded up by a huge police squad and brought in for questioning. All these PKK sympathizers were questioned at length, but again nothing damaging was brought to light. Their houses and apartments were ransacked by police technicians, but nothing worthwhile was found, and no person was charged with any crime.[13] This was the police-master's worst-case scenario. He knew well that the prosecutors would try to use the failure of Operation Alpha to topple him; he also knew that his position with the government had gradually been weakened. Some of the more clearheaded Social Democrats, like minister of justice Sten Wickbom, were already questioning his activities.

But Holmér still had influence where it counted, and his determination and egotism made him confident of success. Together with the prosecutor Zeime, he announced another of his grand press conferences. The world's press was there, hoping that he would finally announce that the murder had been solved. But the conference was yet another farce. Holmér told the press that all the Kurds had been released but added that he still believed, with 95 percent certainty, that the PKK had murdered Palme. Zeime retorted that he would put the credibility of this theory closer to 5 percent. The press conference descended into a sordid squabble between the two, and the Swedish press finally realized that their idol Holmér had feet of clay. In his heyday, his intellect had been compared with that of Sherlock Holmes, and his rugged looks with those of Clint Eastwood; now, he was unflatteringly compared with Inspector Clouseau, of Pink Panther fame. The contempt shown for the hapless police-master by the Swedish and international press further weakened his position with the government. Could they really support a man who was widely accused of turning the murder investigation into a farce and causing the Swedish police to be branded the most incompetent in the world by the foreign press?

During several weeks of intense negotiations, Holmér desperately tried to save himself. He wrote a bombastic appeal to the Swedish police, blaming the prosecutors for all that had gone wrong. He also spoke to both prime minister Ingvar Carlsson and minister of justice Sten Wickbom, scheming to maintain his position of authority over the murder investigation. But the opposition forces were too strong. Chief of national police Holger Romander and chief prosecutor Magnus Sjöberg had been forced to obey Holmér when he was regarded as the savior of the nation, but now they changed sides, joining forces with Wickbom and Zeime against the beleaguered police-master. Still, prime minister Ingvar Carlsson was very reluctant to lose Holmér. In spite of all the police-master's failings, the leading Social Democrats seemed to have their own reasons for keeping him in the post as long as possible.

The prime minister himself negotiated a compromise: Holmér and his friends Per-Gunnar Näss and Tommy Lindström were to form an "operative staff" directly under Romander, leading the murder investigation. Holmér accepted, knowing that he could dominate Näss and Lindström, and that Romander would soon retire. But this agreement turned out to be a trap. As the reorganization of the Palme investigation was unveiled, it became clear that the operative staff had almost no power at all, and the disgruntled Holmér resigned on March 5. Wickbom, Romander, and Sjöberg had won their victory, and from that point on, the prosecutors would—at least officially—be in charge of the murder investigation. The government arranged for Holmér to get a well-paid sinecure position at the United Nations office in Vienna, as a narcotics expert.[14] This was far from his enemies in Stockholm, and the ongoing murder investigation, but as the Swedes would find out to their detriment, it was not far enough.

EBBE CARLSSON'S SECRET INVESTIGATION

What Hans Holmér left behind was the wreck of a police investigation. Since mid-1986, the police work had been devoted to the investigation of the PKK, and all other leads, including vital testimony from witnesses at the crime scene, had been ignored. Had it been the intention of prime minister Ingvar Carlsson and his government that the murder investigation should regain lost time and close in on the killer, it would have made sense to appoint a high-ranking detective as Holmér's successor, someone who had the skill and experience to work with the prosecutors to digest the enormous amount of information at hand and find new worthwhile leads. But the Social Democrats seem to have reasoned that if they could not have their own favorite super-sleuth to lead the investigation, the hunt for the murderer could just as well be left to collapse. Ulf Karlsson, a "loyal" police administrator, was appointed the new leader of the official hunt for the murderer. Karlsson, who lacked experience in practical police work, and who was apparently quite affected by his predecessor's much-publicized fall from grace, chose to keep a very low profile indeed. With little in the way of leadership from him, four police departments (the secret police under Per-Gunnar Näss, the national crime squad under Tommy Lindström, and two different squads of detectives from the Stockholm police) conducted their own separate investigations, sometimes questioning the same witness independently. Although the prosecutors now had the resources to investigate their lead about the man waiting outside the Grand cinema, the murder investigation lacked direction and initiative.[1] Indeed, the Social Democrats seemed more interested in a secret investigation that had been started by their own undercover operators.

From the very first days of the search for Palme's murderer, Hans Holmér had been assisted by a certain Ebbe Carlsson, who had been a close friend of Olof Palme's. At an early age, Ebbe Carlsson had become a convert to Social Democratism, or at least to the excellent career prospects for an intelligent young man within this vast and brontosaurian organization, with its chronic shortage of brainpower. By the mid-1970s, he had risen to the post of assistant political secretary in the Department of Justice, where he was working closely with his friend Carl Lidbom. He became renowned as a political fixer and spin doctor, with an obsessive interest in secret police work.

At this time, the Social Democrats were trying to prevent the communists from taking over parts of the trade unions. They did so by illegal means, monitoring the communist sympathizers through a vast network of spies. Ebbe became a leading player in this secret organization, with access to Palme himself and other leading Social Democrats. Together with Hans Holmér, he once defused a potentially dangerous situation, when spies had been tapping the phones of a radical communist phalanx. The two troubleshooters were again called into action in 1975, when a Social Democratic spy was accused of monitoring communists at a large hospital in Gothenburg. Through blatant lying and falsification, Holmér and Ebbe Carlsson managed to persuade the authorities that the spy had been on a secret mission to investigate claims that adherents of the notorious terrorist Carlos had infiltrated the Gothenburg hospitals.[2]

In 1976, Ebbe left politics for undisclosed reasons; there are hints that he did not resign by his own free will.[3] He became the editor of a provincial Social Democratic newspaper, but the paper went bankrupt after a couple of years. Ebbe then started a career in book publishing, being employed as a senior editor by the Bonniers publishing house. Ebbe Carlsson seems to have kept his position in the Social Democratic elite and his access to Palme and many of his ministers, and it was speculated that he was a leading political spy, using his position in the publishing company as a cover for other, more sinister activities.

Ebbe Carlsson had many friends among the Social Democratic ruling class, but minister of justice Sten Wickbom was not one of them. He told Holmér that such a disreputable character should not be allowed to infiltrate the Palme Room. With chagrin, the police-master told Ebbe to make himself scarce from the official police investigation. But in secret, Holmér kept his old friend informed of every new development. Holmér even lived in Ebbe's apartment for some time, and once questioned Lisbet Palme there. Although he was officially only an editor at a publishing company, Ebbe knew literally everyone who mattered in Sweden and had access to some very senior people. When Holmér fell from grace, Ebbe held several nighttime meetings in his apartment with his friend the police-master, Social Democratic minister

Anna-Greta Leijon, and the prime minister's political secretary, Kjell Larsson. The objective of these meetings was to formulate a strategy to save Holmér, but in spite of all Ebbe's scheming, his old friend had to resign in disgrace, and the PKK lead seemed at risk of being discarded altogether. After Holmér's forced departure, Ebbe remained on the outskirts of the murder investigation, pondering what to do. In the fall of 1987, he decided to build up a secret Palme task force to continue investigating the PKK conspiracy. He was supported in this unconventional initiative by another decidedly strange Swedish politician, ambassador Carl Lidbom.

Carl Lidbom was another key player in the Palme drama, one who until this point made his moves behind the scenes. As an ambitious young public prosecutor during the 1960s and 1970s, he had joined the Social Democrats and enjoyed a distinguished career. A clever, educated man from an upper-middle-class background, he had more than one thing in common with Palme himself. He was instrumental in formulating the strict laws against tax evasion and property crime, and this earned him a fair amount of unpopularity. Being of an arrogant and haughty disposition, and lacking the common touch, Lidbom was less of an asset to Palme and the Social Democrats during the years the party was out of power. In 1981, the post of Swedish ambassador in Paris became vacant. Lidbom was not a professional diplomat, but he was a Francophile who spoke the language fluently, a rare accomplishment in Sweden. He liked French culture, French wine, and French cuisine (*and* French women, his detractors were quick to add). Lidbom was such an obvious candidate that Palme was able to secure him the post. The assignment could be seen as honorable retirement for this grizzled party veteran, but there may well have been another purpose. Lidbom's strong position among the Social Democrats remained unchallenged, and he might one day be needed to serve the party again. Carl Lidbom fully shared Ebbe Carlsson's enthusiasm for intrigue and secret police work. He also shared his suspicions about the PKK, or at least the conviction that this was a very "suitable" solution for Sweden's national trauma.

In 1979, a former police sergeant named Stig Bergling had been arrested as a Soviet spy. He had been spying for the Soviets for many years and with considerable success, and had caused the Swedish armed forces irreparable harm. In 1987, Bergling was allowed out of prison, unaccompanied, on day release. Not unreasonably, the spy lost no time in escaping to Moscow. This was not exactly what Sweden needed after the murder of Olof Palme and the fall of Hans Holmér. That Sweden's state prisoner had been allowed to escape with such ease caused general outrage. Prime minister Ingvar Carlsson used minister of justice Sten Wickbom as the scapegoat, replacing him with Anna-

Carl Lidbom.

Greta Leijon, a popular and respected Social Democratic politician. The prime minister was also dubious about the leadership of the secret police, whose task it had been to keep Bergling under surveillance. In particular, he had concerns about the capability of its recently appointed director, the afore-mentioned police administrator Sune Sandström, who had cut such a sorry figure the night Olof Palme was murdered. Carl Lidbom was a valued old friend of Ingvar Carlsson, and the dynamic ambassador was offered Sand-ström's job. Lidbom preferred his leisurely life in Paris, however, and Sand-ström's career was saved once more. The prime minister instead appointed Lidbom to chair a state committee investigating the shortcomings of the Swedish secret police. This was excellent news for Ebbe Carlsson: not only had his enemy Wickbom been removed from power, but his friend the am-bassador had been appointed to a post of considerable power and influence.[4]

Ebbe Carlsson's murder hypothesis was somewhat different from that of Holmér and strongly colored by his own unconventional approach to secret po-lice work. Ebbe boldly claimed that the Swedish secret police and its prime mover, Näss, had known of the PKK's plan to assassinate Olof Palme, but had decided to keep quiet about it. According to Ebbe, Palme had stopped the Swedish arms corporation Bofors from exporting missiles to Iran, and the Aya-tollah Khomeini's regime had decided that Palme must be killed. At a meeting in Damascus, the PKK terrorists had accepted the task of murdering Palme, in exchange for a steady supply of drugs from Iran for their smuggling operations.

Hans Holmér was still in Stockholm at this time, and Ebbe and Lidbom had two lengthy brainstorming sessions with him about the extended PKK conspiracy. Holmér also did much to facilitate Ebbe's contacts with various police dignitaries. Romander's replacement as the chief of national police, Nils-Erik Åhmansson, was completely taken in by Ebbe and Lidbom, believing that the two adventurers must have government sanctions for their secret murder investigation. Lidbom fully realized the political implications of Ebbe's accusations against the SÄPO: Was this not a great opportunity to put the secret police under political control, with a loyal Social Democrat at the helm? In particular, he wanted to get rid of Näss, a free thinker who lacked the necessary loyalty to those in political power. Ebbe suggested a campaign of slander and tried to persuade some journalists that Näss took bribes, or even that he was a KGB agent. But Lidbom and Leijon did not agree with these tactics, since they feared that the mud would not stick. Näss was a competent police chief, and what better way was there to remove him from the SÄPO than to promote him to become police commissioner in Uppsala, not far from Stockholm? Lidbom used his very considerable influence, and Näss agreed to go, perhaps suspecting that if he did not play along, the ambassador would have other, less agreeable plans for his professional future.

Like Holmér before him, Ebbe Carlsson was greatly taken in by the secret police agent Jan-Henrik Barrling and his colleague Walter Kegö. These two had been at loggerheads with Näss, who did not share their fanatical belief in the PKK conspiracy, and who had threatened to relegate them to other duties. In particular, he wanted them to concentrate on investigating the murder of Olof Palme, rather than trying to prove that the PKK was the most dangerous terrorist organization in Europe. After Ebbe and Lidbom appeared on the scene, Kegö and Barrling were again free to indulge in their flights of fancy about the PKK conspiracy, willingly taking on board Ebbe's new theories about the sinister meeting in Damascus and the ayatollah sentencing Palme to death. With Holmér acting as a go-between, Ebbe and Lidbom were provided with large quantities of secret documents about the PKK, unbeknownst to Näss. Appreciating the need to obtain information from PKK turncoats and deserters, the two adventurers persuaded Leijon to increase the reward for the conviction of the murderer of Olof Palme to fifty million Swedish kronor (seven million dollars).

In late 1987, Kegö and Barrling found what seemed to be a new important lead. A police informant in southern Sweden claimed to have important data that directly linked a PKK sympathizer to the murder. The police paid him twenty-eight thousand dollars to persuade him to share his knowledge, and he pointed out a PKK man named Sarikaya as the killer. Kegö and Barrling were delighted, but not for long, since it turned out that Sarikaya had a cast-iron alibi: he had actually been working delivering newspapers in a southern Swedish town the night of the murder. The informant, a decidedly strange character, then admitted that he had gotten his information by means of card divination! Undeterred by this setback, Kegö and Barrling uncovered another lead. A Kurd who had been arrested in France told the French police that he had information to sell to the Swedes, namely that he had in his possession the sixty-two-page death sentence against Olof Palme, signed by PKK leader Abdullah Öcalan. Full of enthusiasm, Kegö and Barrling went to Dijon and tried to question this suspect, but he demanded one hundred thousand German marks just to see them, and much more to deliver the goods. The two secret policemen tried to obtain this sum from Ebbe Carlsson, but they could not beat the Kurd's deadline. Later, the French secret service informed its Swedish colleagues that the Kurd had possessed no worthwhile documents in the first place.

These two debacles did nothing to weaken Ebbe's faith in the PKK conspiracy theory, however. In December 1987, Lidbom approached prime minister Ingvar Carlsson, most probably to lay out Ebbe's theory. Little is known about what was said in this secret meeting, but the dynamic ambassador and his coconspirators appear to have been greatly encouraged by the prime minister's reaction. Ebbe, Lidbom, and Holmér, along with their willing allies Kegö and Barrling, seemed to perceive that they had official sanction to continue their secret police work.

In early 1988, Carl Lidbom spent a fair amount of time wining and dining in Paris, and he often visited his mistress in London. Since he also had to go to Sweden on a regular basis, to chair the SÄPO commission, he had less time for investigating the PKK conspiracy. But the workaholic Ebbe Carlsson was free from any such commitments. He seems to have deserted his desk at the publishing company altogether, and was active almost around the clock, conspiring with police agents and various foreign contacts. A short, bald-headed man with a sinister aspect and demeanor, he ordered politicians and senior police officers around at will. He arranged for the editor of a leading newspaper to publish a series of interviews with Hans Holmér, in his heyday as a supersleuth, in order to persuade the general public of the PKK's guilt.[5] He visited an old friend of his, a wealthy tycoon named Tomas Fischer, and borrowed $210,000 for the expenses of his secret police force and to rent an apartment to house his headquarters.

The weak and foolish police chiefs Åhmansson and Sandström were gradually enticed into Ebbe's sphere of influence and allowed Kegö and Barrling to recruit a team of other policemen for their crusade against the PKK. They also permitted Ebbe to recruit several of Holmér's Baseball Gang cops to be part of his private police force; one of them was to serve as Ebbe's personal bodyguard. Another recruit was a former police sergeant named Carl Östling, who was trying to establish himself as an international arms dealer. He had supplied Holmér with high-tech weapons, armored glass, and bulletproof vests, and Ebbe thought he might well become a useful ally.

Ebbe went to Vienna to meet up with Hans Holmér, who used his influence with the police to help Ebbe keep Åhmansson and Sandström under his control and provided expert advice about the murder investigation. Ebbe also went to London to conspire with mystery man John Edwards, a journalist who had been employed by Yorkshire Television to make a film about the Palme murder. Edwards had been hinting that he could procure secret information about the meeting in Damascus from the MI16, and Ebbe hoped to persuade the slippery journalist to base his documentary entirely on the PKK conspiracy.[6] Ebbe even interviewed Iranian ex-premier Abdulhassan Banisadr in his villa in Versailles, vainly hoping for support for his conspiracy theory. In the London and Versailles expeditions, he was carrying letters of recommendation from Åhmansson and Leijon, stating that he was acting on behalf of the Swedish government in an important secret mission.

Ebbe also wanted to liaise with the DST, the French secret service, suspecting that they had secret knowledge about the PKK and its links to Iran. This time, his friend the ambassador was ready to help in his own unconventional way. In late March 1988, Ebbe went to Paris, staying at the Swedish Embassy as usual. On March 26, Lidbom called the police, saying that the embassy was under threat from international terrorists, and that one of the diplomats had been kidnapped. A squad of gendarmes poured into the embassy courtyard looking for these invented terrorists; just as the dynamic duo had planned, senior figures from the DST also made an appearance. Nor were these French secret policemen unwilling to cooperate with Ebbe's organization. They found the verbose little publisher more than a little odd, but were calmed by Lidbom's presence, indicating approval from the Swedish government. The same day, the two adventurers phoned Anna-Greta Leijon and told her the same bogus story about the terrorist scare. She was put out by their dramatic revelations, and particularly by Ebbe's claim to have dangerous secret information about the murder of Olof Palme. He insisted that they should meet very soon, and he would tell her terrible things. The next day, Leijon met Ebbe at the Bonniers office, where she had to listen to his endless harangues about the PKK for ten hours.[7]

But Ebbe Carlsson had other, more dangerous plans. He knew that a senior member of the PKK hard core named Ali Cetiner had been arrested by the police in Germany. Ebbe had his agents approach this man, and Cetiner agreed to serve as an undercover agent against his own organization. He was clandestinely brought into Sweden and installed in an apartment that had been rented for him with Fischer's money. The plan was to have Cetiner approach the Swedish PKK men and lure them into making damaging admissions about their part in the murder of Olof Palme. For this plan to be at all feasible, Ebbe needed high-tech surveillance equipment, as well as formal permission to use it. He hoped that Åhmansson or Sandström would provide the latter, but the two police chiefs were cautious about putting pen to paper.

Ebbe decided to try yet another bluff. He alleged that the murder was the result of a triple alliance among the Soviets, Iran, and the PKK, aided by a "mole" in the Swedish government! He later named the mole as Pierre Schori, a radical Social Democratic politician. Schori had a communist mistress in Paris, Ebbe claimed, but she turned out to be a respectable middle-aged professor rather than a dangerous terrorist. Ebbe then tried another trick: he suggested that a KGB agent in Sweden had been bugged by the SÄPO, and that this man clearly had inside knowledge of the planning of the murder. But the two police chiefs were still helplessly dithering about allowing Ebbe to use surveillance equipment. By this stage, Ebbe had got to know Sandström, and he rightly doubted whether the hapless bureaucrat had the willpower to make such a momentous decision. As for Åhmansson, he may have been inexperienced and lacking in initiative, but he was a honest man, and had begun to doubt whether it was right that a publisher was being allowed to build up his own private police force. Ebbe threatened him that through Leijon, Ebbe could make sure his career as chief of national police would not be a lengthy one, but Åhmansson did not budge.

Waiting for the police chiefs to make up their minds, Ebbe went ahead with ordering his bugging equipment. Not trusting the SÄPO, he wanted to purchase this equipment from a London specialist store using Fischer's money and then smuggle it into Sweden. In April 1988, a second meeting took place between Ebbe and the DST to set up this smuggling operation. It was arranged that one of Ebbe's police agents would bring the bugging equipment from London to Paris, where a DST agent was to escort him through customs. The equipment was then to be taken to the Swedish Embassy in Paris, and Lidbom would send it to Stockholm through the diplomatic mail, again elegantly avoiding customs. But the delivery from London was delayed, meaning that the merchandise would arrive in Paris when Lidbom was not there to take care of it. Ebbe was not willing to take the risk having some embassy secretary find out about his secret operation, and ordered his agents to smuggle the electronic devices through Swedish customs themselves. This first smuggling operation was carried out according to plan, but a second operation in early June was less successful. Ebbe's agents may have acted suspiciously, or a double agent may have blown the whistle on them: the fact remains that Ebbe's bodyguard was arrested by Swedish customs police carrying several suitcases full of high-tech bugging equipment.

The bodyguard produced his letter of recommendation from Sune Sandström, saying that he was on a secret mission. The customs police phoned the SÄPO headquarters, and Sandström was alerted. Had the police chief acted coolly, or at least had the sense to ask Ebbe for advice, the situation might have been saved. Customs would have released the bodyguard if it had been verified that he was really on a secret mission; the bugging equipment would have been safe, and Ebbe would have had time to think up a suitable cover story. But Sandström lost his composure and cravenly denied all knowledge of the smuggling operation. He then had second thoughts and phoned Åhmansson and Ebbe Carlsson for advice. Ebbe ordered him for God's sake to phone customs again and make sure the bodyguard was released. But the secret police chief's only coherent thoughts concerned his own career. He pleaded with the customs police, who had taken the bodyguard into custody, to leave his own name out of the inquiry and cover up that the goods impounded were bugging equipment. As Ebbe himself later put it, the "stupid damn Sandström" ruined everything. The day after, the newspapers exposed the entire debacle. After the murder of Olof Palme, the fall of the idol Holmér, and the escape of Bergling, Sweden had yet another major scandal on its hands.

As is fitting for a political superspy, Ebbe Carlsson had kept a low profile throughout his career, but his name was now in every newspaper headline in Sweden. There was much speculation who had given him the authority to build up a private police force to provide a solution to the murder of Olof Palme. One newspaper article was more than a little weird, however. Commenting on the recent scandal, it pointedly asked whether it might be a sign of sinister forces at play if the leader of a secret organisation is a vegetarian, when many of his political and police friends share the same dietary predilection. The journalists pondered the significance of these fateful words. *Vegetarian*, indeed! Then it was discovered that Ebbe Carlsson was a homosexual! The newspaper headlines erupted with homophobia and spy-mania, and the next day, the Swedes were surprised and dismayed to read in the tabloid newspaper headlines that a secret network of homosexual Social Democratic spies had infiltrated and corrupted every political office. It was speculated that in the "swinging sixties," Ebbe and his then boyfriend had been notorious for their wild parties, which were frequented by people who later became leading Social Democratic politicians. Had Ebbe used his knowledge of the past indiscretions of these people to gain favors and preferment? And how many members of the government were closet homosexuals, and as such liable to blackmail? The witty Ebbe himself later commented that if all these wild newspaper statements had been true, he would have buggered every government minister and most senior police officials, including the female minister of justice Anna-Greta Leijon!

Prime minister Ingvar Carlsson must have feared that the Ebbe Carlsson scandal would develop into a full-scale Swedish Watergate and bring about the fall of his government. Although evidence shows that Lidbom had kept the prime minister at least partially informed of Ebbe's investigation, Ingvar Carlsson now decided to deny all knowledge of these intrigues.[8] To pull this deception off was not possible without sacrifices. The first to go was his favorite superspy, Ebbe Carlsson himself. Ebbe had acted as a concerned private citizen, the Prime Minister asserted, and should take the full blame for his illegal actions himself. Ebbe was duly tried and convicted for smuggling and illegal possession of weapons and surveillance equipment, as were the police agents in his organization. Among the senior figures involved, Åhmansson and Sandström had to leave their respective positions, since they had been deeply tarnished by Ebbe's intrigues. Minister of justice Anna-Greta Leijon paid a high price for her imprudence in signing Ebbe's letters of recommendation: she also had to resign, her political career in ruins. In contrast, Ingvar Carlsson's old friend Carl Lidbom, who was far more implicated than any of these people, received no punishment at all and was allowed to remain as ambassador. Through these means, the press was silenced, but even the stolid, uncomplaining Swedes took time to recover from this latest scandal. The murder of Olof Palme and Holmér's bungling of the murder investigation had been heavy blows, but Ebbe Carlsson's activities shook the nation to the core and made the Swedes reevaluate their blind faith in the authorities.

In 1988, Hans Holmér published a book about the murder investigation.[9] He skillfully presented himself as the good honest cop fighting the cowardly prosecutors and irresponsible journalists, asserting that he had been right about the PKK all the time, but had been made a scapegoat by the turncoat politicians. The Swedish public once more regarded their idol with admiring eyes, and the book became a huge bestseller. But Holmér would not have long to enjoy its success. Although he was not directly involved in the trials following the Ebbe Carlsson scandal, the state prosecutors had got scent of the illegal bugging operations directed against the PKK Kurds, and both Holmér and Näss were prosecuted. This must have been a very disagreeable turn of events for Holmér; that *he himself* would end up in court as a result of the Palme murder investigation was a worst-case scenario the police-master could hardly have foreseen during the heady days of 1986. Although he defended himself with vigor, he was convicted on several counts. Most unfairly, the honest Näss was tarred with the same brush, although he had acted on Holmér's orders. The government had intended to provide Holmér with another top job, this time at the Interpol headquarters in Lyons, but as a convicted criminal, he was not considered suitable for this position and had to retire early. Spurred on by the notoriety of his first literary work, he became a writer of detective fiction, although without much success.[10]

Carl Lidbom's behavior became even more outrageous after the scandal.[11] He bullied and mistreated his staff at the embassy, and several times got into trouble for serious indiscretions. Once, he brought his mistress along to a party in a French naval base, presenting her as his wife. A Frenchman warned the admiral at the base that young "Mrs. Lidbom" looked rather like a KGB agent, and the ambassador's latest escapade hit the headlines in both Sweden and France. The woman, it turned out, was not a KGB agent after all, but the press still questioned Lidbom's wisdom in bringing an unknown civilian into a top-secret naval base. Not long after, Lidbom acquired yet another lady friend—the wife of the French foreign minister! When they were photographed together at a Stockholm hotel, Lidbom tried to grab the camera, but the bulky ambassador was not quick enough to prevent yet another unsavory scandal. Most diplomats would have been speedily discharged after such indiscriminate womanizing, but not Lidbom. It was as if he wanted to impress people that just like in the Ebbe Carlsson scandal, he was immune to prosecution, and thus could behave exactly as he pleased.

So, what hard evidence points to the PKK's involvement in Palme's murder? After all, not a single murder scene witness thought the murderer looked like a swarthy foreign terrorist, nor is there a single reliable observation of foreign-looking men acting suspiciously near the crime scene. Hans Holmér made much of a witness named Wiklund, who claimed to have seen a foreign-looking character standing on the opposite side of the Sveavägen just minutes before the murder, but the later police investigation concluded that if this witness was at all trustworthy, he had most probably seen one of the passengers in the Morelius car. Holmér also emphasized a sighting of a frantically running, foreign-looking man bumping into a witness not far from the murder scene; it was later found that this witness was probably yet another unreliable character making up stories for the police.[12] The evidence against the PKK is all circumstantial. We know that some of the hard-core members were serious criminals capable of murder, that they had easy access to firearms, and that they had made threats against Palme for branding them a terrorist organization and for not allowing PKK leader Abdullah Öcalan into Sweden. But making bombastic and threatening comments seems to have been something of a national predilection among the PKK Kurds. In their bloodthirsty pamphlets and newspapers, they threatened everyone who had annoyed them, from president Ronald Reagan down to overzealous Swedish traffic wardens. If they had killed everyone they threatened, it would have been a veritable bloodbath.

The conversations between the German and Swedish PKK men, indicating that they were planning a "wedding" (murder), also appear suspicious. There is no direct evidence that they referred to Olof Palme, however. In fact, other surveillance tapes betray that the Swedish and German PKK men were just as surprised as everyone else by the news of the murder. It is also significant that they kept talking about their wedding *after* Palme was shot, something that Holmér actively sought to suppress. It has been suggested that the PKK hard core were planning to assassinate two Kurdish dissidents in Sweden, and that the phone conversations about the wedding referred to the planning of these intended murders.[13] After all, the PKK had killed many dissenters before, but they had never carried out the assassination of a foreign political leader.

A sinister interpretation has also been made of the fact that the PKK leader Hüseyin Yilderim had several times been seen walking in the Old Town not far from the Palme apartment, but he had in fact been on the way to his favorite restaurant. The evidence from the alcoholic Seppo Ahlström may seem convincing, and it was certainly another mainstay in the case against the PKK as formulated by Holmér and Ebbe Carlsson. But Ahlström was not exactly a pillar of strength. He vacillated and changed his testimony, and in January 1987, he withdrew his evidence altogether, saying that he had not purchased any revolvers and had returned the money to Durak. Earlier, when asked to identify the kind of .357 magnum revolver he had purchased, he had picked out a weapon with a very short barrel, one that could not have been used to kill Olof Palme for ballistic reasons.[14]

Hans Holmér remained an adherent of the PKK theory until the end of his days, and kept on speculating about the murder scenario. In 1996, he again expanded the PKK conspiracy: there had been two killers, one of them waiting by the Tunnelgatan stairs to dispose of the murder weapon, and a number of other Kurds waiting nearby. After the murder, the two hit men were themselves murdered and buried in a park in Cologne.[15] The first part of this theory is not supported by any witness observation; the second is mere speculation. The National Audit Office experts concluded that although Holmér had presented a multitude of circumstantial observations, there was still a near-total lack of reliable evidence connecting the PKK with the crime scene. As for the spicy additions to the case by the irrepressible Ebbe Carlsson, the less said the better. No evidence supports the story of a murder-planning meeting in Damascus, nor is it easy for an unbiased mind to find a motive for the

Khomeini regime to murder Olof Palme, who had established friendly relations between Sweden and Iran. As for the "KGB connection," Ebbe made much of an unexplained increase in the radio traffic on frequencies used by Soviet spies just before the murder, but this increase was likely due to its being the last day of the month. Had there been a KGB connection at all, it would have been blown wide open after the downfall of the Soviet empire, when disgruntled former spies sold secret information to the highest bidder.[16]

The European PKK movement functioned in several strata. First, there were the foot soldiers, Kurdish patriots in exile. Many of these men were decent, hard-working people who made efforts to adapt to their new surroundings in Sweden or Germany, through learning the language and obtaining paid employment. The separate PKK groups worked independently, and if some firebrands from the Stockholm phalanx published an appeal against the Palme government, this would not imply that the PKK as a whole had turned against the prime minister. Secondly, there were the not insignificant criminal elements of the movement. Some of these men, like the drug smuggler Durak and his adherents, were gangsters whose political convictions were diluted by their craving for ill-gotten gains. Finally, the official leaders in the PKK Central Committee were men of an entirely different caliber. Intellectual left-wingers, they distanced themselves from the PKK criminals but found them useful to uphold the rigorous discipline necessary in a revolutionary movement.

It is hard to imagine that these PKK leaders really saw Palme as an enemy. Had he not opened Sweden to them as a safe haven from persecution in Turkey, and had the PKK men not been well treated in their new homeland? Palme's radical socialist rhetoric must have had a certain appeal to these men, particularly at a time when conservative forces were dominating European politics. And were they stupid enough to think that their organization had anything to gain from Palme's death? Surely, the PKK would have been hounded out of Sweden and probably Germany if they had been convicted of murdering Palme; they also would have suffered an immense loss of prestige in the international arena. Was this a risk they were prepared to take for a virtually purposeless assassination? The German police successfully prosecuted a number of PKK men in the 1990s and succeeded in breaking the morale of the PKK hard core. Some of the men who were being prosecuted gave evidence against their former comrades to save their own skins, and, as a result, several PKK gangsters ended up with lengthy prison sentences. Significantly, none of these turncoats mentioned anything about the murder of Olof Palme, something that would have been natural if the PKK had really been behind the murder.

The conclusion can only be that the case against the PKK as responsible for the death of Olof Palme is very weak indeed. The prosecutors, who had all the time been expecting Holmér to dazzle them with the impressive evidence against the PKK, were appalled when they found he possessed nothing at all apart from circumstantial observations, a reaction shared by the officers involved in the later police follow-up of the PKK lead. Prosecutor Anders Helin told the 1999 commission that in his opinion, the PKK lead was deliberate disinformation.[17] Helin did not dare to ask why people professing to be loyal Social Democrats would go to such lengths to spread disinformation about the murder of their prime minister. Had Holmér really tried to solve the murder, or just to find a "suitable" ending to Sweden's national trauma? He purposely exaggerated the case against the PKK and falsified the wedding conversations to make them seem more incriminating. And was Ebbe Carlsson not a fearless crusader, but just a sordid spy helping his disreputable friend the ambassador to denigrate the SÄPO and destabilize its prime mover, Näss? The darkest question of all also remains unanswered: What secret knowledge did Holmér, Lidbom, and Ebbe Carlsson possess to convince them that the murder needed a false solution? Did they know, or at least suspect, that the truth about why Olof Palme had to die led to dangerous paths that not even they dared tread?

THE SECOND MAIN SUSPECT

THE BAYONET KILLER

The departure of Hans Holmér had been wholly beneficial for the long-suffering detectives in the Palme investigation. A further improvement came in early 1988 when Holmér's replacement, the inert bureaucrat Ulf Karlsson, was himself replaced with a young, vigorous detective, captain Hans Ölvebro. Following a pattern that the reader will now recognize, his superiors gave no signs of official dissatisfaction with Karlsson, who was in fact promoted to become deputy chief of national police. Ölvebro started cleaning up the mess left behind by Holmér's unconventional approach to cataloguing police files and recruited a group of clever, experienced detectives who more or less started the police work up from scratch. His second in command, Ingemar Krusell, later wrote a book on the murder investigation, contrasting Ölvebro's sober, analytical detective work to Holmér's dilettante approach. From this time onward, the quality of the police work in the Palme investigation would improve considerably, particularly with regard to systematic attention to detail.

From an early stage, Ölvebro and Krusell saw through the PKK conspiracy: it was just a house of cards, containing no criminological substance. They also doubted the various other conspiracy theories about the murder. Instead, they wanted to pursue the hypothesis, first suggested by the prosecuting attorneys Anders Helin and Solveig Riberdahl, that Palme had been shot by a lone avenger. They had been able to ascertain that several witnesses had seen a man behaving suspiciously at the Grand cinema both before and after the late showing of *The Brothers Mozart*.[1] At about 9:00 p.m., before the Palmes arrived at the cinema, a workman had seen a thin man, about forty or forty-five years old, dressed in a dark skiing cap, a jacket, and dark trousers, gazing intently at the entrance of the Grand cinema. As another witness, artist Birgitta Wennerling, emerged from the Grand at 9:00 p.m.; she saw a pale man wearing a dark jacket and a cap staring at the cinema entrance. This was just as the Palmes were approaching the cinema. The man looked worried and tense, and was breathing deeply. Struck by his "sick, nasty glare," Wennerling made a drawing of him shortly after hearing the news that Olof Palme had been killed.

After *The Brothers Mozart* ended, a company director saw a short man wearing a blue parka and a cap, looking into a shop window near the cinema. Two women saw a stoutish, bespectacled, ordinary-looking man wearing a blue parka and a beige cap, looking intensely at the cinema entrance. He looked like a Scandinavian, with blue eyes and light hair; the only remarkable thing about him was his anxious, tense stare, as if he were waiting eagerly for someone to emerge from the cinema. Air-traffic controller Lars-Erik Eriksson, who was waiting to pick up his parents from the Grand cinema, saw a man in a blue jacket and a yellow knitted cap behaving very peculiarly. For more than twenty minutes, this man walked around nervously outside the cinema, waiting for the film to end and looking intensely into the lobby from time to time. At times, he stared at the witness with such a nasty glare that the air-traffic controller became frightened and swiftly locked the car doors from the inside. As we know, Mårten Palme saw a stoutish, scruffy-looking man wearing glasses walk after Olof and Lisbet as they left the cinema. He wore a blue parka and a flat cap. Finally, a Yugoslav immigrant named Ljubisa Najic, working in a hot dog stand not far from the Grand cinema, saw a fat, middle-aged man wearing a worn gray overcoat follow the Palmes. He had blond hair and looked like a Scandinavian.

The prosecutors presumed that many, if not all, of these observations concerned the same man. They thought that this individual, dubbed the "Grand Man" by the press, had seen the prime minister go into the cinema, and for unknown reasons decided to kill him. He had then gone to get a handgun, to be ready to shoot Palme after the film. The Grand Man then followed the prime minister on his final walk, overtook him when the Palmes were looking in the shop window, and stood ready to kill Palme at the Dekorima corner. Some further observations supported this theory.[2] An Italian chef named Nicola Fauzzi had met the Palmes walking along the Sveavägen. He saw a man wearing a blue parka walking after them, and presumed this might have been their bodyguard, although he looked middle-aged and unfit. No other person was following the prime minister. Then Fauzzi heard two loud bangs and turned around, suspecting that someone had shot Palme. Importantly, he could still see the man in the blue parka, who dodged into a doorway and then cautiously looked out.

A seventy-four-year-old woman named Kerstin Nordström was standing at the window of her sixth-floor apartment at the Sveavägen when she observed a

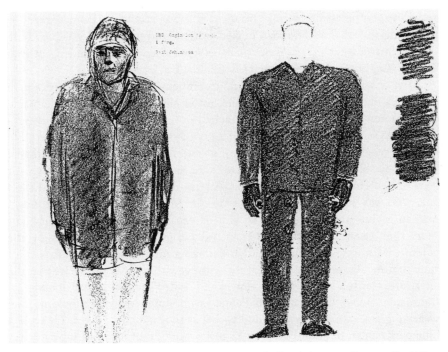

Two drawings of the Grand Man, by the artist Wennerling (left) and the air-traffic controller Eriksson (right). Reproduced by permission of the Swedish National Police Board.

couple crossing the street and a man in dark clothes following them. Then she sat down to knit for a while, before she was startled by two loud bangs. She looked at the clock, which showed 11:22. She again walked over to the window and saw a person lying down, and some others making attempts at resuscitation. Three or four minutes later, several police cars came, and then an ambulance.

At first glance, the testimonies of these two witnesses would appear to strongly support the theory of the Grand Man following the Palmes, but both have important drawbacks. Fauzzi was a very clearheaded, observant witness, but, as the police later admitted, his description of the man he saw fits the witness Björkman very well. The man's behavior after the shots were fired—dodging in a doorway and cautiously looking out—would indicate that this *was* Björkman. As for the old woman's evidence, she herself honestly pointed out that her observation of the three people could have been made at any time during the night. Even if it was made at the "correct" time, she still might have seen Björkman, who was by his own admission walking not far from the Palmes at this stage. It is curious that an elderly pensioner, sitting indoors in a sixth-floor apartment, described the shots as very loud, whereas the two people closest to the killer—Lisbet Palme and Björkman—described them as sounding like fireworks. It is also notable that this witness (who had a clock nearby) not only timed the murder correctly at shortly before 11:22 but also timed the arrival of the police to fit perfectly with the chronology given earlier in this book.

The police had another witness, a rather odd character named Alf Lundin, who told them he was in the habit of taking lengthy nocturnal walks, always alone. His first story, told on April 13, 1986, was that he had seen someone moving in the Adolf Fredrik churchyard; then he had continued walking along the Sveavägen, passing Olof and Lisbet Palme walking down the street not far from the cinema. He then gradually "improved" his story: in late April, he said he had seen a sinister, foreign-looking Grand Man following the Palmes. He also had seen this man a week or so before the murder, together with a tall blond man not unlike the Shadow. In December, he added that the Grand Man had been walking very clumsily. He then told newspaper journalists that he had seen the Grand Man again, visiting the crime scene on the 1987 anniversary of the murder! The police were rather skeptical about this weird witness, who had a history of psychiatric disease, but some details in his story seemed to tally with the descriptions from other witnesses.[3]

As the search for the Grand Man began, the police made a huge trawl for potential suspects: people mentioned in Holmér's old material, men observed in the area at the time of the murder, known criminals, and people who had been behaving threateningly or suspiciously. In March, the police received a hot tip from Thomas Kanger, a journalist with an interest in the murder investigation. A man who worked near the murder scene had been overheard talking to his mother on the telephone; weeping profusely, he had admitted that he had shot Olof Palme! This individual, it turned out, was known to dislike Palme, and he fit the rather vague description of the killer given by the murder scene witnesses. He had told a workmate that he had killed Palme but would never be caught. The suspect was followed by the police and clandestinely videotaped, and his phone was tapped. When formally questioned, the man produced a strong alibi, and in early May, he was entirely dropped as a suspect.[4]

From an early stage, the police had been interested in a gambling club called Oxen, a known hangout for various criminal elements situated near the scene of the murder. It was part owned by a drug dealer named Sigge Cedergren, an objectionable character who dabbled in all kinds of criminal activity. At his club, illegal gambling flourished, drugs were bought and sold, prostitutes plied their trade, and fences touted their stolen goods. Sigge himself had a profitable sideline selling stolen handguns to criminals planning robberies or holdups. From time to time, Sigge was convicted of various wrongdoings. In the United States, such a man would be put behind bars for a very long time, but the Swedish court system was incapable of dealing effectively with professional criminals of this caliber. Even when he was convicted for wholesale drug trafficking, the sentences were ridiculously short, and after just a year or so of rehabilitation in a comfortable Swedish prison, Sigge would emerge to fetch the ill-gotten gains he had stashed away and open another gambling club at a new address.

One of Sigge Cedergren's steady clients was a criminal and alcoholic named Christer Pettersson. During a long and bloody career, this individual had gained notoriety in the Stockholm underworld.[5] Born to a respectable middle-class family, he had studied to become an actor, but left the acting school in disgrace after being caught stealing from the other students. As a teenager, Pettersson drank to excess and used various illicit drugs. In 1967, aged just twenty, he served his first jail sentence for theft. Pettersson got into trouble many times for beating people up in sudden rages. His temper was very short, particularly when he was the worse for drink. A strong, muscular fellow, he carried a formidable-looking bayonet, and the other young thugs in Stockholm treated him with respect.

In December 1970, when Pettersson was a department store buying Christmas presents, two men pushed over his shopping bag. Pettersson went berserk. He pursued the men out of the store and managed to get one of them into an alley. He then brutally stabbed his unarmed opponent to death with his bayonet, twisting his weapon in the wound as his victim pleaded for mercy. This killing took place not far from the Tunnelgatan stairs, an area that Pettersson knew very well. It is amazing that he was sentenced to just six months in a psychiatric facility for this brutal killing; in the United States, he would have been put away for a considerable period of time, and the chapter chronicling his life of crime may well have ended here.

After being released, Pettersson moved into the apartment of one of the women psychologists from the psychiatric hospital, who was apparently prepared to continue his course of psychotherapy in this unconventional way. She may have hoped to inspire him to turn his back on crime and become a hardworking pillar of society, but Pettersson beat her up and returned to his old life as a habitual criminal. He was delighted to find that he had become a notorious figure in the Stockholm underworld. Known as the "Bayonet Killer," he commanded much respect and was sometimes used as a "persuader" by other criminals. Together with another ruffian, he took to robbing drug dealers. His friend would arrange to buy drugs from a dealer, suggesting that they walk into an alleyway. Pettersson then would draw his bayonet and tell the pusher who he was! In New York, the two thugs would have ended up dead very soon after adopting such a primitive modus operandi, but the Swedish drug dealers were a meek lot, unlike their gun-toting American colleagues; it was rare that they put up any resistance when they knew they were facing the Bayonet Killer. Pettersson himself estimated that he and his friend had relieved more than three hundred Stockholm drug dealers of their money and narcotics using this simple stratagem!

Pettersson's reputation as a hard man grew with a series of further brutal outrages. In 1973, he tried to bash a man's head in with an iron bar. In 1974, he stabbed a man in the chest during a drunken brawl and served six months in prison. In 1975, he stabbed a drug dealer with his bayonet but emerged from prison after a year. The year 1977 was to become Pettersson's *annus horribilis*. In June, he attacked a man with an axe in a restaurant and knocked a woman out cold; in August, he stabbed a man in the belly; in October, he cut a man with his bayonet after trying to rob him. In November, he was suspected of murdering his own father. This latter charge turned out to be completely unfounded; the police determined that old Pettersson had fallen over and knocked his head against an iron stove. Pettersson's respite was nevertheless brief. After being released by the police, he went out to buy a thousand white carnations for his father's grave. He then went to a bar to buy some narcotics to steady his nerves, but the drug dealer, who apparently did not know of the Bayonet Killer's reputation, demanded full payment. Without any further ado, Pettersson brandished his bayonet and stabbed the dealer severely, with the words, "Take that for payment, you swine!" The mild and forgiving Swedish justice system had finally had enough of Pettersson's bloody career, and he was sentenced to five years in prison for attempted murder. A forensic psychiatrist examined Pettersson and proclaimed him a dangerous psychopath who should serve the full term without parole.

After he was released from prison in early 1983, the parole board made sure that Pettersson was provided with paid employment—at a youth recreation center in a Stockholm suburb! No one seems to have considered it dangerous to have a convicted killer taking care of children; according to a newspaper article, Pettersson performed his duties well, although his work-shy nature ensured that he did not remain at the youth recreation center for very long. During the following years, Pettersson descended further into severe alcohol and amphetamine abuse. Either the prison sentence or the numbing effect of always being more or less drunk seems to have curbed his aggression, and he committed no further acts of mindless violence like those back in 1977. Instead, he committed many minor offences, mainly petty theft and shoplifting. His friends nicknamed him "the Dasher" for an ingenious trick he devised to steal from the state liquor stores—one that he, by his own admission, used more than a hundred times, always with success. I must warn the reader that this trick is applicable only in Sweden. Pettersson first ordered a large bottle of vodka, then a very expensive bottle of vintage wine. Like a true Swede, the liquor salesman dared not suggest that the scruffy-looking barbarian in front of him could hardly be a wine connoisseur, or even have the money to pay for the expensive wine. As he obediently shuffled off to fetch the wine from the cellar, leaving the bottle of vodka on the counter, Pettersson grabbed the vodka bottle—and dashed off!

By the mid-1980s, Pettersson had become a pathetic figure. The state had rewarded him with a not ungenerous pension, allowing him funds to purchase food, shelter, and enough alcohol to drink himself to death in style. If the weather allowed it, he used to sit in the local park all day, drinking cheap wine with his friends. As the bottles were emptied, the alcoholics got increasingly raucous and cheerful. Pettersson then reeled home to the tiny apartment he had been given by social services, where he continued drinking beer and vodka throughout the evening, sitting alone in the almost unfurnished living room, dressed only in his underpants. Whenever he supplemented his pension by some petty thievery, he could afford to buy amphetamine from Sigge Cedergren at the Oxen club. In early 1986, Pettersson was convicted twice, once for urinating on a shop display window, the other time for trying to steal two cans of spaghetti in a store before being intercepted by the guard.

At the time of the murder of Olof Palme, Christer Pettersson was living in Rotebro, a rough Stockholm suburb. His name entered the Palme murder investigation as early as March 2, 1986, when a computerized search of earlier violent crimes taking place near the Tunnelgatan stairs was performed. No further action was taken regarding him, however. In April, three people independently informed the Palme investigation police that Pettersson was a very dangerous man, certainly capable of murder. Ludicrously, one of these individuals thought he resembled the Phantom; another found him very like the Shadow! The detectives in charge commented that Pettersson was a tall well-built man, and a dangerous psychopath who had killed before. Much emphasis was put on the point that he resembled the Shadow. Pettersson's name thus entered the murder inquiry mainly because of his resemblance to a character that did not exist.

In May 1986, two detectives visited Pettersson, and he told them that the night of the murder, he had visited Sigge Cedergren at the Oxen club, arriving at 7:00 p.m. and leaving just after 10:00. He then walked to the central station, taking the train back to Rotebro and arriving home at 11:30. The next morning, he awoke at 8:00 a.m. and went out to buy the newspaper. When he saw the news that Olof Palme was dead, he sat down at his kitchen table and cried. This story seems to have satisfied the police, at least for the time being.

In October 1986, a certain Ulf Spinnars, a criminal drug addict, was reported to have made confused statements about the murder of Olof Palme; one of them was that he knew the identity of the killer. The police questioned him a month later. He said he had been staying in Christer Pettersson's apartment the night of Palme's murder, and Pettersson was again questioned by the police, this time to give his friend an alibi. The Bayonet Killer verified that when he had come home at 11:30, Spinnars had been sleeping underneath the kitchen table. Again, the police were satisfied the two men were telling the truth.

Sigge Cedergren was a person for whom the words "honor among thieves" had no meaning: he freely "shopped" other criminals to the police, sometimes to save his own skin or to get rid of competitors, other times to ingratiate himself to the narcotics detectives. The police knew well that Sigge might turn out to be helpful, and he was questioned many times, particularly since he himself had started a remarkable rumor just a few weeks after the murder of Olof Palme. Sigge claimed that just at the time Olof Palme was murdered, he and his friend Reine Jansson had been driving back to Sigge's apartment, not far from the murder scene. At the Luntmakargatan, Sigge wanted to take a shortcut, driving the wrong way down a one-way street. A white Volvo drove up to block his way, however, and when Sigge finally managed to negotiate his way past it, the two men heard police sirens nearby. Then, as Sigge parked his car, he saw a tall blond man in a light blue jacket running north on the Luntmakargatan, away from the crime scene.[6]

Sigge was questioned by detective sergeant Thure Nässén, a tough operator in the Stockholm underworld who knew Sigge well from various deals in the past. It seems to have been a rather disagreeable surprise for Sigge that the police took his gossip so seriously, and he found it difficult to explain his story about the running man. He had heard rumors that the hated thirty-three-year-old, who was in custody at this time, was none other than the pop singer Ted Gärdestad, and told the police that the man he had seen looked just like the singer. The police were not particularly interested, since they knew the rumor was baseless and that Gärdestad had been staying abroad at the time of the murder.[7] Nässén made a note that he thought Sigge knew the running man's real identity and was reluctant to tell the police. It is interesting to note that when Nässén mentioned Christer Pettersson's name in the conversation, Sigge immediately said that Pettersson liked Palme and his politics and would never have done anything to harm the prime minister. Sigge was one of the witnesses the police hoped would identify Viktor Gunnarsson in a lineup, but he picked out a policeman instead.

In August 1986, Sigge was himself sentenced to three years in prison for drug dealing and handling stolen goods. Nässén kept questioning him during

Christer Pettersson in April 1986. Pettersson appears at the left of this police surveillance photograph; note the absence of facial hair. Reproduced by permission of the Swedish National Police Board.

this time, since he suspected that the prospect of spending a lengthy period of time behind bars would loosen the tongue of the veteran drug dealer. In this respect, Sigge did not disappoint. He gradually embroidered his story: he had stared the running man right in the eyes, he said, and the fugitive had almost stopped short, believing that Sigge and his companion were police detectives. Sigge then remembered that he had seen four people walking down to the Sveavägen, one of whom was carrying a walkie-talkie. Shortly after, as he encountered the white Volvo, he heard two shots fired! Sigge then suggested yet another identity for the running man: he was Lars-Erik Svartenbrandt, a notorious violent criminal. The police again were unimpressed; although there had been newspaper reports of Svartenbrandt's involvement in the murder, he had actually been in prison at the time.

The tenth time Sigge was questioned, in March 1987, Nässén bluntly declared that the drug dealer's story was a pack of lies. The detectives asked him to search his memory and tell the truth. Sigge then admitted that he had made up his story about Ted Gärdestad after hearing a rumor around town, and that the four people with the walkie-talkies may well have been police detectives. He did not change his story about the white Volvo, the gunshots, and the running man, however. But Nässén had access to the transcript from a secret phone-tapping operation on Sigge's apartment, performed by the narcotics detectives who were investigating the drug dealer at the time, showing that Sigge had been at home already at 11:02, and that he had made several phone calls until 12:57 a.m. The police decided that he was just another liar wasting police time, and lost interest in him for the time being.

In February 1988, Sigge was released from prison. In his usual manner, he purchased another club and another apartment, and went on with his life of crime just as before. Nor did he forget his old contacts within the police, who could turn out to be valuable if he decided to "neutralize" some competitor. He himself asked to see Nässén to deliver further information about the Palme murder, namely that he had read about the speculations about the Grand Man in the newspapers, and that the description fitted his old friend Christer Pettersson very well. Sigge speculated that Pettersson might have gone to see him that fatal evening. If no one answered the door, Pettersson used to roam the neighborhood for hours, checking Sigge's apartment and the Oxen gambling club at intervals. The area in front of the Grand cinema was the perfect place for someone to watch for a light in the window of Sigge's apartment, on the Tegnérgatan just around the corner. An evil-looking character with a nasty glare, Pettersson was the type of person anyone would remember.

Sigge said he could not believe the Grand Man and the killer were the same person, however, particularly since Pettersson had no motive to kill Palme. Yet, he pointed out that Pettersson was a very dangerous man. If he got seriously annoyed with someone, anything could happen, and he was certainly capable of murder. This time, the police detectives were much more satisfied with Sigge's testimony. For Nässén, it formed the basis of a new hypothesis. The night of the murder, Pettersson went to Sigge's apartment but found no one at home. He began walking the nearby streets at random, waiting for the drug dealer to return, and saw the Palmes arrive at the cinema. For reasons unknown, he decided to kill the prime minister and went to get a revolver from some nearby apartment. He waited for Palme outside the cinema, just as the Grand Man was said to have done, and followed him to the Dekorima corner.

In this murder scenario, the obvious provider of the murder weapon would be Sigge himself. The drug dealer freely told the police that in February 1986, he had possessed quite an arsenal of illegal firearms. He had a sawed-off shotgun in a refrigerator next to his bed, a tear gas gun in his toolbox in the kitchen, a .357 magnum revolver underneath the kitchen sink, and a German army revolver hidden inside a clock. Sigge still had the .357 magnum, but the police found that for ballistic reasons, it could not be the murder weapon.

Sigge denied that he had had access to any other .357 revolver at the time. The police were surprised and annoyed that the drug dealer still refused to adapt his version of events to the phone-tap transcript for the night of the murder. He must have known that the police were after Pettersson, since he told them yet another version of the saga of the running man: now it was Pettersson he had seen running down the Luntmakargatan! This was not what the police wanted to hear, however. Although they appreciated Sigge's increasing helpfulness, they pointed out that according to the phone-tap transcript, he had been at home when Palme was killed. In yet another questioning, in November 1988, Sigge's memory had improved further. He now recalled that Christer Pettersson had been one of his old customers for amphetamine, and that they usually met in Sigge's apartment. Pettersson had told him that the night of the murder, he had waited outside Sigge's apartment for a while before going to Oxen. Pettersson had added that he had not told the police the truth about his movements that night, and Sigge had gotten the impression he had something to hide.

The criminal Ulf Spinnars was another key figure among the shady characters surrounding Christer Pettersson. As we know, Pettersson had originally given Spinnars an alibi for the murder of Olof Palme, an alibi that would work both ways. Spinnars was in prison at this time, and the police visited him there, making him presents of pornographic magazines and other things he might find useful. They got a result: Spinnars changed his story and admitted that Pettersson had left the apartment between 6:00 and 8:00 p.m., not at 9:00 p.m., as he had originally said. This latest version meant that Pettersson could have observed the Palmes outside the cinema before the film started. For some time, Spinnars stubbornly persisted that Pettersson had come home between 11:00 p.m. and midnight, thus giving him an alibi for the murder, since the first train to Rotebro departing after the murder arrived at 12:07 a.m. Pettersson did not have access to a car or any other rapid means of transportation. After prolonged discussions, Spinnars finally changed his story: Pettersson had come home at 12:30.

To the detectives' delight, Spinnars had more spicy stuff for them. Pettersson had once become very angry when they discussed what time he had come home, and he had seemed to want an alibi for the murder. Pettersson had also told Spinnars that he was worried because he looked like the Phantom, particularly since he had previously killed a man very near where Palme had fallen.[8] Another criminal alcoholic gave Spinnars some much-needed support: Pettersson had told him that he had been in central Stockholm the night Palme was killed, and the Bayonet Killer had later quarreled with Spinnars about the time he returned home.

A young woman who had been to see *The Brothers Mozart* at the Grand cinema reported to the police that she had had a rather disturbing experience afterward. As she was waiting for the bus home, she was approached by an ugly, scruffy-looking man who appeared to be high on either drugs or alcohol. He was talking to himself in an odd manner, complaining that one of his fingers was bleeding badly. He asked her for a cigarette, and since the young woman was a true Swede, and kind to the unfortunates of society, she handed him one. The tramp, as she supposed him to be, then boldly and optimistically offered to accompany her home, but she firmly told him no. In spite of this rebuff, the man remained in the bus shelter, grumbling to himself about his injured finger. Some young punks then came up to the bus shelter and kicked it hard to frighten the two people inside. The woman was amazed to see that without any hesitation, the tramp drew a large knife and went after them. Although outnumbered five to one, he sent the entire gang of punks running. The woman was relieved to see her bus arriving, and as it drove past the punks some blocks onward, she could see that they were still running hard, with the tramp in dogged pursuit.

The police soon found out that several other people had seen a man fitting the description of this short-tempered tramp at the Grand cinema: he had been reeling around pestering people for a bandage for his injured finger and talking confusedly on the telephone. Since he had been at the cinema at the time of the murder, the tramp could not be the killer, but the police hoped he had seen the Grand Man and wanted to question him. It was far from difficult to track him down. When a police squad raided a bar not far from the Grand cinema during the night of the murder, one of the people they found there was the forty-year-old alcoholic Roger Östlund, and the woman from the bus shelter immediately picked out his photograph.

The police then went on to question Östlund about his observations the night Olof Palme was murdered, but not unsurprisingly, he said that due to his drunken state, he didn't have the slightest recollection of the night in question. A week earlier, he had been released from prison, and he had been tramping around Stockholm in a drug-induced haze, sleeping in various hideouts. When the police told him about the woman and the punks, he admitted that this might well be true, but showed no sign of recollection.

Östlund had been questioned by the police many times in the past, and he must have realized that they wanted something from him, something to do with the murder of Olof Palme. He told a story about a prostitute "girlfriend" of his, whom he claimed to have seen with a revolver of foreign manufacture, but the detectives showed little interest. Later, when he was himself in prison, Roger tried to "shop" a drug dealer whom he claimed had received guns and ammunition in a burglary near the Sveavägen. In November 1988, Östlund told a much more detailed story about how he had gone to the Oxen club the night of the murder, trying to borrow money with which to gamble. After being rebuffed, he kept on drinking at the club. In his intoxicated state, he accidentally cut his finger on his own large knife. He rang the doorbell of Sigge's apartment, but a man came out and said that Sigge was not at home. The man looked like a nasty piece of work, and Roger did not argue, but reeled away toward the Grand cinema. The police asked him whether he knew the identity of this threatening man, and particularly if he had met someone he knew outside the cinema, but in several further questionings, Roger had nothing new to tell.[9]

Throughout October and November 1988, the police kept Christer Pettersson under surveillance: he was videotaped, and particular notice was taken of every person he met. Soon, the police knew most of the alcoholics, tramps, and petty criminals in Rotebro but found no indication Pettersson had any more sinister contacts. It turned out that Pettersson was in the habit of hinting that he knew more that he wanted to tell about the murder of Olof Palme. He told people that he had been at the Sveavägen the night of the murder, and that considering his reputation as a violent criminal, he was lucky not to have been arrested.

Spinnars, too, hinted that Pettersson was somehow implicated in the Palme murder.[10] Just a few days after the murder, the Bayonet Killer had come dashing into the apartment of a friend in the middle of the night after suffering a bad "trip." He was trembling like a leaf and had the delusion that he was being chased by the police. Pettersson then made an effort to move to a desolate village in Lapland, to assist an elderly Finn who had a business pulling down houses. He would actually have gone there had he not quarreled with social services, which refused to pay for his train ticket. This was an odd decision for a man who had spent all his life in the Stockholm area and who had always been reluctant to work.[11]

The police videotapes showed something else that was very interesting. Drunk or sober, Pettersson had a strange, unsteady walk, due partly to alcoholic cerebellar ataxia and partly to an old leg injury sustained when hitching a ride outside a railway carriage, his leg becoming wedged between the train and the platform at a station. Only one murder scene witness originally said that the killer ran clumsily, namely Anders Delsborn. But some of the others changed their stories after Lundin's account of the clumsy man following the Palmes had become known in the media. At the same questioning in which he changed his description of the killer's clothes, Leif Ljungqvist added that the killer had run away with a clumsy, broad-legged gait. Another murder scene witness, cab driver Hans Johansson, had initially said nothing about the killer's strange walk, either to the police or to newspapers. In October 1986, he said that the man he had seen "had run like an elephant." The hot dog seller Najic also "remembered" that the man he had seen follow the Palmes had been walking very clumsily. The police thus had three murder scene witnesses and two Grand cinema witnesses testifying that the man they had observed walked in a similar way to Christer Pettersson.

Yet this "truth" about the murder, echoed in almost every publication, is slenderly supported by the crucial early witness testimonies. We still do not know whether several witnesses somehow belatedly remembered this important fact, or whether they were saying what the police wanted them to say, as in the previous example of the blue parka and the flat cap. The questioning of young Anna Hage gives food for thought in this respect.[12] The police detective asked her to describe how the killer ran, and when she replied that he ran quite quickly, he went on, "Perhaps he ran clumsily or unsteadily?" She replied that he certainly ran very fast, with a determined gait, although he was a tall man with a heavy footfall. The detective then tried again: "Was this footfall not heavy and clumsy?" This she confidently denied, although other witnesses may well have been more susceptible to changing their stories.

On December 14, 1988, the police detectives brought Christer Pettersson in for questioning. They had hoped to keep him under surveillance longer, but the court permission for covert surveillance had been kept in the public record, with the suspect's name on it. Thus it was not difficult for the newspaper journalists to get scent of the news that the police had an important new suspect, and Nässén and his detectives had to make a dawn raid to prevent the ludicrous scenario of Pettersson reading about himself as the prime murder suspect in the evening newspapers. The Bayonet Killer seemed to be in good cheer, and told the police they were crazy to think he had killed the prime minister. He phoned a friend to say he would be back home in three hours, but this was an optimistic estimate, since it would in fact be ten months before he next saw the outside of a prison.

Outside the apartment, journalists were waiting to photograph Pettersson as the cops took him away. The evening papers all had large headlines saying, "The 41-year-old is arrested!" Just as when Viktor Gunnarsson had been arrested, the media did their best to make Pettersson into a monster. Admittedly, this was not difficult considering his blood-spattered curriculum vitae, but there were some dubious and ill-founded additions. The *Expressen* said that he had several times threatened Olof Palme, and the *Aftonbladet*, that he was known for his burning hatred of Palme; neither of these allegations was true, but they certainly added to the image of a sinister killer.[13]

Pettersson's apartment and his safety deposit box at a nearby bank were ransacked by Ingemar Krusell and a squad of police technicians. They hoped to find technical evidence that firearms or ammunition had been kept at these premises, but the search proved in vain. The Bayonet Killer's bookshelf contained a nonfiction work about Dr. Goebbels and also a fascist tract by a disgruntled Swede. Another find was Pettersson's diary for 1986; Krusell found it interesting that he had stopped making entries just after Palme's murder. The police were also curious about a pamphlet from a nearby shooting range. There had been reports of people illicitly using this facility shortly before the murder. Had Pettersson been doing some last-minute target practice? Pettersson liked to steal keys from people, and the police found about thirty keys in his apartment. Most of these were old keys to safety deposit boxes, but not all. It has been speculated that Pettersson stole Sigge's keys to be able to break into his apartment and steal the revolver, but Ingemar Krusell retorts that none of the keys found fit Sigge's locks.[14]

Throughout the day, Pettersson was questioned, but he told the police as little as possible. His own story of what he had been doing the evening of the murder was coherent, although the detectives found it suspiciously detailed, as if he had deliberately invented it.[15] Pettersson said that in the early evening, he had taken the train into central Stockholm to buy some amphetamine from Sigge Cedergren at the Oxen club. The aforementioned Spinnars was left behind in Pettersson's apartment, since the Bayonet Killer had lost the keys to his front door, and was fearful of burglars. Having completed the deal, he spent some time with Sigge and his prostitute girlfriend Lena Åkerman. Along with a gray-haired man he did not know, he signed a legal affidavit for Sigge, to the effect that Sigge and his girlfriend would have a shared bank account. Pettersson very much wanted a drink or two, but the mean-spirited Sigge said he had no vodka to spare. Sigge's girlfriend, who was on bad terms with him, went to get two bottles of vodka, however, and the grateful Bayonet Killer drank several large glasses of vodka and soda. He then took the train back home again without seeing anything of the murder, but since he had drunk more than a pint of strong vodka, he fell asleep and did not wake up until the train had reached its terminus. After taking a couple of deep breaths of fresh air to clear his head, Pettersson boarded the same train going the other way and this time managed to stay awake, finally arriving home just before midnight. Spinnars was eager to get some of the amphetamine, but Pettersson lied that he had not been able to get any. The disappointed Spinnars then left, and Pettersson ended his day by injecting the drugs he had purchased.

The police had been busy preparing for Pettersson's reception, and in the afternoon, the series of questionings was interrupted by two police lineups. The paunchy, repulsive-looking Pettersson was joined by eleven policemen in the lineup, which was first seen by two of the key Grand Man witnesses. Mårten Palme tentatively picked out Pettersson as the man most resembling the Grand Man, although he vacillated between Pettersson and another man in the lineup. The air-traffic controller Eriksson, who had been sitting in his car outside the cinema, vacillated between three men, but finally picked out Pettersson, who gave him the same feeling of revulsion as the man he had seen outside the cinema. The task force police were then very apprehensive, as Mrs. Palme was to see the crucial lineup.

As we know, Hans Holmér had monopolized the early contacts with Mrs. Palme. Firstly, she gave a description of the killer very much resembling the witness Björkman. Not unreasonably, both Holmér and his old adversary Karl-Gerhard Svensson made their minds up that she had never seen the killer's face, only the frightened Björkman taking cover just after the shots had been fired. After the picture of the Phantom had been made public, she described a much more forceful, sinister character. The killer looked fit and had broad shoulders, a rectangular face with staring eyes, straight eyebrows, and thin lips. Mrs. Palme flatly insisted that both times she was describing the same man, the murderer of her husband. Krusell admits that she first saw Björkman but then, when the situation was properly explained to her, realized that the real killer must be *another* man in a blue parka, whom she also clearly saw.[16]

After Holmér's disgrace, and the publication of his interviews about the murder, Lisbet Palme realized that he had never intended to keep his promise to her that her disclosures would be kept secret. There, in black and white, was the confidential information she had given to Holmér only, with the addition that he had not believed her testimony. As a result, her dislike and distrust of the police and prosecutors intensified. Ölvebro met her only once, and when he said he believed the murder of Olof Palme should be treated like any ordinary murder inquiry, she angrily responded that there was nothing ordinary about the murder of her husband. Here the conversation ended, and Mrs. Palme made it clear that she wanted nothing further to do with Ölvebro or his detectives. According to Riberdahl, Mrs. Palme did not try to disguise that she considered the detectives her social inferiors, preferring to speak to the police administrators and prosecutors. Even among the latter, Riberdahl herself was the only one who found favor.[17]

In 1988, Riberdahl and Almblad had several meetings with Mrs. Palme and her sons, informing them about the progress of the investigation. They showed her photographs of various individuals of interest to the murder inquiry, but she never reacted in a way to suggest she recognized them.[18] Riberdahl was surprised that she never spoke of "the killer," just "the person I saw in the Sveavägen," during these information meetings. In a meeting in the fall of 1988, the prosecutors told the Palme family about the main suspects, in particular that one of them was an alcoholic living in a Stockholm suburb, who had committed murder before.

Although her dislike of the prosecutors had somewhat abated during the aforementioned course of meetings, Mrs. Palme would hardly agree even to take part in the lineup of suspects that was intended to bring to justice the killer of her husband. According to Ölvebro, she first said that if the suspect was an alcoholic, it was pointless for her to see him. After much pleading from the prosecutors, who stressed that the procedure was of the utmost importance, she finally acceded. They must have given her the impression that they had a very strong case against the suspect. Even so, Mrs. Palme had a series of demands of her own. She refused to see the suspect live; instead she would view a videotape of the lineup. Nor did she allow the suspect and his legal counsel to be present when she saw this video. The prosecutors were not happy with this arrangement, since it constituted a serious breach of legal formality, but Mrs. Palme was as inflexible as ever. But the outcome when Mrs. Palme was shown the video of Pettersson and eleven policemen must have lifted the spirits of the long-suffering Riberdahl and Almblad. Mrs. Palme immediately said: "Well, it is evident who is the alcoholic! It is number 8!" She then said that number 8 (Pettersson) fit her description with regard to his face, his eyes, and his villainous looks. Two of the other men fit her description in part, she continued, but not as well as number 8, nor did they have his repulsive features. As a direct result of Mrs. Palme picking him out, Pettersson was charged with the murder of Olof Palme.

The newspapers soon got scent of the fact that Pettersson had been picked out by Lisbet Palme and some other witnesses, although this was not formally confirmed by the police and prosecutors. The secrecy was such that some of Ölvebro's closest associates were kept in the dark about what had really happened during the video lineup on December 14. The reason for this secrecy has never been explained, but an uncharitable mind would suspect that the prosecutors still feared that the overbearing Mrs. Palme would refuse to testify in court or retract her evidence. This view is supported by the fact that by late January 1989, a written record of the video lineup in December still had not been made. On January 26, Mrs. Palme was again shown the video, but this time only the part showing Pettersson. The same day, she signed a brief document confirming that she had picked Pettersson out.

This development greatly cheered the prosecutors and police, and the lat-

New police lineup, as seen by Mårten Palme. This time Christer Pettersson is number 3; note his untidy and paunchy appearance and light-colored shoes. Reproduced by permission of the Swedish National Police Board.

ter worked overtime to gather further evidence against Pettersson. Further jubilation came when two more Grand witnesses, the artist Wennerling and the hot dog seller Najic picked Pettersson out as the man they had seen. The descriptions of Pettersson in the newspapers were very detailed, and although he was not named, it was easy for those who knew him to recognize the notorious Bayonet Killer. The media climate thus ensured that a steady procession of damaging character witnesses approached the police: various alcoholics, drug addicts, and jailbirds testified that Pettersson had hated Palme, that he was a Nazi and worshipped Hitler, or that he had made incriminating statements about somehow being involved in the murder.[19]

The police did their best to get a confession out of Pettersson, but without success. Once the alcoholic fumes had cleared from what remained of his brain, Pettersson clammed up completely and gave nothing away. When formally charged with the murder, he reacted as if he had expected this to happen, not showing the feelings of anger or outrage that Krusell would have expected in an innocent man. The main task for the police was to crack Pettersson's alibi, and here they had considerable success. Neither Sigge, nor his girlfriend Lena, nor the gray-haired man Pettersson claimed to have met at the club (Sigge's friend Reine Jansson) had seen him at the Oxen club that

night. The legal affidavit Pettersson said he had signed was been found at the
Oxen club, but it was undated. Sigge said it had been drawn up and signed at
an earlier date. With his usual caddishness, he admitted to the police that its
intended purpose was to enable him to steal the money Lena earned by pros-
tituting herself, since he knew she was using alcohol and drugs to such excess
that she was unlikely to notice the shortage of funds in her account. The police managed to track down the train driver and guard who had been on duty
on the suburban train on February 28, but neither of them could recall seen a
drunk sleeping on the late train to Rotebro and Märsta, or waking him up
when the train reached its terminus.[20]

Another success for the police was that the memory of the aforementioned
Roger Östlund suddenly improved. In January 1989, a friend told him that
Christer Pettersson was the "forty-one-year-old," and at that moment, Roger
realized that the night Olof Palme was killed, he had met Pettersson in the
lobby of the Grand cinema. The police were very pleased with Roger's change
of heart, which would seem to solve the mystery of the Grand Man once and
for all: here was a man who actually knew Pettersson quite well and who identified him as the Grand Man without hesitation. They arranged a direct confrontation between the two ruffians, some sturdy detectives standing by in
case of a fight. Pettersson managed to keep his calm, however. In a convincing
manner, he denied meeting Roger and roundly accused him of lying. It turned
out that although Roger knew Pettersson, they were far from the best of
friends. Pettersson had once tried to steal Roger's amphetamine when they
lived in the same homeless shelter, and on another occasion, they had quarreled when drinking together, and Roger had lashed out at Pettersson with a
bottle. The Bayonet Killer's steely glare must have unnerved the wretched police informer, but prompted by the police, Roger remained convinced it was
really Pettersson he had seen.

The police had obtained another star witness: since Roger actually knew
Pettersson, no one could doubt his identification of the Grand Man.[21] The
problem was that Roger had been hitting the bottle hard in recent months
and using a dangerous cocktail of illicit drugs. Apart from the obvious risk
that he would die from an overdose before testifying, he might also turn up in
court drunk or high on drugs. Even when sober, he was wholly lacking in sen-
sibility and self-control. The police took him to a rural cottage for the dual
purpose of detoxifying him and establishing a positive rapport with this
Swedish Caliban, but Roger brought a supply of drugs, including amphetamine. The project ended in failure after he threatened the cops with a knife
and began demolishing the furniture. Later, when in court for drunk driving
and various drug-related offenses, Roger threatened to withdraw his testimony in the Palme trial if he was not treated with leniency. The police were

pleased that he would have a forced drying out period behind bars, and chose to ignore him, rightly predicting that thoughts of the reward would make Roger appear in court and say what was expected of him.

Due to his gruff and unfriendly manner, and his alarming violent tendencies, Christer Pettersson had never had many friends. But after being charged with murdering Olof Palme, he found more friends than he had ever had before. Not without reason, many Swedes thought him a very unlikely murderer of their famous prime minister. Great men demand great killers, they reasoned, and it would have made more sense if Palme had been assassinated by foreign terrorists, rather than murdered without motive by a violent drunk. The left-wingers preferred a fascist conspiracy involving the police themselves as the ideal murderers. According to their socialist philosophy, Pettersson was an unfortunate let down by society; he should be pitied and supported, and gently reminded of his duty to the People's Home. Their hero Olof Palme had always been so concerned about the outcasts of society; could it really be conceived that one of these people would bite the hand that had fed him such generous social benefits? These left-wingers regarded Pettersson as a political prisoner intended to play the part of Olof Palme's murderer in a trial designed to end Sweden's national trauma. Was this friendless, miserable alcoholic not the perfect murderer, a scapegoat no one would miss when he was led away to prison? As Pettersson was tucking into the generous helpings of nutritious Swedish prison food in his comfortable cell, his supporters saw him as a Swedish Alfred Dreyfus, shivering in a damp, inhospitable dungeon on Devil's Island.

THE TRIALS OF
CHRISTER PETTERSSON

Pettersson's defense counsel was sixty-seven-year-old Arne Liljeros, who enjoyed a good reputation among Stockholm's criminal underworld. Yet he and his assistant, Lars Ekman, were at an immense disadvantage from the beginning. The police and prosecutors had been working as a team for eighteen months, and had had the time to master the huge amount of material in the Palme inquiry. They knew which witnesses to highlight and who should remain "forgotten." The latter group of course included those who had made "inconvenient" observations of the murder scene, as was well as witnesses whose testimony suggested a murder conspiracy. In contrast, Liljeros and Ekman had just a few months to try to master this vast web of contradictory evidence. And Liljeros was quite an old man. Although he was a skillful trial lawyer, his ability to grasp the intricacies of this great case was not the most astute, nor was his memory the most retentive. The aforementioned left-wing conspiracy theorists freely offered their advice, and some of them had detailed knowledge of the murder investigation, but Liljeros knew some of them as oddballs and fanatics and tarred all Pettersson's supporters with the same brush. When the trial began in June 1989, the odds were against the Bayonet Killer.[1]

In his cross-examination of the prosecution witnesses, Liljeros had some initial success. The aforementioned Spinnars, who had been staying in Pettersson's apartment the night of the murder, was supposed to rule out that Pettersson had an alibi, but on this point, his statements in court vacillated wildly. With much more force, he instead testified, still under oath, that the police had lured him with thoughts of the $7 million reward to make him say the right things. Another drug addict, who had characterized Pettersson as a

Nazi who hated Palme, also withdrew his testimony, stating that the police had tried to bribe him with money and later deliberately falsified his evidence.

Sigge Cedergren's evidence, which was supposed to demonstrate that Pettersson had access to a murder weapon, also fell through. The wily old drug dealer changed his story without warning, reverting back to an earlier version, in which he had not owned a second .357 magnum. Liljeros tried valiantly to make him admit that he had been bribed or threatened by the police, but Sigge realized that he had already said too much and kept his mouth shut. An old woman testified that in late September 1988, she had observed Pettersson reeling around at the Rotebro railway station. Trying to exit the station, he furiously kicked the door, yelling, "That damned Palme—I think it's good that he's dead! You should never regret anything, and if he wasn't dead he should be shot again!" Another witness testified that some years ago, he had seen Pettersson reeling along the tracks at another suburban railway station, blind drunk and wearing only one shoe, screaming incoherent curses against the government. Liljeros asked: Was this the Palme government, or the coalition government preceding it? The man had to admit that he did not know.[2]

Questioned by Liljeros, Pettersson stuck to his old story about his whereabouts on the night of the murder. Although as sinister looking as ever, he was surprisingly articulate in court. He said that he had always liked Palme and thought him Sweden's only true statesman. Pettersson gave a realistic picture of his situation in life, saying that for many years, his main occupation had been drinking alcohol and committing petty crimes. When reminded of the killing in 1970, he said, "I may have committed homicide, but I am not a murderer!" Lawyer Claes Borgström, who was following the trial for the state radio station, was not the only person in the audience who thought Pettersson very unlike a calculating assassin.[3] Nor did the prosecution have any success in its attempts to prove Pettersson had a motive or access to a murder weapon.

An obvious line of defense for Liljeros would have been to argue that the murder could have been the result of a conspiracy, and that his client was a very unlikely participant in a planned assassination. After all, the official police investigation had concentrated on this line of inquiry for more than twelve months, accumulating a vast amount of information on the PKK. To the despair of Pettersson's supporters, Liljeros decided not to bring up any of their conspiracy theories. In particular, he has been criticized for not calling Sergeant Rimborn to the stand and questioning him about Lisbet Palme's early observation of two killers. It turns out that Rimborn's written report of his conversation with Mrs. Palme, dated March 1 and not included in the public access material on the Pettersson case, mentions only one killer, however. Thus it is questionable whether calling Rimborn would have done the case much good; according to Krusell, neither the police nor the prosecutors perceived him as a threat at the time.[4]

The only time Liljeros ventured into the realm of conspiracy theories was when he asked the court's permission to call the two PKK fanatics Kegö and Barrling as witnesses for the defense, hoping that they would share their evidence that the murder was the result of an elaborate conspiracy. This was not allowed, however, and Liljeros did not seem to care much about this rebuff. A possibly more fruitful approach would have been to call a number of the people who had seen men carrying walkie-talkies the night of the murder. Quite a few of these walkie-talkie observations were made, although none were of course included in the official indictment of Christer Pettersson. Several people saw men with walkie-talkies near the Palme apartment in the days preceding the murder, but the police investigation has shown that they were probably Polish black market workers restoring an Old Town art gallery owned by a countryman.

A woman claimed to have seen two men with walkie-talkies near the Old Town subway station when the Palmes went to the cinema, but she gradually added to her information and was found to have a history of psychiatric disease. Holmér did not believe her, but the later police investigation suggested that she actually had seen two police detectives, although it was never divulged which two. In particular, it is notable that most of the walkie-talkie observations were in the vicinity of the murder site, and not along the route the Palmes had traveled on their way to the cinema. Perhaps the most mysterious walkie-talkie observation was made by two alert young people at the Olofsgatan, very close to the murder site, just a few minutes after Palme had been shot. A tall blond man was walking away from the murder scene, carrying a walkie-talkie; the police have never found out his identity.[5]

Another curious observation was made by a newspaper photographer, who was listening to the police radio just a few minutes after the murder. He could clearly hear a man say, "Hello up there, how are you doing?" "Damned cold," was the curt reply. Then the first voice said, "The prime minister has been shot." Again, this sinister nighttime conversation has never been explained. It would have seemed an obvious line of attack for any defense lawyer to call these witnesses, the identity of whom was known to the newspapers and to Pettersson's supporters, but Liljeros again was cautious. He distrusted the motley crew of left-wingers backing Pettersson's case and feared that the police had secret evidence to refute the testimony of the walkie-talkie witnesses. To some extent, he may have been right, but if five or six people had testified as to unexplained observations of mysterious men carrying walkie-talkies, it might well have persuaded some of the jurors that the murder was the result of a conspiracy.

As the trial went on, the witnesses from the Grand cinema made a much better impression in court than Pettersson's associates had, and the prosecution side regained its lost momentum. But Liljeros was able to seriously undermine the evidence provided by the silly, muddled Roger Östlund, who more or less admitted that he had been coached by the police. Nor was the hot dog seller Najic very believable. He could not explain his readiness to change his description of the attire of the man walking after the Palmes from a worn gray overcoat to a blue parka, nor could he deny that his original description of the man as corpulent and blond did not fit Pettersson at all. Some witnesses from the crime scene, the ubiquitous Ljungqvist prominent among them, then testified as to the killer's clumsy way of walking, although none of them had been able to pick out Pettersson in the lineups. There was a distressing scene when young Anna Hage described how Lisbet Palme had attacked her when she had been trying to resuscitate her husband. Apparently many would have preferred for this incident to remain conveniently forgotten. The judge sternly admonished her, and the poor girl started crying and had to be taken out of the courtroom.

The authenticity of the transcript from the tapping of Sigge's telephone the evening of the murder was a question that puzzled Liljeros.[6] This transcript was instrumental in placing Roger Östlund at the Grand cinema at a suitable time to see Pettersson there, since the transcript indicated that he spoke to Sigge between 11:15 and 11:21, most probably from the pay phone in the Grand cinema lobby. But neither Roger nor Sigge could remember this telephone conversation. And although several people had seen Roger reeling around near the cinema, they said he had not appeared until 11:30, pestering people for a bandage for his injured finger and talking confusedly on the cinema pay phone until around 11:45. If these witnesses are to be believed, and it is assumed that Roger really phoned Sigge from the Grand cinema, Roger actually provides Pettersson with an alibi for the murder! This is what the pro-Pettersson activists thought; the most audacious of them even accused the police of deliberately forging the phone-tapping transcript to frame the Swedish Dreyfus. The original tape from the phone-tap operation had been destroyed, adding fuel to these suspicions.

It may be objected that Roger could have phoned Sigge from the Grand cinema pay phone at 11:15 without being observed and then gone away before returning to the cinema to call some other person around 11:40. It is also possible that he called Sigge from some other pay phone at 11:15 and then went away, before reeling back to the cinema at 11:40, but this line of thought was spurned by the police, who wanted Roger to be at the Grand cinema at 11:15 at all costs. Impressive-looking documentation verifies that the transcript from the original phone-tap tape was properly done, by two detectives working independently. In addition, Sigge speaks of listening to the police radio in another telephone conversation at around 12:15 a.m., mentioning that certain restaurants were being raided by the police in their hunt for the killer; that this really happened has been verified using police records. This indicates that the phone-tap transcript is from the correct day and correctly timed.

Journalist Gunnar Wall came up with an alternative hypothesis, suggesting that some narcotics detectives had forged both the tape and the transcript, long before this same transcript was used in the Pettersson trial. He speculates that a phone-tap transcript showing that Sigge was lying would dissuade the Palme investigators from scrutinizing Sigge's evidence further and prevent them from finding evidence that Sigge's apartment had been illegally bugged, as had been independently suggested by some other journalists.[7] Wall found that the transcript of Sigge's telephone conversations between 11:02 and 11:21 disagreed with the witness statements from the people he was supposed to have spoken to, and suspected that this part of the phone tap was forged using tapes from other days. In this scenario, the detectives in the Palme investigation acted in good faith, since they had no way of telling the phone tap was a forgery. With reason, Wall questions why it took so long for this important phone-tap transcript to reach the Palme police, when it was being held by another squad of detectives. In 1986 and early 1987, Sigge's tale of his car trip and the running man was considered an important lead in the murder investigation—was this just because the detectives did not cooperate with each other, or was it because there was another, original tape and transcript confirming Sigge's statements?

But this theory has some serious drawbacks, mainly a lack of solid evidence for its various suppositions. Apart from an article in an evening newspaper, nothing attests to the fact that Sigge was bugged at all. As we know, the police undertook many covert surveillance operations against the PKK, but Wall fails to persuade the reader that the same secrecy should have been observed with regard to the bugging of a mere drug dealer, even if the Palme police were behind it. Also, would not the guilty consciences of the detectives involved in such a cover-up operation have prompted them to make the forgery known when the tape they had faked was used as evidence to convict an innocent man in the trial of the century?

I have discovered some further material indicating that there was something strange about the narcotics surveillance operation against Sigge Cedergren the night Olof Palme was murdered.[8] Firstly, Ingemar Krusell told me that the detectives involved went home at 9:00 p.m., instead of staying until 1:00 a.m. in keeping with their instructions. No written report was made of the stakeout, and the forms used to document the phone tap were haphazardly filled in. A similar phone-tap operation directed against the Oxen club was of course of interest to the police, but amazingly, the narcotics detectives refused them access to the tapes involved, saying that there was nothing on these tapes that would interest the Palme investigation. When the Palme task force officers replied that it was up to them to judge what was interesting or not, the response was that the tape had just been demagnetized, and that there was no written record of its contents!

This extreme reluctance to share information, and the evident carelessness of the detectives, raises the question of whether the phone-tap operation worked according to plan that night. Had there been some mistake, and had the detectives tried to cover this up some days later, by forging part of the surveillance tape and transcript? This is an intriguing hypothesis, although it should be noted that according to information gleaned by Wall, the tapes were running around the clock, independently of the presence of a detective to listen to them live. Thus, we do not know more than Liljeros did back in 1989: something is definitely odd about the phone-tap transcripts, but it is hard to pin down exactly what and impossible to prove them forgeries.

In June 1989, a witness came forth at the last minute to give Christer Pettersson an alibi. A sixty-seven-year-old man named Algot Åsell, who worked as a janitor in a homeless shelter, had suddenly remembered that he had been at the Märsta railway terminus at 11:30 on February 28, 1986, and seen Christer Pettersson waiting there. Åsell himself had a background in the Stockholm underworld and recognized the silent Bayonet Killer, who was sitting on a bench smoking a cigarette. Knowing Pettersson's reputation, he did not dare to approach him. If true, this story would support Pettersson's account that he had left Stockholm shortly after 11:00 p.m. and give him a cast-iron alibi for the murder.

But as Åsell was basking in the newspaper publicity, and even the cautious Liljeros anticipated a breakthrough for his client, the police were busy finding out more about this last-minute witness. They soon had ten character witnesses ready to testify that Åsell was a liar, cheat, thief, and drunkard. His life had been full of disreputable acts, the low-water mark being reached when he deserted his wife and sold all their belongings when she was in the hospital giving birth to their child. The police also found several contradictions in Åsell's story of what he had done the night of the murder. He claimed he had purchased some chocolate in a shop at the railway station at 10:00 p.m., but the shop closed at 9:30 every night. He also claimed that he had spent the night listening to country and western music on the radio, but there had been no such radio program that night. Importantly, Åsell said he had only once visited the railway station on February 28. But the police found a guard who had seen Åsell lounging around at the station at a much earlier time, and his testimony was discredited. Åsell cut a sorry figure in court and could not explain why he had taken so long to tell his story when he knew that it was of vital importance to Christer Pettersson.[9]

The biggest problem for the prosecutors was of course how to handle the termagant Mrs. Palme. In the months leading up to the trial, she had been as unhelpful as ever. Helin even doubted the wisdom of going on with the trial, since he thought it unlikely they would be able to get Pettersson convicted. Only with difficulty were his colleagues Almblad and Riberdahl, who both had a fair amount of their professional prestige invested in the Pettersson prosecution, able to persuade him to continue. One can only imagine the dismay and despair felt by the prosecutors when they learned that without consulting them, Mrs. Palme had written a letter to the court saying that she would refuse to testify unless a list of demands was fulfilled. She wanted the courtroom emptied of journalists and spectators, and photography and tape recording prohibited; nor was she prepared to allow Pettersson to be present when she gave evidence. The judge met none of these demands, but summoned her to testify like any other witness. She did not show up. The long-suffering prosecutors again had to use their negotiation skills, persuading Liljeros to allow Pettersson to be excluded when Mrs. Palme gave evidence (except when she was to identify him as the killer) and the judge to forbid tape recording of the proceedings. With great difficulty, they got Lisbet Palme to allow the spectators to remain, on the condition that none of them be allowed to see her face. She particularly disliked Helin, a man she had never before met, and this led to the ludicrous situation that although Helin was the prosecutor running the trial, they were barely on speaking terms outside the courtroom.

Arne Liljeros's strategy was to concentrate on Lisbet Palme's testimony. Knowing well that her evidence was the mainstay in the case against his client, he cross-examined her at length. He had to tread carefully, since if he gave the impression of insulting her or implying that she was lying, the cause of his client would suffer immensely. His worst-case scenario was probably that the grieving widow would start to cry, and that the jury would think he was bullying her. Liljeros need not have worried, however. Lisbet Palme appeared as tough as ever, and, far from breaking down in court, she gave curt and uncompromising answers to his questions. Liljeros seems to have adapted his tactics accordingly: he pretended to be foolish and was repetitive in his questioning, and Lisbet Palme lost her composure and angrily snapped back at him. Liljeros played the part of the somewhat muddle-headed but courteous old gentleman to perfection, and the prosecutors must have ground their teeth as he made Lisbet Palme seem rude and unbalanced. At regular intervals, she said, "I hear people talking behind me; that is very annoying!" and, "I cannot tolerate people coming and going in this courtroom!"

Helin was astounded by her behavior in court and her obvious distrust of the people who were doing their best to convict the man she had pointed out as her husband's killer. He described her as a woman in deep crisis, adamant that no one should be able to observe her reactions or facial expressions, and immensely frightened to show her feelings. When asked why he had not demanded a recess during the trial and told Mrs. Palme that she must stop behaving in this way, for tactical reasons, Helin responded that this would not have been possible and would have merely served to permanently alienate Mrs. Palme.[10] When cross-examined by Liljeros, Mrs. Palme asserted that she had been a very calm, collected witness, and that her training as a psychologist had helped her to assess the situation at the murder scene. She was aided by a dubious new recruit to the cause, our old friend the Skandia Man. As Ingemar Krusell has admitted, it was quite a gamble for the prosecutors to bring this man, whom the police knew had invented large parts of his story, into court. Helin had an excellent reason, however: the Skandia Man was the only murder scene witness who thought Mrs. Palme had appeared calm and collected!

There was excitement in the courtroom when the time finally came for Mrs. Palme to confront the man she had identified as her husband's killer. After she had, with 100 percent certainty, identified Pettersson as the murderer, the Bayonet Killer suddenly stood up, glaring at her.

"Hello there, let me say something!"

"Shut up, you!" the judge retorted.

"Up in Heaven, Olof Palme does not like what you are saying now! All I wish to say is that if you really believe what you are saying, then it is OK. But if you do not believe what you are saying, then it is not OK! That is all I have to say."

"Take that man out of court!" the judge snapped.

But the worst was yet to come for Mrs. Palme. Liljeros called several witnesses from the murder scene, and they unanimously testified that Lisbet Palme had been running around in a state of shock. It must have been galling for the haughty lady as Liljeros repeated each unflattering epithet from the witnesses: "Completely hysterical," "screaming and shouting," and "impossible to get through to." In his summing up, Liljeros alleged that she had been coached by the police, and that the absence of any tape or film documenting the lineup in which she identified Pettersson was a serious breach of legal formality. Mrs. Palme's ill-judged comment that she could see who was the alcoholic indicated that the police had given her this information beforehand. Liljeros ended with the ringing words, "The way Lisbet Palme has acted throughout the police investigation, the scenes at the lineup confrontation, her extraordinary letter to the court, her excessive demands and remarkable behavior, all this calls for caution. Her arrogance, self-sufficiency, and lack of respect for established legal practice disqualifies her as a witness."[11]

But the verdict of the court was that Pettersson was guilty, and he was sentenced to life imprisonment. There was a great eruption of joy and relief from the establishment newspapers: the murderer of Olof Palme had finally been caught and punished. There was an equivalent outburst of fury from the supporters of the Swedish Dreyfus over what they perceived as an unparalleled miscarriage of justice. When Krusell read the legal documents, some paragraphs gave him grave misgivings, however. The verdict was not unanimous: the five jurors had all found Pettersson guilty, but the two judges had both wanted to acquit him. Liljeros made an appeal to the high court, requesting another trial in which all the jurors would be legally trained and thus less likely to be impressed by Mrs. Palme's emotionally charged identification of her husband's killer. Instead, they would be receptive to Liljeros's arguments that her identification of Pettersson in the lineup was legally flawed.

Before the high court trial, the errant Sigge Cedergren had been given a severe talking-to, and he now told the correct story from the police point of view; yet again changing his evidence, he testified that he had really possessed another .357 magnum revolver shortly before the murder. Otherwise, both prosecution and defense testimony was much the same, with some important exceptions, the majority of them benefiting Pettersson. The crime scene witnesses were reinforced with a valuable new recruit, namely Gösta Söderström, who said that Lisbet Palme had been completely confused and hysterical, and that she had tried to strike him as he ushered her to his police car to sit down.[12] In the first trial, Liljeros had asked Mrs. Palme why she had not allowed him to be present when the video lineup was shown. She had replied that the lineup confrontation following Viktor Gunnarsson's arrest had been very traumatic for her, with a lot of people milling around and the defense counsel talking incessantly. Liljeros smartly called Gunnarsson's defender, who testified that he had said only a few words, and that Mrs. Palme had manifested no displeasure with his actions at the time.

Liljeros also made valiant efforts to ascertain how Mrs. Palme had found out that the prisoner was an alcoholic. Mårten Palme honestly admitted that this information had come from the prosecutor Almblad, who had told the Palme family that one of the prime suspects was an alcoholic from a Stockholm suburb who had committed murder before. Mrs. Palme did not deny this, although unwilling to explain the circumstances further.[13] Another scene of courtroom drama came when Liljeros called lieutenant Jerker Söderblom, the author of a secret police document stating that the murder was the result of a conspiracy and hinting that the PKK were the culprits. But the effect was not what the veteran defense lawyer had wanted. The cop freely admitted that the contents of the document were a deliberate falsification, intended to strengthen the case against the PKK! A more damning argument against the PKK conspiracy is hard to imagine.

Liljeros allowed the scoundrel Åsell to make a second, equally unsuccessful attempt to persuade the court of the veracity of his yarn about Pettersson's alibi. Åsell was joined by a second purported alibi witness. Enar Holm, another low-life Swede with a liking for alcoholic beverages, told the police he was in the habit of taking long, solitary walks through Stockholm, stopping at the liquor stores for some sustenance on the way. When traveling home on the suburban train late on February 28, and passing through Rotebro, he realized that a friend of his known as "Big Jerka," who owed him twenty dollars, was living nearby. Leaving the train, he went looking around the blocks of apartments nearby to find Jerka's front door, but without success. On his way back to the station, just before midnight, he saw a familiar figure approach: it was Christer Pettersson returning home.

Unlike Åsell, Holm was not taken in a lie by the police. It turned out that Jerka had been in an alcoholic's home at the time, and that Holm himself had been hitting the bottle hard in February 1986, but he might still have been telling the truth. Holm asserted that he had known all along that Pettersson had an alibi, but he had quarreled with the police in the small town where he lived, due to an ongoing dispute about a vicious Doberman he owned, and did not wish to have any further contact with them. This ludicrous explanation served to discredit Holm's veracity. The high court gave no credence whatsoever to either Åsell or Holm, bluntly stating that Pettersson lacked an alibi. Some authors have pointed out that this may well have been an unfair verdict, since no conclusive evidence shows that Holm was lying.[14]

In the high court trial, two expert witnesses evaluated Mrs. Palme's testimony. Witness psychologist Dr. Astrid Holgersson told the court that she believed Mrs. Palme's mental picture of the killer been manipulated by the police through the phantom image. There was a marked contrast between her early descriptions of the killer, which included no details about his face, and the unrealistically detailed description she made more than two months later.[15] Another psychologist, professor Lars-Göran Nilsson, had the opposite view: Mrs. Palme had seen the killer when fearing for her life, and his image was forever imprinted in her memory. Of the two experts, Holgersson was by far the more lucid and persuasive. Hans Ölvebro and Solveig Riberdahl have eloquently described their reactions to these two expert witnesses. In spite of their conviction that Pettersson was guilty, they could not help being impressed when Holgersson persuasively described how Lisbet Palme's view of the killer had gradually evolved as a result of outside pressure. They realized the case was lost when Nilsson treated the court to a lengthy dose of academic claptrap, of which they themselves could understand very little.[16]

The outcome of the trial was what Krusell had feared: a unanimous court set Pettersson free, giving the reason as grave doubts as to the validity of Mrs. Palme's identification. There was a chorus of groans from the anti-Pettersson phalanx. Some newspapers deplored that such a villain had been allowed to go free and petulantly hoped that Pettersson would swiftly drink himself to death on the money he would be given as compensation. Others made high-handed comments praising Swedish justice, saying that it was better to have a hundred murderers walking the streets than one single innocent man incarcerated. Pettersson's supporters were exultant, commenting that the true spirit of the People's Home had prevailed, defeating the conspiracy against the Swedish Dreyfus. They sent bunches of flowers to Pettersson and belatedly showed some appreciation for Liljeros, the Swedish Emile Zola, who had wrested their hero free from his persecutors.

That same afternoon, the hopes of some of his supporters that Pettersson's enforced ten-month drying-out period would permanently convert him to teetotalism were cruelly dashed, as the Bayonet Killer went to the liquor store to buy large quantities of beer, vodka, and Bailey's Irish Cream. His favorite drink, a neat mixture of Bailey's and vodka with a slice of pickled cucumber, has since been known as "the Killer Drink" in the Stockholm bars. At a press conference the day after the trial, a red-eyed Pettersson remained in a good mood: in front of a huge posse of journalists, he obtusely spoke of the People's Soul that was never wrong, and went on to say that he wanted to hug Lisbet Palme because he shared her loss. Although Liljeros gestured to him to be quiet, Pettersson gave some imprudent hints as to where the murder weapon could be found: "The killer, say I was the killer, would only have had to dump it in a river or a storm drain." When asked by a journalist whether he had killed Olof Palme, Pettersson smiled and said, "Only the People's Soul knows!"[17]

Lisbet Palme, returning home from the trial, is reported to have attacked and struck an impudent newspaper photographer.[18] For her the tragedy was complete. She had suffered the indignity of being disbelieved in court, and the man she had pointed out as her husband's killer was free to walk the streets—and to strike again, possibly against herself. In the newspapers, she seemed to take over her late husband's role as an object of hatred and abuse. The pro-Pettersson publications saw her as a wicked Jezebel giving false evidence against their hero, and the anti-Pettersson phalanx blamed her upper-class arrogance and queen-like attitude in court for letting the guilty man walk free.

THE SCAPEGOAT IS
NEVER TARRED

Before the high court trial, the Swedish newspapers debated what would happen if Christer Pettersson were acquitted. His ugly face was known by almost every Swede—how was some late-coming Swedish Jack Ruby to be prevented from murdering him? Some said that Pettersson should be given money to move abroad, or provided with a cottage in some desolate Lapland village. Other journalists proposed that the Swedish Dreyfus be given a new identity, and that the world's leading plastic surgeons be challenged to change his repulsive looks.[1] But Pettersson wanted none of this. After his release, he moved back into his Rotebro apartment and continued his old life as a drunkard and habitual petty criminal as if nothing had happened. He fully realized the financial advantages of his situation, however, and charged journalists twenty-eight hundred dollars per interview. One of them reported that although Pettersson spent hours sitting on the toilet seat reading the Bible to his cat in a stentorian voice, he spent very little money on cat food, and the half-starved feline had to rely on kindhearted neighbors for its daily sustenance. Pettersson's short temper was not improving with time, and he regularly beat people up after minimal provocation.[2] In 1990, he knocked down a neighbor and kicked her dog, ending up in prison for a year. In 1992, he beat up an old woman who had refused to give him a cigarette and went to prison for four more months. He then almost killed his girlfriend in a frenzied attack and was sentenced to two and a half years in jail.

   Christer Pettersson earned considerable amounts of money doing media interviews, particularly with a private television company called TV3, whose unscrupulous reporters repeatedly tried to trick him into confessing to the murder. Two of them, Robert Aschberg and Gert Fylking, even hinted that they would give him seventy thousand dollars if he confessed live on prime-time television, but Pettersson was wise to this trick. In 1994, he instead collected a large sum to take part in a televised polygraph test conducted by an elderly German professor. The professor announced that the test showed with 80 percent certainty that Pettersson had not murdered Olof Palme and knew nothing about the murder weapon.[3] The anti-Pettersson phalanx who had of course been hoping for the opposite outcome of the test, countered with accusing the professor of being a quack and his machine a completely outdated version.

Another television documentary appeared the year after. An enterprising journalist asserted, before a record number of viewers, that Pettersson had gone into Stockholm to shoot his drug dealer, Sigge Cedergren, but had forgotten his glasses and shot Palme by mistake! Pettersson had stolen some drugs from Sigge some time earlier, and it was speculated that after Sigge had put out a contract on the Bayonet Killer, Pettersson had decided to kill Sigge as a preemptive strike. This theory's only merit is that it explains an otherwise motiveless act of violence. As we know, Sigge was not a man of violence: had he wanted to get rid of Pettersson, he would have shopped him to his friends within the narcotics police. Nor is there any firm evidence that Sigge and Pettersson were really enemies at the time of Palme's murder. And although it is true that Sigge himself had a passing resemblance to Olof Palme, his thirty-year-old prostitute girlfriend was very unlike Lisbet. Any presumptive murderer naturally makes sure he is killing the right person, and if Pettersson was really the man standing outside the Grand cinema, he should have been able to recognize his victim without difficulty.[4]

The spirits of Ölvebro's detectives received a glancing blow when Pettersson was freed in 1989. They realized that in the eventuality of another murder suspect being brought to justice, his defense counsel could simply point out that Lisbet Palme had identified Pettersson as the killer with 100 percent certainty. Some of the detectives left the Palme task force in disgust, but others, including Ölvebro himself, remained to fight another day, hoping to find more evidence against Pettersson for an appeal to the Supreme Court of Sweden. It irritated them that the prosecutors talked about starting the investigation from the beginning and even spoke of Pettersson as no longer being of interest in the inquiry, since he had been judged innocent. The forthright Ingemar Krusell made it no secret that he still considered Pettersson the main suspect. When a journalist asked him why the police were still persecuting the Swedish Dreyfus, who had after all been freed by the court, Krusell gruffly replied, "*We* have not freed him!" This ill-considered remark, more suited to Dirty Harry than a politically correct Swedish detective, caused considerable backlash in the press, and even from Krusell's police superiors, but the veteran detective did not budge. Soon after, Krusell transferred to a precinct in suburban Stockholm, and the Palme task force lost one of its prime movers.[5]

With time, it became increasingly apparent to the beleaguered police detectives that no murder weapon and no technical evidence would ever be found. The only way to convict Pettersson would be to "break" him so that he would finally confess the murder. There have been two attempts to do so, one by relatively fair means, one by foul. In 1998, the task force made an appeal to the Supreme Court for a third trial, claiming that new evidence against Pettersson had been discovered. And indeed, several witnesses had come forth at this late stage. Most interesting was a friend of Sigge Cedergren's who claimed to have seen Pettersson at the Grand cinema at 9:00 p.m. She was seconded by one of the original Grand cinema witnesses, who had seen a strange man near the line to *The Brothers Mozart* at about the same time but had failed to pick Pettersson out in a police lineup. This woman now claimed to have recognized Pettersson's photograph as that of the man she had observed.

It is sad but true that the witness Ljungqvist once more changed his story. In 1996, he appeared on television claiming that he had recognized Pettersson all along, but had been frightened to tell the police because of the risk of revenge against his family! The passenger in Ljungqvist's's car completely disagreed, however. There was no chance Ljungqvist could have seen the killer's face, and Ljungqvist had added to his story little by little, possibly so that he could claim part of the reward. Piling sensation on sensation, the passenger then said that he himself had been in the same class as Pettersson at school, and that although he had not seen the killer's face either, he had recognized his old school friend from the way he walked!

Also coming forward as witnesses were a motley crew of criminals, alcoholics, drug addicts, and lunatics, many of whom had no doubt been attracted by the reward money.[6] Some of these individuals had remarkable tales to tell. A drug addict said that he had seen Pettersson on the Sveavägen four times the night Palme was killed, and that he had actually seen him commit the murder. The reason he had driven away as fast as he could, instead of giving evidence, was that he had thought the shots were intended for himself! Two individuals independently claimed to have seen Pettersson running away on David Bagares Gata, but neither of them had been observed by the real witnesses Nieminen and Jeppsson, nor did they claim to have seen each other. Of similarly dubious value was the testimony from several jailbirds who claimed that Pettersson had confessed to them behind bars. Finally, slimy old Sigge Cedergren told the final version of his tale shortly before dying of cancer. He was now certain that he had given Pettersson a magnum revolver some weeks before the murder, and he had lied in court to protect his old friend. The TV3 reporters were quick to exploit this latest sensation, arranging another live polygraph session with a more alert American expert and an up-to-date machine; the result showed that Sigge was most likely telling the truth.[7]

The police and prosecutors must have realized that with witnesses such as these—some of them the very dregs of humanity, others obvious liars attracted by the reward—the chances for a successful appeal against Pettersson were very slim. In 1998, when the appeal against Pettersson hung in the balance, Ingemar Krusell published a book ably summarizing the case against him.[8] Another book on the murder came from an unexpected source. Pelle Svensson was a successful wrestler who had become a lawyer later in his career, taking part in many trials involving wealthy and notorious clients.[9] Among these had been a certain Lars Tingström, also known as the "Bomb Man." Tingström had been sentenced to life imprisonment for blowing up a series of buildings around Stockholm, one of them the house of a district attorney who had previously put him in prison for another bombing. The district attorney had seduced Tingström's girlfriend when Tingström was in prison, turning the mild-mannered electrician into a monster out for revenge, Svensson claimed.

Christer Pettersson was Tingström's best friend in prison, protecting him from bullies and perverts. For reasons unknown, Pettersson firmly believed that Tingström was innocent and that his life sentence was a great miscarriage of justice. The two convicts decided that as a final vengeance against the state of Sweden, Pettersson should first kill the king, then Olof Palme, and finally the minister of justice. Pettersson obeyed his friend's command, Svensson claims, but he started with Palme instead of the king, either from reverence toward royalty or based on the realization that the feeble, powerless monarch did not really amount to much.

Pelle Svensson was himself a rather strange character, however. Obsessed with publicity, he had previously accused several other people of killing Olof Palme, one of them a well-known politician; this would not appear consistent with his allegation that he knew the identity of the killer all along, but kept it quiet on Tingström's insistence. When involved in a trial concerning a member of the Scientology Church, Svensson had claimed to have secret information that this sinister sect had been plotting the murder of Olof Palme. It was also suspected that some incriminating documents purported to have been written by the Bomb Man were in fact forgeries. And would a loner and psychopath like Pettersson really kill a man for someone else? The TV3 journalists again tried bribing Pettersson to confess, but all they got out of him was that if he had really killed Palme, he had forgotten all about it by this point. He had received a blow to the head as a teenager, he claimed, and this had led to a kind of brain damage that was responsible for his subsequent life of crime.[10] Not long after he made this statement, the appeal against Pettersson was quashed by the Supreme Court.

In late 2001, Pettersson was staying with a friend after being evicted from his own apartment. He was living on beer and fried eggs, not a diet conducive to a long and healthy life, but the now fifty-four-year-old alcoholic seemed to live on forever, as an unprepossessing reminder of Sweden's national trauma. As Pettersson was swigging his beer, reeling around among the sterile blocks of apartments in the dire Stockholm suburb he inhabited, another, more insidious plot was being hatched to break him.

It had started when Ulf Dahlsten, the Social Democratic politician who had once been Palme's political secretary, published a book of memoirs in which he strongly supports Mrs. Palme's testimony in the Pettersson case.[11] Amazingly, Dahlsten describes Lisbet Palme as an exceptionally calm, clear-headed witness. In a newspaper interview in April 1986, Dahlsten said that she had certainly never seen the killer's face; in his memoirs, he asserts that she had had a good look at her husband's killer, and that she was 100 percent certain it was Christer Pettersson. Even more sensational, Dahlsten claims that a few weeks after the murder, Mrs. Palme told Hans Holmér that the murderer had looked like an alcoholic, and that she felt certain he had killed a person before. Fifteen years had passed since the murder, and people were beginning to forget what had happened back in 1986; as a result, no journalist objected to these blatant falsifications.

The psychologist Lars-Göran Nilsson, who was still smarting from his defeat at the hands of his colleague Astrid Holgersson at the trial twelve years earlier, also spoke up in several interviews. He demanded a retrial, saying that his report on Mrs. Palme's state of mind had been overlooked. Then Lisbet Palme herself spoke to the newspapers, accusing judge Birgitta Blom, who had presided in the second trial against Pettersson, of being biased by her hatred of the Palme family and particularly of Lisbet herself. She fully concurred with Dahlsten's dramatic revelations about her conversation with Holmér, but this intriguing addition to the case was promptly denied by Holmér himself and has no support whatsoever from the original police files.[12]

As the newspapers were full of these dramatic stories, TV3 journalist Gert Fylking was busy trying to make Pettersson confess. Fylking was not a crime journalist but specialized in low comedy. He dressed up in odd costumes and behaved in an earthy and burlesque manner that was considered funny by many Swedes. In a popular television advertisement, he farted inside a car to test its air conditioning. His most amusing stunt was to attend the meeting of the Swedish Academy, dressed up as a pig to annoy the stodgy academicians, and shout, "Yes! He finally got it!" when they announced yet another obscure writer with an unpronounceable name as the Nobel laureate in literature. Fylking made it no secret that he had cultivated Pettersson's friendship throughout the 1990s, and that they had often drunk and reveled together. Whether Fylking was actually plying his "friend" with booze to make him confess is not known, but it would not seem unlikely. At one of these drinking sessions, Fylking wrote a confession on his typewriter, and Pettersson signed it with a shaky hand: this document was published in a tabloid newspaper only a few weeks after Mrs. Palme's appeal.[13] Pettersson received only $280 for his part of the deal, but Fylking must have assured him that the best was still to come, and that in Sweden, it paid well to murder prime ministers.

Fylking's document generated a great deal of publicity, with the establishment newspapers celebrating that the killer had finally confessed. The buffoon Fylking bragged that he had accomplished what the police had failed to do for fifteen years: he had solved the murder of Olof Palme. The police and prosecutors were discussing how a retrial could be arranged, but Pettersson avoided them. The plan was that he would confess live on a TV3 talk show called, ironically, *The People's Home*, after Palme's idea of a utopian Sweden. Fylking paid Pettersson thirty-five thousand dollars to take part in this show, and he was kept well supplied with alcoholic beverages. But when he was pressed to confess, Pettersson told his tormentors, "Fuck off!" He said he had never killed Palme, and had only signed the confession for the bribes he had been offered. It is unknown whether this had been Fylking's plan all along, as another of his media hoaxes, or whether the old actor Pettersson had decided to change the ending of this macabre television farce at the last minute. The media reaction to these latest installments in the Palme soap opera was equally bizarre. One would have expected the media to question Dahlsten's motives and Mrs. Palme's own unsubstantiated accusations, and particularly to attack Fylking for his dubious journalistic methods. And who had orchestrated this well-planned attack on Pettersson—was it the successor of Ebbe Carlsson? But instead, the media focused their general outrage on Pettersson, who had broken his promise to confess; his actions had only reopened the old wounds of Sweden's national trauma.[14]

In the following years, Christer Pettersson's health gradually deteriorated. His habit of drinking several pints of moonshine vodka in one go provided him with some unpleasant near-death experiences, and an accident deprived him of the use of one arm. On September 16, 2004, Pettersson had caused an angry altercation at the Sollentuna social services, and the police were called. Two uniformed officers arrested Pettersson, who was sitting on a bench with his drinking companions. They twisted his injured arm behind his back, and

Pettersson screamed with pain. The cops took him to a nearby hospital, where his injury was treated. He seemed in good cheer and talked with the nurses at the emergency department, before being sent off to another hospital to sleep off his intoxication. But in the morning, the nurses at this hospital noticed that Pettersson was unconscious. He turned out to have a severe fracture of the skull leading to an extensive intracranial hemorrhage. In spite of emergency surgery, he never regained consciousness and died on September 29. In the newspapers, there was outrage that Pettersson had never confessed but kept what was termed his guilty secret until the end. The best an enterprising journalist could do was to suggest that toward the end of his life, Pettersson had expressed a desire to meet Mårten Palme to tell him something very important, but for reasons unexplained, this meeting had never taken place. What this important secret was, Pettersson did not want to disclose. The creature Fylking re-emerged with his story that Pettersson had confessed the murder to him, with the added twist that after killing Palme, Pettersson had run through the streets of Stockholm at breakneck speed, taking several turns until he finally reached the main railway station. Now when Pettersson is no longer alive to contradict the various fortune-hunters who come forward with tales of confessions and imaginative reworkings of the murder scenario, there is likely to be further speculation along these lines. A distasteful addition was provided by several articles detailing Pettersson's degraded lifestyle and repulsive habits, and breathing a general satisfaction that he was dead. Rather as an aside in this media furore, the state prosecutors assured the Swedish people that the Palme murder investigation continue in spite of Pettersson's death; the police added that although Pettersson had probably fallen down and hurt himself, they would investigate his death with their usual efficiency.

If today one assumed the role of prosecutor, and built up the case against Christer Pettersson as the murderer of Olof Palme, the mainstay of the case would be Lisbet Palme's recognition of him as the killer of her husband. She picked him out in the video lineup without hesitation and many times reiterated that she was absolutely certain he was the man, without faltering in the slightest. To Ulf Dahlsten, she later eloquently described her reaction to seeing Pettersson in the video lineup. Distrustful of the police and dubious about their capacity to catch the killer, she had been astounded to see the man she remembered from the scene of the crime actually standing in front of her on the video screen. Dahlsten adds that as a psychologist, she had forced herself to be calm and analyze the situation; this would, he asserts, explain the ill-judged comment about which man was the alcoholic.[15] If Dahlsten is telling the truth about these matters, it is doubly fatal that no proper record was made of the lineup, since Mrs. Palme's reaction would have been of vital importance in the case against Pettersson. Tommy Lindström adds some other telling observations. The prosecutor Almblad described to him how Mrs. Palme had stiffened in her chair when she saw Pettersson in the lineup; this had convinced him that Pettersson was the guilty man. After the lineup, Lisbet Palme phoned one of her sons, saying, "Now we can finally relax—the police have got the right man!"[16]

A second mainstay is the Grand Man evidence. The original descriptions of the Grand Man agree quite well in most particulars, and it is reasonable to suggest that there really was a man behaving weirdly outside the cinema, staring into the lobby and waiting for the Palmes to emerge. Nor is it unreasonable to presume that this man had something to do with the murder. As we know, five witnesses identified Pettersson as the Grand Man. The drug addict Roger Östlund, who knew Pettersson, declared himself certain Pettersson was the man. Of particular value is the identification made by the hot dog seller Najic, indicating that Pettersson was actually following the Palmes. The other three witnesses—Mårten Palme, the air-traffic controller Eriksson, and the artist Wennerling—were honest, respectable people, and although their identifications of Pettersson were somewhat tentative, they still add much strength to the case.

Two witnesses from the crime scene also claimed to have recognized Pettersson, although neither did so in a court of law. Yvonne Nieminen, who saw the killer run past her, identified Pettersson when a journalist showed her photographs of Pettersson and three other men.[17] As she was a key witness, it is a pity the police did not include her in the first day of lineups, but no one could have predicted that this foolish journalist would meddle with the investigation. Nieminen's testimony might well have tipped the scales against Pettersson. It should be remembered, however that the journalist showed her only four photographs, and that Pettersson looked like a crook. Finally, as we know, another key witness, Leif Ljungqvist, much later also claimed to have recognized Pettersson as the killer, but he had changed his story before, and it is unlikely he actually saw the killer's face.[18]

A good deal of circumstantial evidence has been accumulated against Pettersson. He burned clothes on his balcony in April 1986: Was he destroying the technical evidence against him? After all, Holmér had just appeared on live television, lecturing on the importance of detecting gunpowder residue on the jacket of Viktor Gunnarsson. Any murderer with a sense of self-preservation would have made sure to destroy all compromising evidence after the helpful commissioner had alerted him to the marvels of modern forensic technology.[19] Pettersson's behavior after the murder, signing two books of condolence and stealing a framed photograph of Palme to take home with him, was out of character. One witness even testified that he saw the normally tough Pettersson crying in his kitchen the day after the murder, with a candle lit in front of the photograph he had stolen.[20] Clandestine police photographs show that Pettersson grew his moustache just after the murder: Was he disguising his appearance?

According to early rumors in the Stockholm underworld, Pettersson either had committed the murder or knew the identity of the murderer.[21] Just a month after the murder, a young man told his mother that he knew that Christer Pettersson had murdered Palme. This individual, who may well have heard the rumor from Spinnars, had a history of alcoholism and psychiatric disease, and both he and his mother refused to testify in court.[22] Pettersson told some people he had been very near the murder scene, and he told a friend the exact words Lisbet Palme had screamed out when her husband was shot: "No, what are you doing!" Witnesses have also claimed that Pettersson has privately confessed the murder, both drunk and sober, both inside prison and out of it. Two former female friends of Pettersson's told Ingemar Krusell that they were convinced he had murdered Olof Palme but had been too frightened of him to testify in court.

It is a strong argument against Pettersson that several clever, experienced police detectives and prosecuting attorneys remain totally convinced he murdered Olof Palme. Among the former are Hans Ölvebro, Ingemar Krusell, and Per-Gunnar Näss; among the latter, Jörgen Almblad and Solveig Riberdahl. Both police and prosecutors felt a considerable amount of anger and bitterness about Mrs. Palme's behavior in court. They were amazed someone of her education and social standing could behave in such an irresponsible way: in their minds, her refusal to cooperate with the police and her arrogance and rudeness in court were instrumental in allowing her husband's killer to walk free. The forthright Krusell said that if Mrs. Palme had cooperated fully with the detectives instead of treating them like something the cat had dragged in, and if she had acted responsibly in court instead of demanding preferential treatment, Pettersson certainly would have been put behind bars.

The police investigation made it perfectly clear that Pettersson did not have an alibi for the time of the murder, that he had lied to the police about his activities, and that the two men purporting to be alibi witnesses were most likely a pair of irresponsible liars out to enjoy their moment of notoriety. It is important that unlike Viktor Gunnarsson and the vast majority of other suspects, Pettersson had the killer instinct: he had demonstrated that he was capable of brutally murdering a man and certainly had the strength and toughness needed to kill Palme.

Whatever is thought of the moral fiber of the drug dealer Sigge Cedergren, the latest version of his evidence states that Pettersson had access to a

.357 magnum in February 1986. Ingemar Krusell has argued that Sigge must have known all along that Pettersson was the killer, and that he himself had provided the murder weapon. Panicking when he realized this, the frantic drug dealer invented his story of the running man to draw off suspicions. Sigge was used to lying when questioned by the police, yet he gradually adapted his story toward the truth, namely that he had provided Pettersson with the gun when Palme had just two hours left to live.

Concerning a motive, Krusell maintains that with his extremely short fuse, Pettersson did not need one: maybe he had approached the prime minister on his way to the cinema and been ignored or rebuffed. Full of hatred toward the man who represented official Sweden, Pettersson then went to get Sigge's revolver, standing ready to follow the prime minister outside the Grand cinema. A stronger case can be made against Christer Pettersson as the murderer of Olof Palme than against any other named person.

Going back to the murder scene evidence, it is clear that Lisbet Palme and the witness Björkman looked at each other, and that her earliest description of the man in the blue parka fits Björkman perfectly. She then saw the witness Jeppsson looking at her from the Tunnelgatan. She may well also have caught a glimpse of the killer escaping, but it is questionable whether she saw his face. The descriptions of her confused and hysterical state suggest she did not; even five minutes after the murder, she had not been able to make her own identity known to the police or bystanders. The claim made by Mrs. Palme herself, and later by her supporter Dahlsten, that she was a particularly alert and clearheaded witness, does not appear to have much foundation in reality. Witness psychologist Astrid Holgersson's criticism of Lisbet Palme's descriptions of the killer—as gradually becoming more detailed and incorporating some of the features of the Phantom—has been corroborated by leading international experts and is in my view fully valid.[23] It has also surfaced that in the witness confrontation arranged when Viktor Gunnarsson was a suspect, Mrs. Palme came close to picking out another man, a smuggler who had been arrested because he resembled the Phantom. She said that of the people in the lineup, this man most resembled the killer, but instead of pressing her to say exactly how sure she was that he was the killer, the detective in charge chose to end the session.[24] It is important to note that this smuggler did not look particularly like Pettersson; nor did a Chilean contract killer whose photograph Lisbet and Mårten Palme showed to Hans Holmér as greatly resembling the murderer.

As for her identification of Pettersson in the lineup, evidence shows that Mrs. Palme believed that the police had had a very good reason to arrest Pet-

The witness Anders Björkman. He fits Lisbet Palme's earliest description of the killer. Reproduced by permission of the Swedish National Police Board.

tersson, and that she wanted to do all she could to pick out the right man.[25] Her statement about which man was the alcoholic would indicate that her identification was built on analytical reasoning rather than instant recognition. As we know, her sons Mårten and Joakim had been told that the main suspect was a criminal alcoholic as early as October 1988 and had passed this knowledge on to their mother. It is amazing that in 1994, Mrs. Palme admitted to a radio journalist that prior to the lineup, the prosecutor Almblad had told her that the suspect was an alcoholic and habitual criminal, who lived in a Stockholm suburb and who had killed a man before. Almblad suffered a convenient lapse of memory when asked to explain these particulars to the 1999 commission, but his colleague Riberdahl may inadvertently have given the game away. She testified to the commission that as she had accompanied Mrs. Palme up to the room where the video was to be shown, the widow had asked her, "Who am I going to see?" Riberdahl was surprised by this unexpected question and said she could not give any underhand information, since this would render the video lineup meaningless. Mrs Palme then seemed angry and irritated, as if she had been expecting further coaching.[26] This statement would suggest that before she was escorted to the video screen by Riberdahl, Almblad had guided her to pick out the right man. With the information that she was looking for an alcoholic, it would not have been difficult for her to pick out the paunchy, repulsive-looking Christer Pettersson in a lineup filled with fit, able-bodied policemen. A Swedish psychologist later conducted an experiment with the American students he was teaching in Seattle, showing them the video of the lineup after giving them the relevant information; not less than 74 percent were able to pick out Pettersson.[27] It should also be remembered that as a clinical psychologist, Lisbet Palme was trained to recognize the physical stigmata of chronic alcoholism, and these were only too evident in Pettersson's sorry figure.

Another curious detail deserves some discussion. As we know, Ulf Dahlsten claims to have spoken to Lisbet Palme shortly after the lineup. Her alleged words were, "It was him! More down-at-heel than at the time of the murder, a few pounds leaner, and with a moustache!" If Dahlsten is to be relied on, the main point here is that she thought Pettersson looked thinner than at the time of the murder. I found this comment somewhat surprising, since Pettersson was addicted to amphetamine, a potent appetite suppressant. Evidence shows that he used much less amphetamine in 1988 than in 1986, possibly because his old supply route through Sigge had been blocked by the latter's imprisonment. Instead, he drank quantities of strong beer and sweet wine, just the things to fatten him up. We also know that Pettersson spent the period from September 1986 until March 1987 in prison: Did the nutritious Swedish prison food not serve to increase his bulk further? In fact, he gained thirty-two pounds from February 1986 until December 1988![28] This adds yet another argument against Mrs. Palme's recognition.

As Liljeros demonstrated in court, if Mrs. Palme's recognition of Pettersson as the killer falls through, so does the rest of the case, like a house of cards. And while Mårten Palme was an honest, upstanding witness, it must be stated that prior to tentatively identifying Pettersson as the man he saw outside the Grand cinema, he had done the same for at least six other people, some of whom were completely unlike Pettersson. The same goes for the witness Wennerling, who did not rule out Viktor Gunnarsson as being the Grand Man. As for the hot dog seller Najic, he at first failed to identify Pettersson in a lineup, being extremely nervous when the lineup was shown. He then returned to say he had known who the Grand Man was but kept quiet out of fear for his family. Najic had previously given a description of the Grand Man that was quite unlike Pettersson: a fat, middle-aged man with blond hair. Had he seen Pettersson's face in a newspaper photograph and decided to do his bit to get Palme's killer convicted? Najic was a very dubious witness who changed his testimony to what was expected of him; even his original observation is surrounded by doubt.[29]

It is also notable that the two witnesses who had had the best look at the

Grand Man, two young women who observed him for some time as he was staring into the cinema lobby, and who gave a description of him that tallied almost exactly with those of Eriksson and Mårten Palme, were not included among the witnesses in court. The reason? They did not just fail to pick out Pettersson's photograph, but positively denied he was the man they had seen![30] The drug addict Roger Östlund was not a particularly honest, upstanding witness, and he cut a sorry figure in court. He had not appeared particularly convincing in the video documentation of his meeting with Pettersson, and it has been speculated that the reason why the high court gave his testimony any credit was that, astoundingly, they had not bothered to view this video.[31] And if Pettersson had really been observed staking out the cinema by a person he knew, would he not have become somewhat reluctant to carry out the murder? As for Sigge Cedergren, he was the most despicable actor of all in the Palme drama: a drug dealer, a vampire preying on vulnerable people, and a conniving scoundrel and perjurer, who had entertained the police with his falsehoods for months before finally delivering the correct pack of lies. Even his final version of the story is unsatisfactory, since he said he had given Pettersson the gun several weeks before the murder, not the same evening, implying that Pettersson had been carrying it around for quite some time.

Not a few leading police officials have firmly announced their conviction that Pettersson is innocent: apart from the inevitable Hans Holmér, these include the clever Tommy Lindström and leading criminologist Leif G. W. Persson.[32] As for the hypothesis that Pettersson approached Palme at the Grand cinema and was rebuffed, thus giving this walking powder keg a motive to kill the prime minister, it must be remarked that no witness saw the incident in question. Surely, it would have been natural for the scores of people outside the cinema to notice a dangerous-looking character approaching the prime minister. Furthermore, knowing Pettersson's alarming violent tendencies, would he not more likely have struck or kicked Palme as an immediate retribution for this alleged rebuff? The sly and cunning behavior of going to Sigge's apartment to get his hands on the heavy revolver is hard to reconcile with Pettersson's character. And if Pettersson was standing very near the Palme family outside the cinema, would they not have noticed such a dangerous-looking character? It also seems likely that Lisbet Palme would have been alarmed at the sight of Pettersson lurking outside Dekorima, but Morelius testified that neither she nor Olof shrank away from the shadowy figure who was awaiting them.

Christer Pettersson had no clear motive to kill Olof Palme, no solid evidence proves he had access to a murder weapon, and not one shred of technical evidence against him exists. Although a habitual criminal, he had never actually planned a crime or used a firearm. All his previous convictions were either for minor misdemeanors or for sudden bursts of aggression using blunt instruments, knives, or his trusty bayonet. Was it really possible that such a drunken barbarian could plan and execute a murder in such a skillful manner and then make a clean getaway? The night of the murder, he was dressed in his old blue parka, and although this attire matches that of the Grand Man, it does not match that of the killer. Pettersson made it a habit never to wear a cap or hat, however cold the weather, whereas there is agreement that the Grand Man wore a beige cap and some indication that the killer wore a blue or black knitted cap. Nor was Pettersson ever in the habit of wearing an overcoat. It is interesting that the witness Jeppsson, who lived in Rotebro and who had seen Pettersson many times, was convinced Pettersson was not the man running past him up the Tunnelgatan steps.[33] It is also questionable whether Pettersson would have had the physical stamina to run up the eighty-nine steps with such agility and then outrun his pursuers. With all the evidence taken into account, the case against Pettersson is not as strong as some have presumed. The high court probably was right to acquit him.

CONSPIRACY THEORIES

The murder of Olof Palme shocked Swedish society to the core. The police investigation of the murder was harshly criticized, particularly after the idol Holmér was found to have feet of clay, and many Swedes despaired of these bungling detectives ever catching the killer. Others saw more sinister motives at work, and wild rumors and conspiracy theories began to grow in number.[1] Quite a few people decided to start their own private murder investigations. These "Palme Detectives" were constantly at loggerheads with the police, who accused them of meddling with the detective work and harassing the witnesses.[2] More than one murder scene witness had to change his or her phone number after being contacted by inquisitive amateur detectives. The Palme Detectives retorted that the reason the police wanted to suppress their activities must have been that they themselves were involved in the murder conspiracy.

Many people have speculated that the murder was the result of a police conspiracy, and that the reason for the amazing blunders in the early police response to the crime was that the cops were helping the murderer, one of their own colleagues, to escape. Quite a few of the observations of mysterious men with walkie-talkies remain unexplained. They were something of an embarrassment for the police when the cops were concentrating on the theory of a lone killer, but a great asset for the enterprising Palme Detective constructing a conspiracy theory. Hans Ölvebro has blamed the sense of moral outrage in Stockholm for this profusion of conflicting testimony regarding walkie-talkies: if the police had made an appeal for observations of a man carrying a hockey stick on the Sveavägen, the result would probably have been the same.

The basic police conspiracy theory is relatively simple. From the earliest stages of the murder investigation, witnesses made observations of policemen and police cars acting suspiciously near the site of the murder.[3] Palme was undoubtedly hated by many right-wing policemen, and tendencies toward racism and Nazism did exist within the Stockholm police force. It is sad but true that some Stockholm cops celebrated openly when they learned that the hated Olof Palme was dead; two of them even made a champagne toast, exulting "Now the bastard is dead!" The Palme Detectives found out that the evening of the murder, the crew of one of the police vans in central Stockholm had been cruising in the area of David Bagares Gata. The stated reason for this was that one of the officers had to move his car, which was illegally parked. This was given a sinister interpretation: Had the cops not been doing a last-minute reconnaissance of the killer's escape route? And why did the officer who owned the car vomit after a relatively mild exertion when pursuing the killer up the Tunnelgatan stairs? Was this not a sign of nervousness and a guilty conscience?

The Palme Detectives also questioned how Lieutenant Dalsgaard and his driver could have arrived on the scene so early. And why did they not stop the witness Jeppsson in their pursuit of the killer? The Palme Detectives also pointed out that the very last observation of the killer was near the officer's parked car: Had the killer used this vehicle as a hiding place? One of the young officers pursuing the killer and Dalsgaard's driver were former members of the Baseball Gang. The police conspiracy theory had a firm adherent in television journalist Lars Borgnäs. In a series of provocative television documentaries, he made the most of these unexplained sightings of policemen and police vehicles, as well as the sightings of men with walkie-talkies, as indicating a murder conspiracy. He was a constant thorn in the side of Ölvebro and his detectives and delighted in depicting them as stupid and culpable in his controversial documentaries, which were instrumental in persuading a considerable proportion of Swedes that the police had killed Olof Palme.

The rumors of police involvement have been fueled by some remarkable statements from lieutenant Gösta Söderström, the first officer to arrive at the scene of the crime. Both before and after his retirement for ill health, he has alleged that he received the alarm at 11:28 and arrived at the murder scene as late as 11:30, almost nine minutes after the murder. Söderström has gone on to argue that the police alarm was deliberately delayed to help the killer escape, and that his own police colleagues were involved in the murder conspiracy.[4] From an analysis of the taped telephone conversations with the emergency services, as presented earlier in this book, it can be deduced that Söderström's allegations are clearly absurd, however. It is yet another minor mystery why this experienced police officer would alienate his superiors by making such a scandalous claim. The police have of course suggested that he wanted to cover up his own tardiness at the crime scene, but although his en-counter with Lisbet Palme was somewhat farcical, Söderström appears to have acted reasonably competently. Even before the murder, he was known as a stubborn, difficult character, noted for his persistent opposition to women being allowed into the police force.

A spectacular addition to the police conspiracy theory came from televi-sion producer Lars Krantz. The night of the murder, he had been traveling home on a bus. Not far from the murder scene, he saw a man boarding the bus and then exiting. This individual looked sinister and acted suspiciously, and Krantz later suspected he had seen the killer escaping. On March 3, he con-tacted the police, but they showed little interest. Krantz's son, a newspaper journalist, then told him about a tip he had received that the notorious Base-ball Gang officers were involved in the murder. At this very time, two Base-ball Gang cops were suing the state television station over an accusation that they had beaten a drug addict to death. They ended up winning their case and receiving substantial damages. One of the spectators at the trial was Lars Krantz, who claimed to recognize one of the cops, Thomas Piltz, as the man he had seen boarding the bus. The excited producer visited Hans Holmér to tell his story, but the police-master formed a low opinion of Krantz's abilities.

The driver of Krantz's bus, it turned out, had also seen two men acting suspiciously not long after the murder. When Krantz showed him photo-graphs of Baseball Gang cops Leif Tell and Thomas Piltz, he identified them as the men he had seen trying to board the bus. But the police made a note that the bus driver seemed quite insane, and that he "improved" his story with each questioning. In the end, he maintained that one of the cops had been made up to look like Viktor Gunnarsson, and that this same man had traveled on the bus several times that evening, once with another man dis-guised as a woman! The crazy bus driver kept pestering the government, claiming the reward for catching the killer. It is curious to note that a third witness also claimed to have seen Piltz near the murder scene, carrying a walkie-talkie, but this was yet another low-quality witness, whom the police roundly accused of having invented his story after Krantz's sensational accu-sations had become known.[5]

That the Swedish police had murdered Olof Palme was a pet theory for many Swedish left-wingers, and the editors of three communist magazines were audacious enough to publish the names and pictures of the men they be-lieved to be involved. Very unfairly, the list of policemen accused of complic-ity included Lieutenant Dalsgaard and his driver. Dalsgaard, an honest cop with twenty-eight years of service, was no likely participant in a right-wing conspiracy. His "early" arrival at the scene is not strange, since, as we know, Jeppsson waited for some time before pursuing the killer. Nor would it be a particularly logical move for the killer to hide inside a parked car in an area that would be swarming with police within minutes. As for Tell and Piltz, they both had moderately solid alibis for the night of the murder. The police-men sued the communist magazines, earning substantial damages. The crazy bus driver made an appearance in court, this time taking back all his previous evidence; his behavior was so unbalanced that the judge had to remind him he was testifying under oath. Tell and Piltz then challenged the imprudent Lars Krantz, who had written a sensational book naming them as being directly in-volved in the murder. Krantz had to settle out of court to the tune of fourteen thousand dollars.

From an early stage, veteran Stockholm journalist Olle Alsén took a vigor-ous interest in the murder investigation. Unlike most other Palme Detectives, who jealously defended their own pet conspiracy theories, Alsén flitted from one murder solution to another. At first, he was a leading player in the at-tempts to incriminate the police, speculating at length about sinister police planning meetings preceding the murder. He then became a convert to the Pettersson theory, adding the spectacular twist that after killing Palme, Pet-tersson had doubled back through the side streets. Alsén speculated that he was the frantic, red-faced man observed on the Sveavägen itself five minutes after the murder, literally running into a witness yelling, "This is terrible! Olof Palme has been shot!"[6] The argument that such ostentatious behavior, and such a speedy return to the crime scene, would hardly be logical was lost on this Palme Detective.

After Pettersson was freed, Alsén sought new pastures. He speculated that a CIA agent called "Razin," also known as Oswald LeWinter, had dangerous secret knowledge about the planning of the murder, and that a lodge of sin-ister Italian Freemasons had sent a telegram saying, "Tell our friend Bush the Swedish tree will be felled" shortly before the murder. The police retorted that LeWinter was a well-known international con artist, and that the story of the telegram was entirely bogus.[7] Alsén then proposed that a French for-eign legionnaire named Louis Bernard had gone to Stockholm and killed Palme. When the police found out that this man had in fact been serving time in an African prison, the ever-optimistic Alsén suggested that a double must have been installed in the Togo prison cell to give the sinister legion-naire an alibi.[8]

In 1992, after six years of persistent amateur detective work, Alsén finally hit the jackpot. He met two young Finnish women who had a remarkable story to tell. The night of the murder, they had been to see a film in central Stockholm. Just a minute or two before Olof Palme was murdered, one of them saw a tall man standing at the Dekorima corner. Recognizing him as a fellow countryman she had once met in a suburban gym, she walked up and asked him the time. The man tried to ignore her, but the persistent woman grabbed him by his brown leather jacket and repeated her question. Then there was a noise from a walkie-talkie underneath the man's jacket, and a voice said, in Finnish, "Now they are coming!" The man replied, also in Finnish, "I have been recognized! What am I to do?" A voice from the instrument responded, "Don't mind that, and do what you are supposed to!" The other woman found this turn of events very frightening, particularly as she saw that the man was holding a large revolver underneath his jacket. She urged her friend to stop trying to find out the time from this sinister character. Not long after they had left him, they heard two shots fired. The morning after, they read all about the murder of Olof Palme in the newspapers. Although convinced they had seen the killer, they decided to keep quiet about it, fearing for their own lives.

The mysterious "Dekorima Man" made headlines in every newspaper in Sweden, and various suggestions were put forward about his identity. Was Olle Alsén going to solve the murder that had confounded the police for seven years? The veteran journalist managed to track down the gym the woman had mentioned, and found some evidence that it had been frequented by a bodybuilding Finn who fit the woman's description. The Finn was a Stockholm police sergeant! This discovery gave the police conspiracy some much-needed bolstering, with people speculating that this sinister Finn had been the chosen hit man in a team of police assassins.

But when Ölvebro and his detectives questioned the two women, considerable doubts emerged as to their credibility. The women contradicted themselves, and no other witness had observed them at the murder scene. The film they claimed to have seen had premiered more than a year after the murder. And was it not strange to hire an assassin who could speak only Finnish, and who stood in the street with his revolver and walkie-talkie fully visible? The policeman from the gym had an alibi, nor did he fit the women's original description. The police investigators suggested that the women's acquaintance might have been another gym visitor; it was never divulged exactly who, since the women refused to cooperate with the police any further.[9] The Dekorima Man joined the crowd of phantoms hovering around the murder site on dark February nights.

In 1996, the police conspiracy theory was revised and extended when two academics, brothers Kari and Pertti Poutiainen, published a book on the subject.[10] More clever and persistent than the aforementioned Palme Detectives, these two devoted many years of research to scrutinizing the early response to the murder, rightly suspecting that there was something fishy about the official chronology. They clearly demonstrate that the police alarm was delayed at police headquarters, and their research has withstood the whitewashing efforts of the 1999 commission. Deservedly, their book became quite widely known, and it rekindled the rumors that the police had been involved in the murder. Senior Social Democratic politician Kjell-Olof Feldt wrote that the Poutiainen book had made even him speculate that the Swedish police force might have been involved in a conspiracy to murder Olof Palme.

The later parts of the Poutiainen book are wayward and speculative, however. They suggest that the alarm was deliberately delayed to facilitate the escape of the killer, as one part of a large conspiracy led by senior officers from the SÄPO. But they ignore that the delay can be explained by natural means, namely that the police radio operators were very busy that night, and that the individual taking the call from the cab company may have felt a need to double-check that the incident had really taken place in Stockholm. Two minutes is a narrow escape margin, and one of the police vans actually came very close to catching the killer, had it not driven off seconds before he came running up the Tunnelgatan stairs. And what if Gösta Söderström, whom nobody could accuse of being part of the conspiracy, had been just a little closer to the Tunnelgatan, in a position to hear the shots and pursue the killer? And what about the young officers who nearly succeeded in intercepting the killer in their squad car?[11]

The Poutiainens are correct that several officers at police headquarters lied about their activities, but this would imply little more than a desire to cover up the series of disastrous mistakes that had been committed and to save their own careers. In particular, the argument that officers from the SÄPO were behind the plot is a feeble one, since they seem to have been just as surprised and unprepared as the rest of the Swedish police when they learned that Olof Palme had been murdered. Furthermore, these officers have no formal authority over the uniformed and detective police.

The government commissions investigating the Palme murder inquiry have found little to support the theory of a police conspiracy, and it must be admitted the evidence is very weak.[12] What we know about the Stockholm police the night of the murder does not suggest that they had the determination, courage, and organizational skills to plan and commit the murder and then make a clean getaway without anyone suspecting them. The evidence at hand speaks of a shocked, feeble police response on almost every level, not a team of ice-cold professionals covering their tracks. Also, such a conspiracy would have involved dozens of police of every rank, some of them carrying out the murder, others delaying the alarm at headquarters, yet others making sure that the killer's escape was unimpeded. Swedish policemen are not particularly well paid, and in a conspiracy involving twenty or thirty police, some of them lowly uniformed officers, the temptation to turn in the coconspirators and claim the reward would have been overpowering.

Whereas the evidence supporting a large-scale police conspiracy is feeble, it is worthwhile to examine various leads involving individual police officers. As rumors flew, more than one Stockholm policeman found himself accused of complicity in the murder, but generally with very little foundation. It is remarkable that several people claimed to have observed the two Baseball Gang officers Tell and Piltz behaving suspiciously near the murder site. This lead was actually taken quite seriously by the police for a while, but it soon became apparent that at least one of the cops had a reasonably solid alibi, and that the witness observations were extremely low quality. Although the two Baseball Gang cops were tough customers who had many times been accused of police brutality, no solid evidence points to their having had a grudge against Palme, nor did they have any history of political violence. Neither cop had a license for a magnum revolver. They have both spoken out firmly against the various fanatics accusing them, and one of them is still a Stockholm police sergeant.

Yet another sinister Stockholm cop, employed as a bodyguard or police agent by both Holmér and Ebbe Carlsson, was a right-wing officer named Per Jörlin, formerly accused of police brutality and known for his familiarity with firearms. He seems to have executed his duties to the satisfaction of both Holmér and Ebbe, but he resigned from the police force some years later. He started a security guard company that speedily went bankrupt, but this did not prevent the former Baseball Gang cop from living well and gambling excessively. In 2000, he was convicted for brutally killing his girlfriend, thus proving he had the killer instinct. Yet the many rumors surrounding this individual are not supported by evidence linking him with the crime scene.

Curiously, the most interesting lead involving the police comes from the trial against Ebbe Carlsson and his private police force. Not the least surprising fact that emerged at the trial was that many of the policemen employed by Ebbe and Holmér were right-wing extremists, a strange choice for two people purporting to be loyal Social Democrats. After the collapse of Ebbe's investigation, the apartment of one of his agents, former police sergeant Carl Östling, was raided by the police. Östling was setting up shop as an arms dealer at the time, together with a right-wing army major, Ingvar Grundborg. The apartment was found to contain numerous photographs of Östling and Grundborg performing the Hitler salute in various Stockholm locations, one of them the main Jewish cemetery. On Östling's bookshelf was *Mein Kampf* and many other racist and fascist tracts. Östling also had a huge arsenal of weapons in his apartment: pistols, revolvers, high-velocity rifles, and two grenade launchers. One of his handguns was a .357 magnum, with an ample supply of ammunition.

On investigating the matter further, the police found that they had previously received several tips suggesting that Östling himself had been involved in the murder of Olof Palme! Quite a few people knew him as an unbalanced right-wing extremist who had many times told them how much he hated Palme's politics and even made threats against the prime minister.[13] A police colleague had been amazed by the vehemence and hatred with which Östling had spoken about Palme; another officer added that he had heard the sergeant discussing the murder with another policeman; they had said that they knew who the killer was, although his identity would never be made public. Another unexpected finding was that Östling had access to an apartment rented by Grundborg on the Regeringsgatan, not far from where Palme's murderer was last seen; had this apartment served as a refuge for the killer?[14] Per-Gunnar Näss thought not, since he knew (or rather thought he knew) that the murder scene could not have been chosen beforehand. This made Östling much less interesting as a suspect from his point of view.

On investigating Östling's alibi, the police found out that he had been in the hospital following surgery for a burst appendix. According to hospital staff and other witnesses, he had by no means recovered by the day of the murder; although he was capable of locomotion, his steps were faltering and he was in a lot of pain. This did not prevent him from suddenly leaving the hospital against medical advice the same afternoon, however, alleging that he would rather stay in his own apartment than share a room with a lot of smelly old cripples. The police learned that Östling had had some visitors later the same evening, and these individuals, mostly police colleagues and right-wing cronies, confirmed his story, although none of them gave him an alibi for the hours surrounding the murder.

For medical reasons, it can be ruled out that Östling committed the murder himself, since it is impossible for a person who has recently had fairly major abdominal surgery to quickly run up eighty-nine steps. This led to the police losing interest in him as a suspect, which may have been a bit premature; this man, with his hatred of Palme, contacts within both the official police and the underground network of political spies, knowledge of the arms trade, and easy access to firearms, could well have been a key player in a murder conspiracy. He might have left the hospital in such a hurry to provide the killer with the murder weapon. It may also be significant that the Baseball Gang cop Piltz was at one time been employed by Östling's company, proving a link between these two.

Another persistent conspiracy theory is that a phalanx within the Social Democrats decided that Palme had to be killed. It has been speculated, but without much solid evidence, that some of his political colleagues thought that Palme was nearing the end of his career and was becoming a liability. The Social Democratic conspiracy theory explains the lack of a vigorous police response: the police in the field were only following the orders given by their own superiors. It has been speculated that Hans Holmér, Carl Lidbom, and Ebbe Carlsson were in charge of the conspiracy, and that this disreputable trio deliberately tried to frame the PKK Kurds.

Veteran journalist Sven Anér has devoted much time to this theory. In a series of books, he has tried to prove that the Swedish police are still covering up this huge conspiracy, involving some of the highest in the land.[15] One of his theories is that Hans Holmér never left Stockholm the day of the murder; he was there the whole time, supervising the planning and execution of the murder. According to Anér, the dastardly police-master forged an alibi that he had been staying at a hotel in Borlänge on his way to the ski race.[16] The hotel staff gave conflicting testimony as to whether they had seen Holmér in Borlänge, and one hotel receptionist resolutely denied he had ever been there. After some newspapers became interested in the ex-commissioner's whereabouts at the time of the murder, the police had to investigate. They found another hotel receptionist who testified that she had definitely seen Hans Holmér the morning after the murder, and also obtained what was purported to be the commissioner's hotel bill and receipt. The hotel manager and receptionist who had previously said they had not seen Holmér retracted their testimony, claiming they had made their original statements only to get rid of the Palme Detective who had been pestering them.

Anér retorted that the bill and receipt were certainly forgeries, planted by the police conspiracy to hide the truth behind the murder, and that the police had harassed the hotel witnesses to make them change their story. The bill definitely looks odd, since it gives February 28 as both the day Holmér checked in and they day he checked out. But the explanation is that 1986 was a leap year, which confounded the computerized hotel billing system for February. Another mystification was provided by an alcoholic police sergeant who had sometimes acted as Holmér's driver. This man declared that the evening of the murder, he had been driving Holmér and some friends of his around central Stockholm, finally taking the Commissioner past the murder site a few minutes after Palme was killed. But when formally questioned by the police, the sergeant denied everything. The 1999 commission found no evidence that he had served as Holmér's driver in February 1986.

If Sven Anér's arguments about Holmér's whereabouts appear feeble, he is on somewhat firmer ground in another of his sensational books, in which he claims that Carl Lidbom and Ebbe Carlsson also lied about their actions the night of the murder.[17] Far from going to pick up Olof Palme's son, they were busy masterminding the murder plot. There is definitely something odd about Lidbom and Carlsson's alleged journey to Chamonix to fetch young Mattias Palme, although it is hard to say exactly what. These two were quite unscrupulous, deceiving men, and several matters concerning their activities the night of the murder remain unexplained. Lidbom has added to the sense of mystery by making a series of enigmatic comments hinting that he has dangerous secret knowledge about the murder. Once, he said that it would be best for all concerned if the murder of Olof Palme were never solved.

The official story is that Lisbet Palme telephoned Lidbom's wife at the embassy in Paris, asking that her youngest son Mattias, who was on a skiing vacation in Chamonix, be informed about his father's death by the ambassador himself. Mrs. Lidbom then phoned her husband, whom she knew was making a nocturnal visit to a French lady friend of his. The dynamic ambassador leaped out of bed when he got this momentous news about the tragic death of his old friend and political patron. He contacted the French secret police and air force, commandeered a jet from President Mitterand's private wing, and set off for Geneva with Ebbe Carlsson in tow.

The latter individual, who first claimed to have been in Paris to celebrate Lidbom's birthday, later changed his story, saying he had been there on publishing business. Whatever this business was, it was not important enough to prevent him from flying off into the night with his friend the ambassador. Fairly solid independent documentation shows that Lidbom really was in Chamonix, where he and a prefect named Cailly met Mattias Palme and gave him the sad news. But here the stories start to diverge. Sven Anér found evidence that young Palme had already been informed of his father's death by the tour guide of the skiing trip. According to another story, he was notified by some other youths shouting and reveling that the hated Olof Palme was dead, and ordering champagne for a toast!

The quickest and most rational way for Mattias Palme to return home would have been to fly from nearby Geneva directly to Stockholm, using the ticket he already had. Several witnesses, including members of the Palme family, said that he had done exactly this, and that his brother Mårten had met him at the airport. But Lidbom and Ebbe claimed they had brought young Palme with them to the Paris embassy, and that Ebbe had later accompanied him home on a commercial flight from Paris to Stockholm via Copenhagen. The persistent Anér found evidence that Ebbe Carlsson's Air France ticket from Paris to Copenhagen had in fact never been used; yet there is independent corroboration that Ebbe and Mattias Palme came to Stockholm on a plane from Copenhagen to Stockholm, and that they were met by a bodyguard and taken to the Palme apartment. This of course raises the question from where Ebbe had been traveling to Copenhagen.

When the authorities managed to produce what were purported to be the lists of passengers on the French government flights from Paris to Geneva and back again, the names including Lidbom, Ebbe Carlsson, and young Palme, the audacious Anér again cried forgery. But by now, the Swedish establishment had had enough of him. His book about the Chamonix conspiracy received some scathing reviews from the big daily newspapers, and he was called a sick, fanatical conspiracy monger. Mattias Palme, who had refused to speak to Anér, freely told the reviewers that he had come to Paris with Lidbom and Carlsson. The investigation by the 1999 commission has supported Anér in more than one particular: people at the Paris embassy had deliberately been lying to him, and less was known about the movements of Lidbom and Carlsson than had previously been supposed. In particular, it is surprising to find it confirmed that Carl Lidbom was the only Swedish ambassador in the world not to officiate at the memorial reception in Olof Palme's honor in their respective host countries. Such a reception was really held at the Paris embassy in the days after the murder; it was attended by many distinguished French politicians, but no one saw Lidbom there.

With admirable energy and persistence, Sven Anér has devoted many years of hard work to investigating the murder of Olof Palme. He has been given little or no encouragement by the Swedish media, but has had better luck abroad: his theories have been accepted in two prestigious German television documentaries and given an airing in both Germany and France.[18] The main drawback for this and other huge conspiracy theories is the aforementioned seven-million-dollar reward. Any conspiracy theory involving scores of people, lowly police officers among them, must be viewed with great skepticism. There was no clear-cut motive for Holmér, Lidbom, and Carlsson to kill Palme, nor did any of them have anything to gain by his death—in fact they had more to lose, since he had been their political patron.

As for their whereabouts at the time of the murder, there may be other reasons why Lidbom and Carlsson were not completely honest about their activities. A trivial explanation, one that is vastly more likely than Anér's conspiracy theory, is that Ebbe Carlsson found it embarrassing that he had been partying at some Paris nightclub the night Olof Palme was murdered. With his usual need to be the center of attention, he started bragging to his friends about his great influence in government circles, inventing the untrue story that the Palme family had asked him to go to Chamonix to pick up young Mattias. It is suspicious that just as the early official accounts of the journey to Chamonix do not mention Ebbe being present, Ebbe's earliest version of events does not mention Lidbom. When the story of Ebbe's journey to Chamonix was repeated in the newspapers, Lidbom had to concur with Ebbe's lies when the suspicious Anér came snooping around, adding the twist that they had actually traveled together.[19]

Another theory is somewhat more sinister, and will delight those with an interest in conspiracies. There have long been rumors that Carl Lidbom needed to visit Geneva soon after the murder of Olof Palme, to arrange some urgent banking matters. If he went there from Chamonix, he could have covered up his activities by claiming that he accompanied Ebbe and young Palme back to Paris. This version would have support from the fact that Lidbom was actually not seen at any official function at the Paris embassy *for several days* after the murder of Olof Palme. Another puzzling matter concerns an alleged burglary at the Paris embassy in April 1986. Carl Lidbom was widely quoted in the French and Swedish press saying that he and his wife had been gassed by the burglars and spent the entire night and morning lying unconscious in their beds. The burglars had spurned money and valuable art but stolen some trivial items.[20] The official investigation concluded that there had probably never been any burglary at all, hinting that the ambassador might have been drinking too much French wine at the time. But perhaps something was really stolen from the embassy that night, something that Lidbom could not readily divulge he possessed, since it related to his secret mission in early March.

Television producer Lars Krantz, who had started out as a witness in the murder investigation, became an inveterate Palme Detective. He suggested that Palme had planned the murder himself as a concealed suicide, aided and abetted by the Social Democratic establishment. Aware that his career was nearing its end, he decided to go out with a bang rather than a whimper, thus benefiting both his own reputation for posterity and the Social Democratic opinion polls. At first, Krantz left it undecided whether the prime minister had let off an explosive device underneath his overcoat or employed one of the crooked Baseball Gang cops to shoot him dead. Later, in a live radio interview following his prosecution for libeling the policemen he had previously accused, Krantz came out with an audacious new theory. The silly radio interviewers had hoped to make fun of him, but the elderly Palme Detective turned the tables on them by calmly saying that he knew exactly who had killed Olof Palme. Prompted by the interviewers, he revealed the identity of the killer: it was Lisbet Palme herself who had shot her husband in the back with a small-caliber pistol! Palme's son Joakim had acted the part of the murderer, firing two blanks at his father just as Mrs. Palme pulled the trigger and then running up the Tunnelgatan steps.

Krantz has gone on to claim that a huge conspiracy of freemasons, homosexuals, and feminists has been covering up the truth ever since, masterminded by the sinister Mrs. Palme.[21] One of his foremost pieces of evidence is a photograph allegedly portraying Mrs. Palme arriving at Sabbatsberg Hospital in a police car. In this photograph, she is wearing a different coat than the one she wore at the time of the murder. According to Krantz, Mrs. Palme left the ambulance and stepped into a waiting police car, leaving her coat to be shot at in the police laboratory; she faked her own injury in order to be eliminated as a suspect. Unfortunately for Krantz and his theory, this photograph also shows three additional police cars. But there was no police presence at Sabbatsberg when the ambulance arrived at 11:30, indicating that this photograph actually depicts Mrs. Palme *leaving* the hospital.[22] The reason she is wearing another coat in the photo is of course that her own had been taken as evidence by the police.

Krantz's theory is not supported by either of the two people who actually saw the murder committed, namely Morelius and Björkman, nor by any other murder scene witness. He has tried to bolster it by testimony from various dubious authorities: for example, Olle Alsén heard from someone that Lisbet Palme dropped her handbag at the hospital. Inside her bag was a small pistol. But Alsén seems to be a rather mischievous character who liked feeding disinformation to the more gullible among his fellow Palme Detectives. It is in fact remarkable that the Palme family have not sued Krantz for libel. Probably they think he is such a buffoon that nobody would ever take him seriously, but here they are clearly wrong. Krantz was clever enough to set up a Web site about his solution of the murder of Olof Palme, and his controversial theories and uncompromising language have ensured that this site has had more than 170,000 visitors since 1996. Ludicrously, schoolchildren sometimes use this site when collecting information for school projects about Palme and the murder; in all earnestness, one of them even wrote to Mrs. Palme asking why she shot her husband!

Just like the Kennedy assassination, the murder of Olof Palme has become surrounded by far-fetched conspiracy theories. It has been speculated that Hans Holmér murdered Palme, that either of Palme's sons committed the murder, or that Ebbe Carlsson found out that Palme had another boyfriend on the side and killed him in a fit of jealousy. In a manuscript submitted to the Palme task force, the ever-audacious Olle Alsén reaches new lows. He speculates that Palme was bisexual, had been infected with HIV by his boyfriend Ebbe Carlsson, and decided to conceal his guilty secret by planning his own murder. This distasteful speculation is as baseless as Alsén's other imaginative concoctions. Author Ernst Lindholm agrees that Palme had caught HIV from his lover Ebbe Carlsson, adding the twist that a huge conspiracy, involving almost everyone who counted in Sweden, decided that the prime minister had to die; the spy Stig Bergling acted as the hit man.[23] Just like Krantz, this audacious individual has little good to say about Palme: he was a homosexual and a schizophrenic who took bribes and stashed away money in a Swiss bank account.

These extreme conspiracy theories from unbalanced Palme Detectives can be seen as a continuation of the campaign of vilification against Palme during his lifetime. Even more hair-raising is the suggestion that Palme had become bored with politics and wanted to retire from it all. Assisted by the ubiquitous Ebbe Carlsson, he faked his own murder, substituting the body of a dead homosexual for his own in the ambulance on the way to Sabbatsberg Hospital, and escaped to sunnier climes! According to an Internet message board, he has been spotted on the Isle of Rhodes, selling ice cream at a tourist resort in the daytime, and chasing men in the local gay bars at night.

Some conspiracy theorists have suggested that the motive for killing Olof Palme came from his involvement as a mediator in the Iran-Iraq war. One theory says that president George H. W. Bush ordered Palme killed, as a result of his meddling in the arms supply to the Middle East, and that the murder was performed by a CIA hit squad led by colonel Oliver North. The Web site of journalist Anders Leopold advocates a slightly different version: Bush and the CIA signed Palme's death warrant, and their chosen hit man was Viktor Gunnarsson, assisted by two Chilean assassins.[24] It was of course the CIA that finally silenced Gunnarsson after he had moved to the United States. This theory leaves unexplained why the CIA would involve such a blabbermouth as Gunnarsson, who seems to have had a constitutional aversion to keeping anything a secret, in a life-or-death conspiracy. Nor can an unbiased mind find a solid motive for the CIA to kill Olof Palme. The prime minister was known to be anticommunist in spite of his left-wing rhetoric, the days of the Vietnam War were long forgotten, and the Bofors arms export to Iran was really very small. As we know, Ayatollah Khomeini's Iran featured largely in Ebbe Carlsson's audacious murder scenario. Other conspiracy theorists have pointed the finger at Saddam Hussein's Iraq, but neither of these two states had a convincing reason to want Palme dead, nor were they in the habit of sending their death squads as far north as Scandinavia.

There has also been much speculation that the South African government had Palme killed as a result of his firm antiapartheid stance. This theory has more in its favor than any other foreign conspiracy theory.[25] Palme was recognized as South Africa's greatest enemy in European politics, and just a few days before his death, he had made a speech condemning apartheid's racism more fiercely than ever before. At an early stage, a Swedish journalist reported that according to one of her South African sources, the murder of Olof Palme had been the handiwork of three South African agents. They had purchased a station wagon converted into a camper in Germany and lived in this vehicle after entering Sweden. This lead was never properly investigated by the police, since it emerged when all resources were being devoted to the anti-PKK campaign.

But in 1996, the South African conspiracy became headline news. The South African former police officer Eugene de Kock was on trial for serious crimes committed while serving under the apartheid regime. He testified that an agent named Craig Williamson, head of a South African murder squad called "operation Longreach," had masterminded the plot to kill Olof Palme. The murder had been committed by one of Williamson's agents, Anthony White. Colonel de Kock turned out to be a shady character, himself convicted of murder, and his detailed information made little sense. Nevertheless, Williamson was arrested in Angola shortly after de Kock's trial.

The police ascertained that Craig Williamson knew Sweden, that he saw Palme as a danger to the regime he supported, and that he had previously pulled off audacious undercover operations. In 1980, he had infiltrated the European support organization for the African National Congress (ANC), claiming to be a South African refugee who had become disgusted with apartheid. He soon became a leading official, handling large amounts of money donated by antiapartheid Swedes. But instead of sending the checks on to the ANC, Williamson embezzled large amounts of money, which he actually managed to divert back into the bank accounts of the South African secret police. Thus, instead of funding children's homes and hospitals through the ANC, the donors were sponsoring the torture camps of the police; two of these loathsome establishments were in fact erected using money stolen by Williamson. The wily South African sent kind thank-you letters back to the donors, saying that the money had been well spent and that he hoped for their continued support. It is sad but true that this despicable charade went on for three years, and that brave antiapartheid campaigner Stephen Biko was arrested and tortured to death based on information gleaned by Williamson. When this South African spy was finally found out, he made a quick getaway and was given a hero's welcome back home.

After the South African conspiracy became headline news in Sweden, several people claimed that they had seen Craig Williamson in Stockholm at the time of the murder, but like the sightings of the Phantom, these observations remain controversial.[26] A huge mountain of a man, with a receding hairline and a walrus mustache, Craig Williamson bore little resemblance to Palme's killer, and it is out of the question that he committed the murder himself. Although he was a master of the dirty tricks played by the South African secret service, his denial of any involvement in the Palme murder sounded convincing. With regard to the story of the three agents in the camper car, he asked how three South African agents, trained for desert warfare rather than snow and subzero temperatures, could live in the Swedish outback for three months without attracting suspicion. Anthony White was also questioned and denied all involvement in the murder with vehemence. He blamed de Kock and another shady South African named Riian Stander for spreading disinformation to help their own cases. Rumor had it that a Swedish secret agent employed by Williamson had been the hit man, but no progress was made in finding this individual, if he ever existed. The only Swede known to have been employed by the South African secret service was a former army lieutenant named Bertil Wedin, a right-wing extremist who was living in Cyprus at the time of the murder.

The most intriguing part of the South African connection is an investigation that took place in Maputo, Mozambique, in 1997.[27] The Swedish ambassador in this country learned that a mysterious South African had been behaving oddly, hinting that he had inside knowledge of the murder of Olof Palme. Shortly after, this very man was arrested for smuggling and arson by the Mozambique police. The Swedish police were alerted and sent a man down to Africa, where some very interesting information came to light. The arrested man, whose name or alias was Nigel Barnett, was definitely an agent in the South African secret service. He possessed quite an arsenal of firearms, including at least one Smith and Wesson .357 magnum. He may well have been active as an assassin of antiapartheid activists in various African countries. He knew both Craig Williamson and a certain Peter Casselton, who had been rumored to possess dangerous secret information about the murder of Olof Palme and who himself died mysteriously in early 1997. Not the least curious thing about Barnett was that as a child, he had been adopted by a part Swedish family; he had visited Sweden several times and could speak the language.

In Barnett's possession were some videotapes concerning the Palme murder and an airline ticket from Johannesburg to Stockholm dated May 9, 1986. He also had photographs of a blond woman and various Stockholm buildings and sceneries, including a Saab station wagon that had been converted to a camper van. Since the Mozambique police considered Barnett a serious criminal, he was subjected to a polygraph test. During questioning, he claimed to have a good idea which of his secret service colleagues was behind the murder of Olof Palme, but he avoided going into detail. His denial when he was himself accused of the murder tested on the polygraph as a lie. Bullets from Barnett's revolver did not match those that killed Olof Palme, but the package in which they had been sent from Maputo to Stockholm showed signs of having been tampered with. The Swedish police found no evidence to suggest that Barnett had been in Sweden in February 1986, and the investigation regarding him was closed, perhaps prematurely.

In January 2003, the South African conspiracy again became headline news in the Swedish papers.[28] International businessman Kent Ajland claimed to have found out the truth about the murder when traveling in South Africa; he had then worked closely with maverick police chief Tommy Lindström and two senior Social Democratic politicians to accumulate further evidence. The killer's name was Roy Allen, a former captain in the South African army who had emigrated to Australia in 1992. Ajland produced what was purported to be Allen's travel invoice to Stockholm for "Operation Slingshot," as the murder of Olof Palme was called. Lindström and two politicians were enthusiastic, but the Palme police commented that there was little new in Ajland's information. Some experts on South African secret police operations added that it was not the practice within this organization to leave implicating travel invoices lying around; all payments were made in cash, and all documents shredded. Ajland had made a sinister implication of the initials "OP" in the documents, but this was in fact a reference to "Observation Person," the individual the covert operation was directed against. Then it was divulged that the two men who had sold the information to Ajland, major general Tai Minaar and former secret agent Riaan Stander, had both been convicted for wholesale fraud and forgery in the United States. The newspapers turned on Ajland himself, accusing him of being a penniless adventurer trying to recoup nonexistent "expenses" from his alleged secret police work in South Africa. Tommy Lindström and two politicians hastily withdrew their support. The ending of this farcical story was that Roy Allen himself spoke up, describing Ajland's documents as forgeries and indignantly denying any involvement in the murder. Stander was a scoundrel who had previously tried to implicate him in another murder, he said, and no doubt these unscrupulous South Africans had been after the Palme reward.

THE POLICE INVESTIGATION KEELS OVER

In June 1993, it was decided that the murder investigation should take advantage of the recent advances in criminal profiling. This method of systematically analyzing serial criminals had had some spectacular successes in the United States, leading to the arrest of several serial killers and rapists. There is less evidence that profiling is helpful in solving one isolated murder, particularly when performed more than seven years after the event, but the police had run out of leads and were desperately clutching at straws. Detective lieutenant Jan Olsson and psychiatrist Ulf Åsgård were set to work writing the profile of the murderer of Olof Palme, with support from the FBI's Behavioral Science Unit; their 116-page document was finished almost a year later, in May 1994.[1]

The two profilers make a promising start, rightly pointing out that the Palme case offers plentiful research opportunities for the witness psychologist. Several witnesses clearly invented their stories, others added further data in questioning after questioning, yet others clearly altered their testimony under the influence of external information from the police and media. Olsson and Åsgård lament that little is known about whether Palme was involved in any secret discussions or negotiations at the time, and hint that he might have played a vital role in deals between states and private companies. Another passage of interest is a comparison of the murder of Olof Palme with other assassinations of prominent politicians. It is unusual that the murder took place late at night, that the victim's wife was also attacked, and that there was no clear motive for the killing. In particular, the profilers express amazement that the assassin could have come so close to the Palmes.

After analyzing the murder at length, the profilers declare that it was the motiveless act of a disturbed lone attacker. The killer was around forty years old, a sociopath and loner without any higher education, quite possibly on long-term unemployment or retired on medical grounds. He might well have been an alcoholic and/or drug addict, had problems with authorities in general, and committed crimes of violence in the past. It is further speculated that he might have shown an abnormal interest in the murder investigation, or even approached the police with false testimony regarding his observations the night of the murder. The Swedish police approved of the profile, and decided to make it a mainstay in the continuing murder investigation.

The National Audit Office experts were critical, however, objecting that in many respects, the two experts seemed to have written a profile of Christer Pettersson, not a profile of the killer of Olof Palme. In a television interview, FBI profiler Greg McCrary said that the Swedes had told (or rather misled) him that Palme had not at all been a controversial politician, and that they had ignored profiling characteristics that did not fit Pettersson. Distinguished American criminologist Robert Ressler accepted the conclusion of the Swedish authorities that the killer was a lone attacker, although he did not share their belief that he was necessarily a sociopath or a known violent criminal. In his opinion, it was likely that the killer was not an alcoholic or a drug addict, but rather a depressed, introverted loner, for whom Palme had become the symbol of everything that had gone wrong in his life. Ressler was amazed that this lone killer could have escaped after the murder; this was an extremely improbable outcome and made the murder of Olof Palme the crime of the century.[2]

The police made a huge trawl through the material in their hands, comparing the characteristics of a vast array of lunatics, alcoholics, known violent criminals, and people with an obsessive interest in Olof Palme with the profile. In reality, it was one last try to fish out a potential killer from a huge pond full of criminals before time ran out. One of the individuals caught in the net was Alf Lundin, a former witness in the case against Christer Pettersson. As we know, he first claimed to have seen Olof and Lisbet walking down the street the night of the murder and the assassin hiding in the bushes nearby. He then gradually improved his story: he had seen the Grand Man follow the Palmes, and in his latest version, had actually seen the murder being committed. He saw the Pettersson lineup but picked out one of the policemen. This ended his usefulness for the police, and he was not called as a witness in the trial against Pettersson; the prosecutors considered his credibility as a witness to be so low that he might actually damage the case.

In 1994, after the Profile had been written, the police detectives realized that this bogus witness actually fit it himself. He had lied about his activities the evening of the murder and shown an abnormal interest in the murder investigation. He had worn a blue parka and steel-rimmed glasses at the time. A rather pathetic creature, previously convicted for indecent exposure, he lived off temporary odd jobs. By this time Ölvebro was becoming desperate, and he decided to try a bluff. He made a series of ostentatious statements to the newspapers, claiming that he expected the murder to be solved within a few months, and then gave a description of the new suspect that would be easily recognized by the man himself. It was hoped that Lundin would try to flee the country, dig up the murder weapon, or even confess the crime.

All that happened was that Lundin admitted he had made up his entire story. When Olof Palme was shot, he had been sitting at home watching television, he said. The police got no further, and it soon became apparent that this pathetic little man could not be the killer.[3] Ölvebro had to publicly recant and lost a fair amount of respect because of this ill-advised move. This debacle was in fact the beginning of the end for Ölvebro, who had never been popular among his subordinates. Some of his own detectives anonymously reported him for tax evasion and for illicitly using a police vehicle. These were still heinous crimes in Sweden, and for quite some time, Ölvebro was himself under secret surveillance! The accusations turned out to be unfounded, but Ölvebro nevertheless decided to resign, disgusted with the lack of loyalty shown by his detectives.

More than a few of the suspects brought to light by the profile were obviously mentally ill. By this time, the murder investigation had distanced itself so far from what had really happened when Palme was killed that no one seems to have questioned whether a lunatic was capable of killing a man in an accomplished manner, making a clean getaway, and then keeping his dark secret for almost ten years. The police knew that several people, psychiatrists prominent among them, had pointed out a thirty-five-year-old man with severe schizophrenia. He had been obsessed with Olof Palme and used to call himself Palme's Crown Prince. More than once he had behaved oddly in public, making confused remarks about Palme. He looked something like the Phantom but was very thin. Some witnesses thought they had seen him lurking around outside the Palme apartment, or outside the government building in which Palme worked. When this man was finally interviewed by the police, he accused his own brother of killing Olof Palme, in league with the leader of the Swedish conservatives. He wanted to marry Princess Anne, he said, and claimed to be the chosen successor of Boris Yeltsin.

Another mentally disturbed character caught the interest of the police when several people testified as to his extreme hatred of Olof Palme. He himself boasted that he had several times followed Palme around and sneaked up to Palme's front door and put excrement in the mailbox. He had once knocked down a man who spoke favorably of the prime minister. The day after the murder, he expressed delight that Palme was dead and later boasted that he had been at the murder site and pursued a man who was running away. He had brought with him a handful of buttons, which he had thrown at the murder site to confound the police. Later, he had defaced Palme's tombstone by throwing grease over it. It turned out that this individual had several times been convicted for assault and battery, but never anything more serious. No buttons had been found at the murder site. Still, the police took this man seriously as a suspect and even bugged his telephone for a month's time. They saw him spit at the memorial plaque at the murder site. When questioned, he claimed to have been in Copenhagen the night of the murder. In the early 1970s, he had possessed a small-caliber handgun, but never a .357 magnum.[4]

A somewhat more likely suspect was a Yugoslav gangster, who had previously been sentenced to three years in prison for attempted murder after shooting a man from a rival gang. He claimed to have been wrongfully convicted, having acted in self-defense, and for some obscure reason blamed Olof Palme. He cursed the prime minister in front of the other convicts and swore he would kill Palme as soon as he was set free. After being released, he joined a foreign gang smuggling heroin into Sweden. He still hated Olof Palme and made threats that he would kill the prime minister. The Yugoslav once visited the municipal archives to recover a letter he had previously written to the prime minister. He acted threateningly, saying, "You will all die, I am not joking," and one of the archive assistants saw what looked like a pistol in his bag. The Yugoslav later returned to his country of origin, and it was difficult for the Swedish police to track him down when, based on the profile, he was singled out. As late as 2000, he was questioned by the police; he denied having any involvement in the murder and claimed that he had been in Montenegro at the time.[5]

The most valuable part of the post-Pettersson police investigation was the systematic search for the murder weapon. In 1986, some early attempts were made to trace the .357 magnum revolver used by the killer. Every Swede with a license for a .357 magnum was told to report to the police; an enormous amount of data was accumulated, but nothing that advanced the murder investigation. Hans Holmér realized that it would be impossible to examine every .357 magnum in Sweden, but he planned a test shooting of all such handguns within the county of Stockholm. A hundred thousand rounds of ammunition were purchased, but this ambitious project was preempted by the great campaign against the PKK. Late in 1989, the police continued where Holmér had left off, and a test firing of 429 out of 620 revolvers took place, but without anything worthwhile being discovered. The police were able to rule out many of the remaining revolvers for various reasons.

The police also made some headway with regard to the ammunition used by the killer. In 1990, they wrote to the Winchester Western factory, enclosing data from the lead isotope examination of the bullets. The factory replied that this ammunition had been manufactured in 1979 and packed in boxes marked "PM." Hoping to track down the actual batch of ammunition used, the police then wrote to arms dealers all over Scandinavia, asking for ammunition samples and details of the boxes the bullets had been packed in. Nine bullets matched the lead isotope characteristics of the Palme bullets; four of these had been packed in boxes marked "3 PM 7," indicating that they came from a batch manufactured in November 1979.

In particular, the police were interested to find that an arms dealer in Lapland had a half-empty box of this kind of ammunition. They knew that in 1983, a .357 magnum revolver and ninety-one rounds of Winchester metal-piercing ammunition had been stolen in a burglary in Haparanda, Lapland. The burglar, a Finnish criminal, later joined forces with two countrymen and used the revolver to rob a bank. All three were later caught by the police and convicted for both the burglary and the bank holdup, but they had passed the revolver on to other criminals. The police also knew that two masked men had robbed another bank, in Mockfjärd, the month after the other robbery. One of the robbers had been brandishing a large revolver, with which he shot one of the bank customers in the leg. The police dug the bullet out of the bank wall and found that although it was too deformed for its markings to be compared to those of the Palme bullets, the lead isotope readings were an exact match.

The man who had stolen the revolver suspected that the Mockfjärd robbery had been the work of two Finnish brothers. One of these men was later arrested for the crime but released without charge due to lack of evidence. Both Finns were hardened criminals and very reluctant to speak to the police. According to rumors, the revolver had been test fired at a telephone pole once, but when the police got there, the pole had been taken down. The Finnish gangsters had thrown the revolver into a certain lake, according to other rumors, but ambitious police diving operations found nothing worthwhile. One of the Finns then approached the police, saying that he had sold the revolver to a drug addict he knew. He demanded fourteen thousand dollars to divulge this man's name. The police drew up a document saying that he would be given the money if his tip proved worthwhile to the Palme investigation, and showed him a briefcase with fourteen thousand dollars in cash to entice him, but the stubborn Finn insisted on being paid in cash up front, without any stipulations. The police did not take him up on the offer, and the whereabouts of the Mockfjärd revolver are still unknown. Ingemar Krusell, who strongly suspects this revolver was the one used by the killer of Olof

Palme, speculates that it was traded for drugs and ended up in the hands of Sigge Cedergren.[6]

Another Smith and Wesson .357 magnum and ammunition was stolen from an apartment belonging to a certain Jens Sucksdorff. This gun had originally belonged to Sucksdorff's father, who had bought it in 1954. In 1989, twelve years after the burglary, the burglar himself approached the Palme police anonymously, telling them that he had passed the revolver on to a well-known illegal arms dealer, who had sold it to another criminal. This last individual sat playing with the revolver one day and accidentally fired a shot through the heel of the shoe of a friend of his. Sobered by this narrow miss, he decided to keep away from loaded firearms and returned the revolver to the arms dealer. The police approached both these men, but without eliciting much more information.

It may be that the revolver was bought by a man who accidentally shot himself dead with it on Christmas Eve 1984; it may also be that it was bought by a drug dealer who knew Sigge Cedergren. The latter hypothesis was of course the most interesting for Thure Nässén and the police, who wished to believe this was the gun handed over to Christer Pettersson just before the murder.[7] In 2002, a forty-seven-year-old criminal told the police that he knew where the Sucksdorff revolver was kept; he wanted to do a deal to get his sentence reduced for various crimes he had committed. For several weeks, the media dwelled on the possibility that the murder weapon had finally been found. One paper even interviewed Christer Pettersson, who said that the police would never find a .357 magnum with his fingerprints on it. He got angry when Lisbet Palme was mentioned, saying that she would lose her soul for lying about him. He ended the interview by saying that only three people knew the truth about who killed Olof Palme: he himself, the murderer, and God. Not long after, the 2002 revolver was ruled out as the murder weapon for ballistic reasons.[8]

In August 1993, the police double-checked the list of .357 magnum hand-guns in the county of Stockholm. They found that a then forty-seven-year-old man had failed to turn up for the planned test shooting in 1989. A detective had tried to track him down at the time, but had mistakenly interviewed a different man with the same name. In early 1994, the police managed to find this suspect. A decidedly odd character, he had quit his job in 1980 after a large gambling win. He started playing the stock market, but gradually lost his money. In 1992, he decided to sell his .357 magnum for financial reasons: a foreign-looking man he met in a bar paid $760 for it. The night Palme was killed, the man had been suffering from the flu, he said, and had been in bed in his apartment. He had been expecting the police to contact him after the murder, since he had a .357 magnum and lived just fifteen minutes from the murder site, but this had not happened.

The police found out that this suspect was a loner with few friends. As the years went by, he had become increasingly bitter and morose. He was an expert shot and an experienced hunter, and had blamed the Palme government and its excessive taxation for his financial ruin. His story about selling the revolver did not have the ring of truth: Who would buy a powerful handgun from an absolute stranger and pay twice the market value for it? The suspect had a criminal record, but only for kicking a dog that had annoyed him with its barking. A tall, well-built man, he fit the description of Olof Palme's killer quite well. Interestingly, the police found evidence that he had been lying low for a while after the murder, and that he had detailed information about the murder investigation.

The National Audit Office experts were impressed with the case against this individual and called him the second main suspect after Christer Pettersson. Prosecutor Jan Danielsson and captain Ingemar Krusell were more circumspect: in a newspaper interview, they pointed out that no witness could tie the new suspect to the murder scene, and that there was no way his revolver could be tracked down. He did not resemble Christer Pettersson, who had after all been identified as the killer with 100 percent certainty by Lisbet Palme. The 1999 commmission blasted the police for their incompetence, pointing out that if someone failed to appear for an obligatory test firing of his revolver, they should not wait several years to contact him. If he really did sell the revolver in 1992, it would have been possible to examine the weapon had he been approached back in 1989.[9]

After the appeal against Christer Pettersson was quashed, the murder investigation went into what can only be called terminal decay. As it became obvious no killer would ever be caught, the Swedish establishment instead began searching for scapegoats: What exactly had gone wrong, and who was to blame for these mistakes? As we know, two state commissions on the investigation of the murder of Olof Palme had been active in 1987 and 1988, but they had concentrated on the early response to the murder and events preceding the downfall of Hans Holmér. In 1993, mainly because of the persistent rumors of police involvement in the murder, it was decided to appoint a third state commission. Throughout 1994 and 1995, this commission slowly and steadily plodded away. Its chairman was a certain Sigvard Marjasin, a former trade union leader and Social Democratic politician who had become a provincial county governor. It is reasonable to suggest that Marjasin was not selected for his superior intelligence, nor in the hope that his independent mind would lead to trenchant criticism of the murder inquiry. He was a loyal bureaucrat in the service of the ruling Social Democrats and would do as he was told. Marjasin even went so far as to forbid other members of the commission to see secret documents and made it clear that one of the commission's objectives was to demolish the conspiracy theories that were flourishing about the Palme murder; they were to educate the citizens that the state and the police could still be trusted.

Marjasin was certainly right about this kind of propaganda being sorely needed. In 1996, the murder investigation suffered one disaster after another. This was the year the South African conspiracy theory gained prominence and the Poutiainens published their book revitalizing the police conspiracy theory; the police and prosecutors failed to present a coherent response to either of these outside challenges. The year was also full of turbulence for more than one member of the Palme task force. First Ölvebro resigned after being (falsely) accused of tax evasion. Then it was the maverick Tommy Lindström's time to go; he had set up a bogus firm for providing unmarked police cars and been convicted for fraud and forgery. The prosecutor Almblad handed in his notice after being accused of using a police car outside work hours and buying alcohol with taxpayers' money.

The authorities may have hoped that the trusted Marjasin and his commission could do something to reestablish the public's faith in the rather shoddy individuals charged with investigating the murder of Olof Palme. But then a journalist found evidence that in his duties as a county governor, Marjasin had managed his finances in a rather unconventional manner. He had made it a practice to cut up his receipts so that no one could trace what he had purchased and had sent duplicate invoices to be paid twice for certain expenses. The press gloated over this miserable display of dishonesty and crowed over Marjasin's lengthy shopping lists for alcoholic beverages for his parties. After being prosecuted for fraud, Marjasin had to leave the Palme commission in disgrace.[10]

The remaining members of what would become the 1999 commission agreed that Marjasin's departure was probably a good thing. One of them arranged for two experts from the National Audit Office to write a critical appraisal of the murder investigation, giving them access to all police files. The experts' 260-page report provides an astute and independent view of the murder. They discuss two possible scenarios: either a small, close-knit conspiracy of a few professionals, or a lone attacker who spotted the Palmes outside the Grand cinema before the film. Far from being convinced about Pettersson's guilt, they add to the debate several arguments in his favor, although they cautiously avoid attacking the testimony of Mrs. Palme. Had the 1999 commission followed in their footsteps, its report would have been valuable indeed. It still is one of the main sources for any historian writing about the murder, but more due to its extensive factual contents than to elements of analysis and criticism. The 1999 commission made a habit of never questioning the police or double-checking information; its report has a firm anti-Pettersson bias and avoids addressing many of the minor mysteries discussed in this book.[11]

DID OLOF PALME
KNOW HIS KILLER?

The greatest mystery surrounding the murder of Olof Palme is the murder site. Holmér, Näss, and Lindström were all amazed at how the killer seemed to have known which way the prime minister would be walking home from the cinema.[1] Holmér told his journalist confidante Åsheden that unless it was assumed that the Palmes were followed from the cinema, everything became "insufferably enigmatic." He later commented that one of the extraordinary features of the murder of Olof Palme was that the murder site had been chosen by the victim and not by the murderer; when asked to explain what he meant by this obtuse comment, he reluctantly volunteered that he had "referred to the scenario preceding the murder." Näss thought the murder site "impossible": How had the killer been able to stalk the Palmes and escape up the Tunnelgatan stairs as if this was a premeditated plan? Foreign minister Sten Andersson made a similar comment: if we know why the Palmes crossed the Sveavägen, we also know the motive for the murder.

Firstly, it must have been completely unexpected for Palme to be walking home at all, instead of taking the subway or a cab as most people would on a freezing cold night. Secondly, even if the murderer or murderers had calculated that the prime minister might walk all the way home, the route chosen by the Palmes was a very illogical one. The natural way for the Palmes to walk from the Grand cinema to the Old Town would have been via the partly pedestrianized Drottninggatan, directly leading onto the Västerlånggatan, where they lived. Not only was this the shortest route, but these were safe, well-lit streets where few hooligans would be lurking. Instead, the Palmes chose a route that would have taken them past the Monte Carlo restaurant, the Haymarket, and the Sergels Torg, three notorious trouble spots in Stockholm nightlife. Few middle-aged couples would have been eager to walk through these parts of the capital after 11:00 p.m. on a Friday.

Thirdly, even if the killer or killers had predicted the way the Palmes were walking home, how could they know that their prey would suddenly and unexpectedly cross the street and continue walking on the other side—the side opposite the one they would eventually need to be on to make their way home? This scenario would have to involve either a huge gang of murderers, patrolling every street corner in central Stockholm, or a lone avenger who had the extreme good fortune to be in the right place at the right time, armed with a powerful handgun. The former of these alternatives has virtually been excluded by the police investigation; the second is equally far-fetched and unlikely.

The mystery deepens when the testimony of the witness Inge Morelius is taken into account. There is no doubt this man was a very reliable witness, acknowledged as such by the police. Morelius tells us that the killer stood at the Dekorima corner for several minutes, calmly waiting for his victim, with a heavy, loaded handgun ready in a side holster underneath his coat. He looked up and down the Sveavägen once or twice, as if waiting for someone to arrive. The exact amount of time Morelius saw the killer waiting for the Palmes is a very important point. He himself said that he had seen the killer waiting for at least two minutes, quite possibly for as long as four minutes. Here he is supported by the times printed on his friends' ATM receipts, which demonstrate that Morelius parked his car at about 11:16:40, thus more than four minutes before the murder. Morelius also testified that far from hiding in the Dekorima entrance, the killer stood calmly waiting on the sidewalk, like any other person waiting for a friend to arrive or sheltering from the bitter wind.[2]

Three other witnesses put an upward limit to the amount of time the killer could have waited outside Dekorima. First, two women who had been to the Grand cinema walked past the crossing of Sveavägen and Tunnelgatan at around 11:17 or 11:18. For a short while, they stood discussing whether they should walk up the Tunnelgatan stairs, deciding against it because the entrance looked sinister and desolate. At this time, there was no other person nearby. Secondly and more importantly, the alert and reliable witness Nicola Fauzzi walked past the Dekorima corner just before 11:19 and saw no man waiting there.[3]

But another witness would seem to support Morelius's testimony that the killer was waiting for his victim for about two minutes. This man made his existence known in early 1988, claiming that he had walked past the Dekorima corner at about 11:20 and seen a man standing there. He reported this to the police in Helsingborg, a precinct in southern Sweden, and the aforementioned Thure Nässén was dispatched there to question him. Reporting back to his boss Ingemar Krusell, Nässén said that the man's story made good sense. The witness said that he had torn up a check he had been writing and thrown the pieces into a trash can just at the crossing of the Sveavägen and the Tunnelgatan. Had the police technicians noted the contents of this container at the time, there would be firm evidence the witness had really been there. But as Krusell found out to his chagrin, no one had bothered to take such an obvious step. Until a relatively late stage, the task force considered calling this witness in the Pettersson trial, but the prosecutor Helin decided against it.[4]

Another important point is that although several witnesses agree that a man was watching the Grand cinema in a conspicuous manner, his looks and clothes did not match those of the killer. The killer was tall and well built, and wore dark clothes and a dark overcoat; the Grand Man was shorter, more stocky, and wore a blue parka and a beige cap. No evidence shows that the Grand Man followed the Palmes further than the hot dog stand; nor is it likely he would have been able to overtake them on their walk to the Dekorima corner. This distance takes about two minutes and thirty seconds for a swift walker and four minutes for someone walking very slowly. The Palmes were agile and fit people, and when questioned in court, Lisbet said that they had walked quite fast. This statement has support from the witnesses Björkman and Fauzzi, both of whom testified that the Palmes were walking significantly faster than Björkman. The Palmes should have managed to walk this distance in less than three minutes thirty seconds, allowing for the brief stop outside the Indian clothing store. Since Morelius saw the man waiting at the Dekorima corner for at least two minutes, the Grand Man would have needed the superpowers of Batman or Spiderman to make up the distance. Furthermore, a frantically running man would have attracted attention, but neither Mrs. Palme nor Fauzzi noticed any such activity at the time.

In fact, Fauzzi's evidence strongly suggests that no one (apart from the witness Björkman) was following the Palmes during the latter part of their walk down the Sveavägen. It might be argued that the Grand Man could have turned into the Luntmakargatan, running parallel to the Sveavägen to reach the Dekorima corner, but then he would have encountered Jeppsson, who did not notice anything untoward. The clinching argument again comes from Morelius, who had ample time to observe the killer. He did not see a panting, nervous man who just about had time to get his gun ready: the killer was calm and collected, and stood patiently waiting for his victim. In Morelius's own somewhat agitated words: "It was a planned assassination—an execution! The killer was ice cold! He just stood there—he knew they were coming that way!"

The only theory that explains this puzzling murder scenario is that Olof Palme had arranged to meet somebody at the Dekorima corner that night, and that this meeting was a trap to lead him to his death. Surely, the reader might object, Palme would not have gone to a meeting with an unknown man in the middle of the night. But Palme was an extremely unconventional politician who often used informal means of communication. We know about his inside knowledge as an intelligence agent and his distrust of the official secret police. Palme was also a very brave man, with a disregard for danger and a fatalistic approach to his own longevity. Furthermore, it may well be that Palme knew the man who had contacted him: perhaps an intelligence agent or policeman, or a part-time spy from Ebbe Carlsson's network of acquaintances. Palme would certainly never have agreed to meet a blackmailer or an old enemy, but he would not have hesitated to set up a meeting with a person claiming to have urgent political information.

The reason for a private meeting may well have been that Palme was to receive some important documents from his mysterious contact. If the meeting called for immediate and clandestine action, Palme might well have taken advantage of his planned visit to the cinema to arrange a brief encounter outside the Skandia building. This was an obvious meeting place, being a well-known Stockholm landmark, as well as having the advantage of being located just between the two cinemas—the Grand and the Spegeln—that the Palmes had been choosing between that evening. The meeting could easily have been set up over the telephone either before or after Palme had returned home from work. There was no obvious reason for him to tell his wife, or any other person, about this secret mission.

So, what do the murder scene witnesses say about a possible contact between Palme and his killer? They say little that is controversial in the official indictment and trial of Christer Pettersson, but this is due to clever doctoring of the information. Several of the original witness statements suggest a completely different murder scenario. As we know, the cab driver Anders Dels-born, the same man who was clearheaded enough to phone for help, saw Olof Palme and his wife standing on the sidewalk with the killer shortly (fifteen to twenty-five seconds) before the fatal shots were fired. The Palmes were facing the killer and having a conversation with him. Christina Vallin, yet another murder scene witnesses, remembered seeing three people standing together a short while before the shots were fired.

Anders Björkman, who was walking not far behind the Palmes, also saw the killer talking to them. The three of them were walking together for a short distance, and the killer was speaking to Olof with his arm around his shoulders. All of a sudden, he pulled a gun and shot Palme in the back. Björkman first thought a woman had been shot, since he found it unnatural for a man to embrace another man in this manner. Even in a later questioning, under hypnosis, he repeated that a woman had been murdered, not a man.[5] Cab driver

Jan-Åke Svensson, who had a quick glimpse of the three people together before the shots were fired, told a journalist he had perceived them as being in a group and thought the murder "a family drama."[6]

Another murder scene witness, Cecilia Annerstedt, was sitting in the same car as Anna Hage and Karin Johansson, with a good view of the Dekorima corner. She saw three people, the Palmes and the murderer, walking from the advertisement pillar at the corner of the Sveavägen and the Tunnelgatan toward the Dekorima display window. The killer was considerably taller than Olof Palme. She said the three people seemed to be together, adding the vital information that they stopped near the Dekorima window. It is regrettable that she then turned her eyes away from them and thus narrowly missed seeing the murder being committed. All of a sudden, one of Cecilia's friends cried out, "God, what are they doing!" and another said, "Typical of those drunks!" When she turned back to the three people, it seemed as if one of them had knocked the shorter man down.

Cecilia's two friends also had interesting things to say. Sven Åke Larsson, the youth driving the car, clearly saw the three people standing together before the shots, and got the impression they were quarreling. "Look over there, they are having a fight!" he said to his friend Elizabeth Johansson. When Elizabeth looked, only two people were there, but they certainly seemed to be fighting: one was holding the other by the collar. They then both saw the shorter man falling down, but neither of them heard the shots fired.[7] Some other youths driving past the murder scene in a car made very similar observations. One of them, Johnny Falk, saw two people, Olof Palme and the killer, standing together just seconds before the shots were fired. They appeared to be having a discussion. Then Palme threw his hands up in the air and waved them around in a strange manner, before falling over.[8]

An important murder scene witness who would appear to contradict that a brief meeting between Palme and the killer took place is the aforementioned Inge Morelius. But it is clear that his attention was divided between the prelude to the murder and various other matters: he was keeping an eye on his girlfriend, who was withdrawing money from an ATM, and was also watching out for the police, since his car was illegally parked. He was not watching the killer the whole time; he only looked that way a few times to see if the man was still standing there. One of several indications of this is that Morelius said a crowd of young people had walked past the Palmes just before they reached the advertisement pillar at the corner of Tunnelgatan and Sveavägen. If this had been true, these people would have been perfectly placed to see the murder, but the police investigation shows that they had in fact walked past several minutes earlier.

Morelius was certainly right that the killer had stood there patiently waiting for his victim for at least two minutes, but his other memories seem rather

The killer walks up to the Palmes. In this official photo of the police reconstruction of the crime, note the short (blue) parka worn by the killer—the police had already made up their minds as to how he was dressed. Reproduced by permission of the Swedish National Police Board.

fragmented. Nor is there any question that like many other witnesses, he was affected by the moral panic in Sweden after the murder, and unconsciously adapted his evidence to Hans Holmér's 'official' version of how the murder had happened. It would appear that Morelius had one clear memory of the killer approaching the Palmes near an advertisement pillar at the corner of the Sveavägen and the Tunnelgatan, and another memory of them closer to Dekorima, where the gunman pulled his revolver and shot the prime minister.[9] Morelius also provides the information that after the killer walked up to the Palmes, Lisbet released her grasp of her husband's arm and walked ahead—to allow the other two to talk in privacy? The police reconstructions provide another vital clue. The alert witness Nicola Fauzzi, who testified that no one (apart from Björkman) had been following the Palmes, also told the police exactly where he had met the prime minister and his wife. By timing Fauzzi's walk that night, the police were able to determine that the Palmes stopped for at least thirty seconds—most probably to speak to the killer.[10]

The killer runs away up the Tunnelgatan. An official photograph of the police reconstruction of the crime. Reproduced by permission of the Swedish National Police Board.

It is important to note that all these witness observations fit with one another. They indicate that the killer who was seen by Morelius waiting for his victim at the Dekorima corner walked up to meet the Palmes near the advertisement pillar. The reason the killer did not see the potential witness Björkman was of course that the advertisement pillar was in the way. After the killer met the Palmes, the three people walked together toward the Dekorima corner, as observed by Björkman, Annerstedt, and others. Lisbet then walked ahead, leaving the other two alone to have their discussion, as seen by Morelius and others. Suddenly, the prime minister seemed to perceive that something was wrong, and there was a short scuffle, as seen by Elizabeth Johansson and Johnny Falk. The killer grabbed Palme by the shoulder or collar, drew his revolver, and shot the prime minister dead, as observed by Morelius, Delsborn, and Björkman.

The Minutes before the Murder of Olof Palme

11:16:50	Inge Morelius arrives and parks his car.
11:17:20	Olof and Lisbet Palme start walking from outside the Grand cinema.
11:18:00	The witness Inga A. and her friend pass the Dekorima corner and see no one there.
11:18:50	The witness Fauzzi passes the Dekorima corner and sees no one there.
11:19:10	The killer moves into position.
11:19:20	Morelius spots the killer outside Dekorima.
11:19:45	The Palmes meet Fauzzi.
11:20:00	The "Check Man" sees the killer at the Dekorima corner.
11:20:50	The Palmes meet the killer at the advertisement pillar at the corner of Sveavägen and Tunnelgatan.
11:20:55	The Palmes are seen by the witness Delsborn standing facing the killer and having a conversation.
11:21:00	The Palmes and the killer walk from the advertisement pillar toward the Dekorima.
11:21:10	The Palmes and the killer are seen walking together by the witnesses Björkman and Annerstedt.
11:21:20	The killer suddenly pulls his gun and shoots Olof Palme dead.

The only witness to directly contradict that Palme went to meet his murderer is Lisbet Palme herself. She has emphatically denied that she and her husband met anyone. In her version of events, she and Olof were walking along with their arms linked and didn't see anyone outside Dekorima. No one came up to them, and everything appeared completely normal until she suddenly heard what she thought was a firecracker. As she turned to Olof, saying that the children's fireworks were frighteningly loud, her husband collapsed. It is remarkable that she has denied seeing the murderer standing nearby: when she desperately looked around for help after Olof had fallen, the only person nearby was the surprised, staring witness Anders Björkman, who had dodged into a doorway after hearing the shots fired. This is very peculiar, since the forensic investigation shows that the murder weapon was just six to eight inches from Olof when the trigger was pulled; the killer must literally have been breathing down their necks. But when Mrs. Palme was questioned on May 7, 1986, she said the killer had been standing on the Tunnelgatan corner, between eleven and sixteen yards away. This estimate far exceeds the actual distance from the murder site to the corner in question, however, and at the supplementary questioning after the Pettersson lineup, Mrs. Palme changed her estimate to between five and eight yards, without providing any explanation.

All the reliable witness statements agree that just after the shots were fired, Mrs. Palme entered a state of shock; some witnesses added that they had never seen anybody so distraught and hysterical. Her initial description of the killer was certainly that of the witness Björkman. Every point in her description is a direct match: his stocky body, short neck, gray trousers, and short blue parka. She never said anything about this "killer" brandishing a gun. As we know, her description was later influenced by the publication of information about the Phantom; she then portrayed the killer as a much more powerful, sinister-looking person. It is curious that according to Mrs. Palme's testimony in court, she kept looking around after meeting Björkman's surprised stare. She saw a thin man wearing a beige coat standing nearby. He looked frightened and seemed reluctant to help her. This observation remains a mystery, since the police investigation has established that no such man was at the murder scene. Lisbet Palme then saw a person—most certainly the killer— run away into the Tunnelgatan. She also clearly remembered a man standing forty yards into the Tunnelgatan staring at her. This was a minute after the murder, and the man's position and behavior indicate that he was not the killer, but the witness Jeppsson. The testimony of some of the murder scene witnesses, like Björkman and Ljungqvist, would suggest that Lisbet Palme saw the killer's face, but if she did, it does not seem to have made any particular impact on her description of the culprit.

Yet another minor mystery is the exact positioning of the three people involved: Olof, Lisbet, and the killer. According to her testimony in the Pettersson trial, Mrs. Palme was walking beside her husband when the shots were fired. Their arms were linked, and she was dragged down by the weight of her husband when he fell. This is the version that has since been echoed by practically everyone writing about the murder, some of them adding that the reason the killer missed Lisbet was that she was herself falling down when he fired a second shot. But it should be noted that when Inge Morelius was questioned in the same trial, he bluntly denied, when questioned by Liljeros, that the Palmes had walked with their arms linked. Mrs. Palme had been walking a couple of steps ahead of her husband, Morelius said, and when she turned around and saw Olof collapse after the shots were fired, she remained standing for a while before kneeling beside her husband's body.

Morelius told journalist Thomas Kanger another vital detail. When the killer took a few steps up to the body to make sure Olof was dead, he approached the still standing Lisbet. The killer then doubled back, going around the feet of the recumbent Olof, and ran into the Tunnelgatan. It was not until then that Lisbet screamed something, walked back a step or two, and bent over Olof. The witness Jeppsson saw the same scene, but from a different angle. He could clearly see Olof Palme collapse after being shot; at that time, he saw no other person. A moment later, Lisbet came into view and bent over her husband's lifeless body. Several other murder scene witnesses made statements indicating that Lisbet had walked ahead of Olof, or that she had definitely been standing up when her husband collapsed, or that she had walked back a step or two to bend over his lifeless body.[11] In fact not a single murder scene witness supports her version of events.

Has Lisbet Palme been lying about what really took place the night her husband was shot? Some Palme Detectives have speculated that she was in league with the killer, but this is too absurd to even contemplate.[12] Firstly, she had no reason to want her husband dead; secondly, all the witnesses agree that the murder came as a complete shock to her; thirdly, the killer tried to shoot her too. Other authors have speculated that the Palmes might have set up a meeting with an unknown contact, for example a blackmailer who had secret knowledge about the Harvard case.[13] After realizing that this meeting had in fact been a trap to kill her husband, Lisbet decided to lie to the police to prevent the truth about the blackmailing plot from becoming known. The supporters of this theory point out the fact that Mrs. Palme has been unwilling to deliver her husband's diary and private papers to the police: Was this because what they may have contained information about the blackmailing plot? According to a witness statement, Mårten Palme paid a hurried visit to the Palme apartment at about midnight: Did he go there to hide or destroy evidence relating to the fatal meeting?

But this hypothesis suffers from some serious drawbacks, mainly that it would have been illogical for Lisbet to purposely sabotage the investigation of her husband's murder. This would play into the hands of the murderer/blackmailer and put herself at risk; after all, the man had tried to kill her too. And what if the blackmailer had again made himself known, this time demanding money not to expose the entire plot to the press? Much has been made of Mårten Palme's nocturnal visit to the apartment, but this is likely to have a perfectly natural explanation, namely that when his mother phoned him, she was too distraught to tell him she was already at the hospital, and that young Palme presumed they had been attacked back home. Furthermore, very strong arguments can be made against the Harvard case being the motive for the murder. We know that Palme had nothing to hide about this business, and that after he had made his mind up to fight the tax authorities, he had put this matter behind him. Palme did not deny giving the Harvard lecture without a fee, nor did he deny that Harvard had agreed to give his son the scholarship, so it would seem unlikely that a potential blackmailer could have had access to any damaging information. And if Lisbet Palme and perhaps other family members had known the truth about the clandestine meeting, would they have deliberately incriminated Christer Pettersson?

In 1988, journalist Thomas Kanger formulated an alternative hypothesis, which was later considerably added to by another journalist, Gunnar Wall, in a prizewinning book about the Palme murder.[14] Might Mrs. Palme have been afflicted by a phenomenon known as traumatic memory loss? We know that her last memory before the murder was that she was still walking beside Olof with their arms linked, on their way to the Dekorima corner. Then she has a blurred memory of shots being fired. Her first memory after the murder is seeing the surprised Björkman staring at her. She has no memory of the man her husband had arranged to meet, the murder itself, or the vital seconds when the killer was lingering nearby to make sure Olof was dead. In examining Wall's hypothesis further, it is important to scrutinize the early observations of Mrs. Palme after the murder. It is striking that although the killer had been literally breathing down their necks, she told the police she had originally perceived the shots as coming from a distance. When asked about the people standing nearby, the only descriptions she could volunteer were those of Björkman, Jeppsson, and the mystery man in the beige coat. Since no such man was at the murder site, could she have seen him prior to her memory loss?

It is a pity that the observations of Mrs. Palme at the murder scene were scanty and confused, the prevailing impression of most witnesses being her extreme sense of shock and devastation. Ljungqvist and Karin Johansson, the people who had tried to calm her down, agreed that she had been completely hysterical and making very little sense. Although she was talking incessantly, she was just repeating her demands for doctors, ambulances, and an operating room for her husband. A man named Ersson heard her moaning, "Can't you see who he is?" as a reaction to the inability of the bystanders to recognize Olof Palme.[15] The young woman, Anna Hage, who tried to resuscitate Olof told the high court that she had heard Lisbet Palme calling out, "Why did he do it?"—a statement that is of course completely at odds with Lisbet's account of the shots coming from a distance. Anna also heard Lisbet muttering, "That little one . . . he behaved badly . . . he was a nasty person!" and thought she was referring to the killer.

According to Anna Hage, Lisbet Palme was very secretive with regard to her own identity and that of her husband. In her statements to the police, Anna Hage gave the impression that she found Lisbet Palme's reaction to the murder somewhat odd and thought that Lisbet had some knowledge of what had happened that she was unable or unwilling to divulge.[16] Anna Hage spoke to several news reporters, and this may have been the foundation of the early rumor that Mrs. Palme made some confused statement about recognizing the killer. In a news bulletin on March 1, 1986, Hans Holmér was asked about this rumor, and he curtly confirmed that Mrs. Palme had made such a statement, although he did not know what to make of it. To one newspaper, Anna Hage is alleged to have stated, "Lisbet Palme said that she had in some way recognized the man who had just shot her husband."[17] It is also possible to speculate about Lisbet Palme's surprised outcry "No, what are you doing!" Was this directed toward the killer, someone she had not expected to have any hostile intentions?

WHO MIGHT OLOF PALME HAVE MET?

The alternative murder scenario outlined above can fit into a number of conspiracy theories, some of which have been discussed earlier in this book. The scenario begs the question what person Olof Palme would have consented to meet at a very inconvenient time, late on a Friday night. Firstly, disturbed right-wingers like Viktor Gunnarsson and criminal alcoholics like Christer Pettersson can definitely be excluded. Nor would Palme have consented to meet, for example, a disgruntled PKK activist wanting to present a petition. Clearly the meeting outside Dekorima related to some matter of vital importance to the prime minister's private life, or more likely some unresolved business high on the political agenda in early 1986. This matter was something Palme needed to take care of personally and in secret; he could easily have recalled his bodyguards that evening, but chose not to do so.

Are there any observations of Olof Palme during his last day of life that might give vital clues as to who, or rather which organization, might have been behind the meeting outside Dekorima? All evidence agrees that Palme was in a good mood in the morning, but then something happened. At the 1:00 p.m. government luncheon, he was in a terrible state, angry and frustrated, and unwilling to tell anyone why. Minister Birgitta Dahl was surprised that the normally punctual prime minister did not arrive until 1:20. She was even more surprised when she saw how distraught he was, pacing the room and looking quite furious. Palme was normally calm and collected, and she "could see that he must have been through something really terrible."[1] Birgitta Dahl comforted him as well as she could, and Palme gradually calmed down. She and the others found it uncharacteristic that he was unwilling to tell them what had happened; although their boss was sometimes short-tempered, he usually liked to debate the event that had annoyed him with his colleagues.

The explanation for Palme's sudden change of mood is not hard to find. At 11:30 a.m., he met with the Iraqi ambassador, Mohammad Saeed al-Sahaf, who was later to gain notoriety as "Baghdad Bob," Saddam Hussein's ranting minister of information during the 2003 U.S. war against Iraq. In 1999, it was divulged what they had been discussing: the ambassador had informed Palme that the Swedish armaments corporation Bofors was illegally exporting arms to Iran. Whether Baghdad Bob produced documentary proof of these trans-actions is not known, but he may well have done so. It is further recorded that Palme was very displeased to hear this news, which was even more shocking since he was himself the United Nations official arbitrator in the bloody and long-standing war between Iran and Iraq.[2]

In the afternoon, a journalist interviewing Palme urged the prime minister to stand by the window, but Palme declined, saying, "You never know what may be waiting for me out there." This comment struck the journalist as being very unlike Palme. As we know, several people who saw Olof Palme and his wife walking to the cinema thought that one or both of them seemed nervous, worried, or cautious. Also odd was the incident at the bookshop display win-dow, when Olof wanted to read something from the cinema program, but the lights went out. Again, his reaction to this trivial incident was out of charac-ter: he became upset and suspected somebody in the shop had deliberately turned off the lights. Olof Palme seems to have felt worried and threatened that day: yet he was determined to walk all the way home through the streets of Stockholm without any bodyguards.

But why would Olof Palme take the arms export to Iran so seriously? As we know, this was a comparatively minor sale, certainly of little importance to the outcome of the war. Although Palme would have been embarrassed by the Swedish illegal arms export, he could easily have evaded responsibility by pointing out that Bofors had exported the arms behind his back. But Palme's involvement with the rogue arms corporation was much more complex than that. Throughout the 1980s, Bofors had been struggling to secure an immense order, worth 8.4 billion Swedish kronor ($1.2 billion), of howitzers for the In-dian army.[3] French arms corporation Sofma was its major competitor, and seemed to have the upper hand in 1985, since the Indian army thought their howitzers superior to the Swedish ones.

Bofors senior management asked Olof Palme for advice, knowing that Rajiv Gandhi, the prime minister of India, was a close friend of his. Palme agreed to help the Bofors executives; he wanted to support the struggling Swedish export industry, and a failure to secure this vast export order, the biggest in the history of Sweden, would have meant major industry layoffs in an area already stricken by unemployment. In October 1985, Palme met with Gandhi and other senior Indian officials, working closely with the Bofors directors to secure the order. They appeared to have some success, and the pendulum was clearly swinging the way of Bofors. One of the Bofors executives later boasted that their company had employed one sales consultant who had single-handedly determined the outcome of the India deal—Olof Palme.[4]

Rajiv Gandhi had some other things on his mind when he met Olof Palme, however. One of his promises to the Indian people had been to combat corruption, and he knew that widespread bribery was common when foreign companies were exporting weapons to India. He demanded that Palme make the Bofors directors abolish all contracts with middlemen who might serve as distributors of bribes. When prompted by Palme and his political secretary Carl-Johan Åberg, Bofors managing director Martin Ardbo, who had led the negotiation team in India, agreed to this demand. But the situation was much more complicated than Palme could have foreseen. Ardbo was a former naval officer who had turned businessman in middle age. Far from the typical bluff, honest sailor, he was a conspiring, ruthless player in the murky world of international arms trading. He knew well that there was no chance of exporting anything to India without greasing the palms of quite a few people.

At an early stage, he had made contact with two companies that facilitated the contacts between foreign industrialists and the Indian ruling class. One of these companies was led by a certain Win Chadha, a former military man with valuable contacts in the Indian army. His duty was clearly to help persuade the Indian artillery officers that the Bofors howitzer was superior to its French competitor. Bofors had used him in the past and he had proved reliable. A mysterious Swiss company known as Moresco acted as Bofors's second middleman. One can only presume that if Chadha was to concentrate his efforts within the military establishment, Moresco was to facilitate the deal within government circles.

At least by late 1985, no evidence had surfaced that Palme knew about these dubious business deals. Yet some commentators have marveled that he showed such particular concern for the success of the India deal. Lisbet Palme told the police that the Bofors India order had been at the top of her husband's political agenda in late 1985 and early 1986, and Palme's political colleagues agreed. A journalist who met Palme on February 8, 1986, was surprised how strongly the prime minister seemed to feel about the India deal. When they were discussing some other matters, Palme suddenly said, "Damn it, if Bofors do not secure the order, it is not my fault! I have done all I can for them!" After a brief pause, he continued, "This Ardbo, what kind of a man is he really?" This Palme would not live to find out.[5]

The demands from Olof Palme must have been a disagreeable surprise for Martin Ardbo. Not only had Bofors already paid very considerable sums of money to their middlemen, they had also made deals with some very influential characters, who would not easily be fobbed off. Ardbo told Palme that he was busy closing the accounts with the middlemen, but in fact let things continue largely as before, although payments to the two companies were reduced and disguised as "cancellation fees." It is a remarkable fact that on November 15, three weeks after being approached by Palme, Ardbo signed a multi-million-dollar contract with a third company of middlemen, called A.E. Services and nominally based in Guildford, England. The service provided by this company must have been vital to the business deal for Ardbo to have disobeyed Palme's instructions so blatantly.

On January 22, 1986, when he had just a month left to live, Olof Palme again met Rajiv Gandhi, this time at a disarmament conference in New Delhi. He assured Gandhi that Bofors had followed his instructions and that no middlemen were involved in the India deal. On the plane back to Sweden, Palme and Ardbo spoke at length in the business class cabin; unfortunately, we do not know the details of their conversation. The negotiations were still ongoing when Palme had just weeks left to live. On February 18, Palme managed to extract from Gandhi that the price being charged by Bofors was about 10 percent higher than that of its French competitors. This was vital information, and Bofors adjusted its pricing accordingly. On February 20, Palme met with Bofors director Anders Carlberg in an unscheduled emergency meeting about the credit terms for the India deal; the prime minister again spoke to Gandhi over the telephone and then agreed to help Bofors by guaranteeing the financial terms of the loan to India.[6]

On March 14, the Indian government awarded the contract to Bofors. Ardbo hoisted the Indian flag on his flagpole and held a big party at the Bofors factory, becoming a local hero for saving the ailing company. Secretly, he must have hoped that the sheer amount of money involved in the India deal would induce those in the know to cover up the truth. In this respect, the murder of Olof Palme must have formed a welcome diversion. Throughout the remainder of 1986, and well into 1987, there was little speculation about the India deal in either of the two countries involved, and the conspirators used this time well to obscure possible leads. But Ardbo's respite would not be a lengthy one.

Although he seemed to have buried the secrets behind the India deal deep enough to hide them, this unscrupulous man had other skeletons in his closet. Under his leadership, Bofors had many times circumvented the strict Swedish laws prohibiting arms exports to countries involved in war or civil war. Using middlemen in neutral countries as the alleged recipients, Bofors had smuggled guns, missiles, and explosives into various blacklisted countries in Asia and the Middle East. Since the entire company could not be prosecuted, when this information emerged, Ardbo and his colleague Claes Winberg were used as public scapegoats. Both men were sacked from Bofors in March 1987, to await criminal proceedings. In the police investigation of these smuggling offences, some detectives obtained a search warrant for Ardbo's house. The Bofors director was not at home, but the detectives nevertheless ransacked his office. The most interesting find was Ardbo's private diary, partly written in code. One of the entries was a dramatic one: Ardbo wrote that if the full extent of Olof Palme's involvement in the India deal became known, the Swedish government would fall.

In April 1987, Swedish and Indian media alleged that through its three middleman companies, Bofors had bribed Indian officials with very large sums of money. The middlemen in their turn received many millions of dollars when the business deal went through as planned. A full-scale political crisis broke out in India when the Bofors scandal exploded on the newspaper front pages. The opposition parties furiously lambasted Rajiv Gandhi as a hypocrite; he had played "Mr. Clean" and pretended to combat corruption, while at the same time allowing this disreputable Swedish company to bribe its way into a lucrative contract. Anti-Swedish demonstrations were held in the streets, angry students were beaten up by the police, and "Bofors" became a byword for everything unsavory or corrupt: "There is some Bofors in this banana!"

In Sweden, foreign minister Sten Andersson started an anti-Bofors crusade, promising that the truth about the India deal would be unearthed at all costs. He soon had evidence that far from following Palme's instructions, Bofors had paid millions of dollars to the three middleman companies. But Olof Palme's direct involvement in the India deal seems to have troubled Andersson considerably. When meeting Bofors director Anders Carlberg in August 1987, Andersson ordered the Bofors man to leave Palme's name out of things at all costs. This order seems to have had the desired effect. When the police questioned Ardbo about his diary note about Palme's involvement, the Bofors director sat stubbornly silent, giving the impression that he feared his own safety would be jeopardized if he said too much. When challenged with another dramatic diary entry: "Everyone fears I will tell the whole truth," Ardbo replied, "The truth dies with me!"

In September 1987, Sten Andersson met Indian deputy foreign minister Natwar Singh to discuss the Bofors scandal. Singh seemed reluctant to support the naive Swede's crusade to find out the truth, pointing out that Bofors might have information that could be deeply compromising for both India and Sweden. He probably went into further details, since it is recorded that immediately after his return, Andersson demanded to see Carlberg, asking the Bofors executive "whether the party had received any money." It has never been explained exactly what he meant by "the party," but it could only be the Indian Congress Party—or the Swedish Social Democrats. Might this have been a reference to a fund to combat unemployment, set up by the Palme government with money donated by Bofors on the condition that the India deal went through? After this incident, Andersson lost all interest in his anti-Bofors crusade, and the Swedish and Indian governments appear to have decided that the matter was best forgotten.[7] In early 1988, an Indian state commission concluded that no Indian citizen had received bribes from Bofors, and the Swedes meekly disavowed the evidence to the contrary that they possessed.

But Indian journalists Chitra Subramanian and N. Ram, working for the influential newspaper the *Hindu*, discovered one secret after another. Firstly, the truth about Win Chadha's involvement was exposed, and he was arrested for various financial indiscretions before fleeing India in disgrace. Then the journalists learned that the men behind Moresco were none other than the brothers Hinduja, international businessmen of immense wealth, and that Bofors money had been paid into three Swiss bank accounts held by the Hindujas. The greatest sensation of all was that A.E. Services was just a shell company, run by major Robert Wilson, but lacking a board, capital, and even offices, instead operating from a post office box in Guildford, England.

Wilson was reluctant to say what had happened to the money paid to A.E. Services by Bofors, or exactly what services the company performed to earn these immense amounts.[8] A.E. Services was owned by a mysterious Swiss company called Ciaou Anstalt, which was in turn owned by another company, and so forth. Wilson refused to name the ultimate owner of A.E. Services, except to say that it was just one man, who was not an Indian. The crowning touch again came from Ardbo's diary, saying, "Wilson had met with Gandhi truste lawyer." Was this a reference to the ultimate fate of the Bofors bribe? Many Indians thought so, and distressing scenes followed in the parliament, with Communists and right-wingers standing side by side shouting, "Gandhi is a liar!" The Bofors scandal lost Gandhi the 1989 election; he was assassinated by a suicide bomber in 1991.

It has taken the Indian legal system more than fifteen years to bring the Bofors conspirators to trial. The leading suspects are very wealthy and influential people, and clever enough to cover their tracks and use all kinds of legal obstructionism. The Hindujas tried every trick in the book to evade trial, seeking foreign nationality (two brothers became British citizens, the third Swiss), obscuring their financial records, and fighting hard (but unsuccessfully) to prevent access to the three Swiss bank accounts.[9] The Indian authorities were finally able to trace the money paid by Bofors via A.E. Services to a Swiss bank account held by wealthy Italian businessman Ottavio Quattrocchi, who was known for his friendship with Rajiv Gandhi. Just as Wilson had said, here was one man who was not an Indian.

Quattrocchi is very likely the individual referred to as "Q" in Ardbo's diary. One note said that Q's involvement was a problem due to his close link to R[ajiv], another that Wilson promised to figure out exactly what had been said between P[alme] and R[ajiv]. In 1993, Quattrocchi hurriedly left India, where he had been living since 1950, and he has stubborny fought extradition ever since. Of the other conspirators, Chadha is dead, and Ardbo is fighting extradition from Sweden. In June 2002, the charge sheet against the Hindujas were quashed by the Delhi high court, but the month after, the Supreme Court of India found this ruling unsustainable and revived the trial against the brothers. The trial court will now frame charges against the Hindujas but has shown no urgency in doing so: in September 2003, the brothers were still appealing against the trial court order, and in March 2004 a further delay resulted from legal technicalities.[10]

So, will the full truth about the Bofors scandal ever be known? This is very unlikely, since the conspirators have not wasted the respite given them by Olof Palme's death. Not much is known about what had really happened back in 1985 and 1986, in particular what Chadha, the Hindujas, and Quattrocchi did with the money they received from Bofors. Surely, it was not just a gift from the generous Swedes, but something was expected from them in return. The most hotly debated issue is the role of Rajiv Gandhi. His political opponents have accused him of taking bribes and keeping the money himself, but no evidence exists for this, nor is such a dishonorable action consistent with his character. Gandhi's friends hotly deny that he took bribes in any form, either blaming his political enemies for framing both him and Quattrocchi, or alleging that the Italian was himself in on the scam, along with Ardbo and Wilson.[11]

The time has now come to go back to February 28, 1986, and seek the link between the Bofors scandal and the murder of Olof Palme. It seems highly probable that Rajiv Gandhi decided that the howitzer deal should carry a political price. Already in July 1985, there had been a meeting between senior Indian minister Arun Nehru and Swedish diplomat Rolf Gauffin, in which the latter was promised that Bofors would get the contract if they made sure all Indian middlemen were ruled out of the deal.[12] Both men were shrewd operators: Nehru was a cousin and close associate of Gandhi, and Gauffin was no stranger to intrigue and deception. A realistic view of these proceedings would be that Gandhi wanted to redirect the flow of Bofors money into the election funds of his Congress Party. This was why the payments to Chadha and the Hindujas were reduced, and why the A.E. Services deal was made in November 1985. Arriving at such a late stage, this company could have performed no duty but a politically corrupt one. The loyal Quattrocchi could be relied on to transfer the Bofors money into the accounts of the Congress Party and to keep his mouth shut about it afterward.

A fair amount of evidence supports this version of events. According to journalist Henrik Westander, Martin Ardbo himself privately admitted that the A.E. Services money had been a bribe to Gandhi's party. In 1992, another Bofors director told a journalist that Nehru had acted on Gandhi's orders, and that A.E. Services had been a front for the bribes. When asked the reason he was finally telling the truth, he said he had always suspected the murder of Olof Palme was linked to the India deal, and that his conscience had been gnawing at him these six years. Swedish diplomat Bertil Hökby has admitted that he and a senior Bofors director were present when the transfer of the money was arranged.[13]

The Bofors conspiracy would only have winners if the deal went through and the truth was kept hidden. Bofors would sell its guns, the Indian army would acquire useful high-tech equipment, and the Congress Party would acquire a substantial influx of capital. It could even be argued that Gandhi kept his promise to fight corruption, since the money his party acquired would otherwise have been used to bribe private individuals. Olof Palme, who had provided the conspirators with invaluable help by pushing Bofors to reduce the payments to Chadha and Moresco and acting as a figurehead for the deal, would bask in the glory of helping the Swedish export industry, as well as having seven million dollars of Bofors money in a government fund to combat unemployment. Quattrocchi and Wilson would of course be generously paid for their part in the conspiracy. It is true that Win Chadha lost out when some of the money was rechanneled via A.E. Services, but he was still generously paid, and far from nursing a grudge against the conspirators, he arranged a large party in New Delhi to celebrate the deal. To begin with, the Hinduja brothers may also have viewed developments with a disapproving eye, but for them, the money involved was just nickels and dimes. Government favor in India was far more important for them, and they closed a deal to buy India's largest car and truck manufacturer not long after the Bofors contract was signed.

In 2001, none other than Salman Rushdie raised the question of whether Palme's death had something to do with the Bofors India deal: Had the Prime Minister been shot on the orders of a disgruntled middleman?[14] To answer Rushdie's question, it is essential to determine who would have had the most to lose if Palme suddenly decided to withdraw from the India deal. One of the three middlemen can immediately be ruled out, namely Win Chadha, who had no influence outside India and no motive to kill Palme. He had done his job to facilitate the deal, quite possibly through bribing various Indian officers, and was pleased with the reward he had obtained. With regard to the Hindujas, they definitely had the influence and resources to have the prime minister of a small European country neutralized if he threatened their empire. But again, no discernable motive exists for such an act. It is true that they lost money as a result of the A.E. Services deal, but this was a minor amount for some of the world's richest men.

For many years, the Hindujas have acted to facilitate deals between foreign companies and various Indian authorities; their contract with Bofors dates back to 1979. It is of interest that the Hindujas also had a contract with Sofma, the French competitor of Bofors. There has been some speculation that the murder of Olof Palme may have been an attempt to secure the French company the deal. The Palme police received some suggestions along these lines, but from notoriously unreliable sources.[15] The Sofma company had a good reputation, at least compared with Bofors, and no reliable evidence links it or any of its middlemen to the murder. If Sofma had been involved, the murder would have been a totally pointless act of violence, since Bofors got the contract anyway.

It is more fruitful to link the murder to the A.E. Services deal itself. If Gandhi gave the Bofors deal a political price, Palme does not appear to have been aware of it in January 1986. Ardbo may have given him some hints on their flight back from India on January 23, but then he may not have. We do not know what secret negotiations had been going on between Gandhi, Palme, and Bofors during Palme's last weeks alive, but it would appear inconceivable that Palme knew the full truth about the A.E. Services deal. Did Baghdad Bob inadvertently cause Palme's death by highlighting Ardbo's duplicity in the illegal arms export to Iran, thus triggering a furious reaction from the prime minister against a man he already distrusted? If Palme broke with Ardbo and Bofors and threatened to disrupt the A.E. Services deal, the conspirators behind this deal would have had a perfectly valid motive to kill him.

In early March of 1986, the police received a vital tip containing *exactly this information*. Three days after the murder, the secretary-general of the Swedish Civil Defence League, former journalist Karl-Gunnar Bäck, was contacted by an Englishman with contacts in the MI6, who claimed to know who had killed Olof Palme.[16] The man was calling from London but offered to go to Sweden in person. Bäck was intrigued, knowing that this man had provided valuable information to him in the past, and received him the following day. The London mystery man told Bäck that the motive behind the murder was the Bofors India deal, and that a shady company called "A&I Services" had received money from the deal. The leader of this company, whom Bäck's contact knew as "Donaldson" or "Robertson," lived part of the time in London, part of the time in Johannesburg. This "Robertson" was the mastermind behind the plot, and the murder had been arranged by some South African hit men and a Swedish policeman.

Bäck tried to contact the Palme police, but getting through by phone was too difficult: these were the heady days of the Phantom and the Shadow, when every Swede was an amateur detective. Bäck knew one of the police agents at the SÄPO office in Uppsala, and had his secretary deliver a tape with the full story to them. In May, Bäck's secretary was told that the tip contained nothing of interest. Bäck was amazed; he thought the information highly relevant and sinister. He had already made plans to make some private investigations of his own and arranged to interview Martin Ardbo in the Civil Defense League magazine. The meeting with Ardbo did nothing to allay Bäck's suspicions, and he decided to make an appeal in his magazine, boldly stating that there must be a connection between the Palme murder and the Bofors India deal. Shortly after this article was published, he received a phone call from an agitated Martin Ardbo, who said that Bäck's information was totally wrong, and that such groundless speculation would earn Bäck and the Civil Defense League nothing but ridicule.

Bäck's information has been interpreted by the 1999 commission as implicating A.E. Services and major Robert Wilson as central actors in the murder conspiracy. This man has been described as a tough operator in the international arms trade. According to one source, he knew Sweden well, and had for some time been working closely with Bofors and his personal friend Martin Ardbo, providing advice regarding industrial espionage.[17] It is a pity so little is known about Wilson's links with South Africa, particularly whether he knew Craig Williamson or the mysterious Nigel Barnett. The latter is especially interesting, since here we have a rogue South African agent who speaks good Swedish and knows the country: Was he the hit man in the tip received by Bäck? One source says that Barnett was going into business as an arms dealer himself, another that he had excellent international contacts through his friend Peter Casselton. There has been speculation that Barnett knew the sinister Swedish cop Carl Östling and his colleague major Ingvar Grundborg, both of whom had visited South Africa more than once, and had links with Bofors.[18] Just like Barnett, these two were going into business as arms dealers.

With a rough hypothesis as to why the murder happened and who ordered it, it is time to enter the realm of conjecture to reconstruct what happened on February 28. The Iraqi ambassador's comments must shake Olof Palme to the core: the suspicions the prime minister may already have had about the rogue Bofors's business ethics are now verified in no uncertain terms. Baghdad Bob, with good international connections within the arms trade, may mention that rumors are going around in arms dealer circles about gross bribery by the same corporation in its dealings with India. After the ambassador leaves, Palme immediately phones a senior Bofors contact and furiously tells him that the company has gone too far. He himself has done everything he can to help them, but the greedy, irresponsible capitalists still insisted on selling arms to a state involved in war. Palme insists that the arms trade to Iran must cease immediately; he also promises to investigate the allegations of widespread bribery in the corporation's dealings with India.

Stomping off to lunch in a furious temper, Palme thinks of the potential political repercussions of this brewing scandal: Is he, the world's leading proponent of disarmament, and the official UN arbitrator in the Iran-Iraq war, to be caught in a murky web of bribes and illegal arms deals? He also ponders the ingratitude and irresponsibility of the leaders of the Bofors corporation; surely, his decision to help them in their dealings in India has done his reputation little good. Palme belatedly suspects that Gandhi knows more about the Bofors bribes that he has divulged, and that his demand to exclude the middlemen was not altogether sincere. Nevertheless, Palme realizes that both prime ministers are sitting on a political time bomb that threatens to ruin their respective careers.

In the meantime, faced with this potentially disastrous situation, the Bofors director is not sitting idle. He contacts his friend the middleman and tells him about Palme's phone call. Since the middleman will lose millions of dollars, as well as his good name as an operator in Indian business ventures, if Palme makes good his threat and the India deal falls through, he decides on immediate action. The middleman may well have earlier feared that Palme would back out and made some plans accordingly. It is unlikely that an elaborate, prearranged assassination plot exists, since the easiest way to kill Palme would have been with a precision shot from a roof or other hiding place as he was leaving his house or walking through the Old Town. It is much more likely that the instigator of the murder has been anxiously following the developments, knowing that disaster will follow if Palme finds out the truth about the A.E. Services deal. He has made some loose arrangements with a Swedish contact concerning how to take action if the prime minister threatens to disrupt the India deal.

The plan set in motion is simple and effective. The arms trade middleman's Swedish contact, another arms dealer with links to Bofors, has easy access to firearms. He has also spoken to two men who would willingly undertake the mission, since they are right-wing extremists and loathe Palme intensely.

They may be policemen or secret service agents, possibly belonging to the murky underworld of political espionage. Nor can it be ruled out that Bäck was right and that a rogue South African agent, traveling on a fake passport, has been sent to Stockholm several weeks in advance. One of the hit men knows Palme personally, possibly from experience in the secret service or as a bodyguard. In the evening, he telephones the prime minister, claiming to have vital documents about the Bofors bribery allegations. He is afraid for his life, he says, and would not trust the police or the various political fixers surrounding Palme with these dangerous documents, only the prime minister himself.[19] Palme suggests that they meet early the following week, but the man urges him that they have to meet sooner. Palme is disposed to agree: if the political time bomb beneath himself and Rajiv Gandhi is to be defused, immediate and determined action is necessary. Palme proposes that they meet by the Skandia building that same evening, since he is going to the cinema not far away. Thus Palme chooses the site for his own murder, just as Hans Holmér once hinted; the commissioner added that the real solution to the murder would shake Sweden to its foundations.

One of the men contracted to kill Palme is a burly fellow, about forty years old, inconspicuously dressed in a blue parka and a beige cap. He waits at the cinema for the prime minister and his wife to arrive, watching closely to see if any bodyguards accompany them, since this would of course upset the murder plot. Well before *The Brothers Mozart* ends, he comes sneaking back, looking into the cinema lobby to see if any bodyguards are waiting there. (Several of the witnesses who saw the Grand Man were surprised by how carefully he scanned the half-empty lobby.) His attention is also caught by the air-traffic controller sitting in his car nearby. This car is a new Volvo sedan, and the Grand Man suspects that the witness might be a bodyguard ready to pick up the Palmes. That is the reason why he stares so intensely at the car. The coast is clear, however, and Palme and his wife walk the right way, toward the Dekorima corner. The Grand Man follows them for a short while, perhaps as far as the watchful hot dog seller, and then runs up a side street to his car that is parked there. Had there been bodyguards nearby, or untoward activity indicating the presence of the secret police, the man would have walked hastily past the Palmes and alerted the killer at the Skandia building. It is of course also possible that they use walkie-talkie communication.

Having received the signal that the Palmes are approaching, the killer, a tall, well-built man wearing a dark overcoat, dark trousers, and a close-fitting dark blue cap, walks into position at the Dekorima corner, where he is seen by Morelius. In a side holster, he carries a .357 magnum given to him by the arms dealer, who knows that Palme might well be wearing a bulletproof vest for this clandestine late-night meeting; the ammunition from a gun this powerful would penetrate the vest, while that of a small-caliber pistol would not. After waiting about two minutes for the Palmes to arrive, he walks up to greet them. Palme recognizes him and they exchange some words, facing each other as they are observed by Delsborn. They then walk together for some distance, as observed by Annerstedt and Björkman. The killer pulls out a small bag containing the documents, while anxiously checking to see how close Björkman is.

Sensing that her husband wants to speak to the other man in private, Mrs. Palme lets go of her husband's arm and walks ahead of the other two. Seeing that Björkman is no threat, the killer grabs Palme with one hand, pulls his gun, and shoots the prime minister dead with a well-aimed shot. His second shot is probably intended for Mrs. Palme, but the killer is thrown off by the unexpected recoil of his powerful handgun, and the shot only grazes her back. In keeping with the training of a Swedish policeman, the killer holsters the gun immediately after firing, although it might have been more rational to have it ready in case anyone tried to stop him. The agile killer then runs up the Tunnelgatan steps, outrunning every pursuer. He may then take refuge in some apartment nearby; this would explain why the trail goes completely cold after the final sighting at David Bagares Gata. It is also possible that the Grand Man picks him up in the car, and that the two accomplices make their getaway together.

THE CRIME OF THE CENTURY

Seen as a historical episode, the murder of Olof Palme is a tragicomedy. As criminal investigations go, those of the Kennedy assassination, Pan Am flight 103, and the Palme assassination have been the biggest in the world; but the last is in a class by itself with regard to the end result. The incompetence of the early police response, the attempt to frame Viktor Gunnarsson, and the gross exaggeration of the case against the PKK Kurds all make for dismal reading. Some strong arguments support the theory that Christer Pettersson killed Palme, in particular Mrs. Palme's testimony and that of the Grand Man witnesses, as well as a wealth of circumstantial evidence. He is a much more likely murderer than Gunnarsson, having already committed crimes that in most U.S. states would have put him in prison for life. But a multitude of compelling arguments point to Pettersson's innocence, as does the lack of a believable motive and any kind of technical evidence. At the time of Pettersson's death in late September 2004, he had not confessed to the crime in a credible manner, although surreptitiously coaxed and bribed to do so; the debate concerning his guilt is likely to continue.

Following the early phases of astonishment and determination, the reaction to the murder of Olof Palme has reached a third phase, of resignation. A force of twelve detectives is still working on the case, but its activities have regrettable hints of occupational therapy. Once or twice a year, the Swedish public is reminded of the existence of this task force when the newspapers pick up rumors about the whereabouts of the murder weapon, or when some journalist decides to rehash the old police conspiracy theory. The interest is not what it was ten or fifteen years ago, however: Sweden's national trauma has become just another historical incident, and an entire generation has grown up not knowing about the country's great international statesman. Far from sharing Palme's role as the world's conscience, his Social Democratic successors have advocated the principle that the Swedes should mind their own business. While still paying lip service to his socialist ideals, they have been slowly but steadily dismantling the People's Home to make it possible for Sweden to join the European Community.

The murder of Olof Palme is fast acquiring the status of a historical mystery. As I have discussed at length in another book, one of the hallmarks of a true historical mystery, like the disappearance of Louis XVII of France or the riddle of Kaspar Hauser, is that the vast amounts of contradictory evidence enable people to construct extravagant theories.[1] In this respect, the murder of Olof Palme would not disappoint anyone. Compared with the murder of John F. Kennedy, where even the most obdurate conspiracy theorist would find it difficult to disregard the role played by Lee Harvey Oswald, the Palme mystery is even more enigmatic and obscure. As some of the Palme Detectives have demonstrated, the conspiracy theorist can play the game of "pick the murderer" without any constraints. A multitude of suspects, all with believable motives, form a long line of ghostly killers waiting at the Dekorima corner: a lone avenger, a disgruntled Stockholm cop, a right-wing extremist, a CIA agent, a South African assassin, and a PKK Kurd.

At this stage, the reader might well object that I am myself little better than a Palme Detective, choosing certain witnesses to believe to make up a sensational conspiracy theory. And sure, maybe Palme did not walk to meet his killer, and maybe there never was a Bofors conspiracy. But I am sure the reader would agree that it would have been better to *know* about these matters. The meeting scenario outlined above has been largely untouched by the official police investigation. Within a few days of the murder of Olof Palme, it must have been clear to Hans Holmér that the stories of several murder scene witnesses suggested that Palme had met and spoken to his killer. The police may have taken measures in secret to follow up this lead, but one of the main purposes of Holmér's police investigation seems to have been to cover up these politically sensitive facts.

This process appears to have begun at a very early stage. In the early news bulletins the day after the murder, the witness Delsborn was prominently featured, with his story of seeing the killer talking to the Palmes and then firing his revolver. Yet this dramatic story was left out of the evening news, and *never heard again* in the media. Delsborn and Annerstedt were largely ignored by the police investigation, and it is hard not to link this with their tendency to say the wrong things. As for Björkman, whose story was even more remarkable, he was described as an unreliable drunk. Yet, unlike some of the witnesses in the Pettersson trials, these three never changed their stories and refused to be exploited by the media. When approached by journalists years later, they stood firm by their stories, expressing surprise that the police had not taken them seriously.

As we know, Holmér personally took charge of the murder investigation and prevented a thorough examination of the witness testimony from the murder scene and from the Grand cinema. In particular, he himself took charge of interviewing Lisbet Palme, making sure her testimony was not followed up on or investigated and that she did not take part in reconstructions at the crime scene. In one of the questionings, he asserted, she had said that the Palmes had stopped at several shops on their way from the Grand cinema to the Dekorima corner. Mrs. Palme herself denied this when she was interviewed by other detectives a few months later, and again when speaking on oath in the Pettersson trial: they had stopped at the Indian shop only. Was Holmér trying to find a "suitable" explanation for the missing thirty seconds that would indicate a meeting? Mrs. Palme's description of the blue parka was used to put pressure on other murder scene witnesses; her denial that Palme had met someone was used to put the lid on the press speculation. It should be remembered that at this time, the Swedish press stood loyal and united behind Holmér. Was it just misdirected zeal to solve the murder that prompted the publication of the images of the Phantom and the Shadow, and the gross exaggeration of the case against the PKK, or were these deliberate attempts to cover up a truth that might be politically disastrous to the Social Democrats?

Due to the obvious temporal relationship of the Palme murder and the Bofors India deal, the detectives who were already investigating the Bofors bribery offenses built up a dossier with material indicating a connection between these events. They tried to hand over this material to the almighty Hans Holmér, but he several times refused to accept it. In November 1986, they spoke to their own boss, who was astonished that the Bofors connection was not being taken seriously. The detectives were finally allowed to enter the Palme room, where Wranghult and a few others heard their presentation without showing any interest. The morning after, the dossier was handed back to them, with the comment that it contained nothing of interest. The police investigation of the Bofors conspiracy was superficial, credulous, and amateurish, partly because it was actively suppressed under the reign of Hans Holmér. Even so, the police did not even keep up with the steady flow of incriminating information published in the Indian newspapers, nor did they make any attempt to question some of the key figures in the affair. The 1999 commission rightly found their lack of interest in the Bofors conspiracy bizarre and culpable.[2]

But what about the vital intelligence from Bäck, divulged just days after the murder and quickly forwarded to the police? It is likely this information never reached the Palme police. When the story was brought to light by some journalists in 1996, the police found no record of the Bäck tape being delivered back in early 1986. They suggested that Bäck's secretary had not delivered the tape as ordered, but this was later denied by both Bäck and the secretary's family.[3] We will never know whether the missing tape was just another instance of incompetence, or the result of elements within the police actively suppressing unwanted evidence. Thus it can only be speculated what effect a swift and determined investigation of the A.E. Services lead, with its possible extensions to South Africa and to the Swedish police, could have accomplished.

The murder of Olof Palme is now in the hands of the historians. Before long, its status will be similar to that of the hunt for the elusive Jack the Ripper, and various people will propose novel suggestions as to who killed the prime minister, safe in the knowledge that the mystery will never be solved. As some of the Palme Detectives have already demonstrated, these "solutions" will continue to distance themselves from what really happened at the Dekorima corner and the vital early witness testimony. Elaborate conspiracy theories will be constructed, only to be toppled over like houses of cards by the skeptics entrenched around the "ideal murderer" Christer Pettersson. It will be up to the wanderer in Stockholm on a dark February night to feel the faint residue of diabolical energy lingering near the plaque marking the site of the blood on the snow, and sense the memory of a heinous act that drew an awful price, as the shadowy specter disappears up the Tunnelgatan steps.

NOTES

Preface

1. There are three previous English-language books on the murder of Olof Palme. R. Freeman, *Death of a Statesman* (London, 1989) is a wayward and fanciful work that makes a very feeble case that Saddam Hussein's Iraq was behind the murder; C. Mosey, *Cruel Awakenings* (London, 1991) is an amusing anti-Swedish diatribe. H. H. A. Cooper and L. J. Redlinger, *The Murder of Olof Palme* (Lewiston, 2003) is another wayward and speculative study, seemingly ignorant of all Swedish-language standard works on the Palme murder. Its startling conclusion—that Israeli agents killed Palme to put the blame on the Iraqis—is based on a critical reading of the Freeman book, which is assumed to have been authored by the sinister Israelis to point the finger at the Iraqi secret service. This ignores that the Freeman book—which is rightly ignored by all competent authorities on the Palme murder—is stated (*AB*, July 18, 2003) to have been written by a Swede named Eive Tungstedt.

1. Death in Stockholm

1. The best biographies of Olof Palme are B. Elmbrandt, *Palme* (1989) and T. G. Pettersson, *Olof Palme som jag minns honom* (2002). A more hostile and scurrilous account is B. Östergren, *Olof Palme: Vem är han?* (1984). Many official hagiographies appeared after Palme was shot: the best is H. Haste, ed., *Minnesboken om Olof Palme* (1986).

2. On Palme's movements the day of the murder, see NAO, 38–47; GK, 161–67, 861–65; also the relevant section of TV4-CD.

3. The testimony of the various witnesses observing the Palmes on the way to the cinema is in CP, III: note in particular pages 5, 13, 36, 46–47, 56, 69, 73. Also *Exp*, March 5, 1986; *AB*, March 7, 1986; and *Statstjänstemannen* 1987 (2), 10–13.

4. The walk from the Grand cinema to the Dekorima corner is described by NAO, 47–51; GK, 167–71, 865–68; various witness reports are in CP, III:1, 41–53, 80–81, 85–86, 89–94. See also G. Wall, *Mörkläggning* (Gothenburg, 1996), 897–921; and documents reproduced by S. Anér, *Cover-up* (Gothenburg, 1999), 16–58; and *Palme-Nytt* 2002 (3), 6–10.

5. What Morelius saw is reported in CP, III:2, 356–86, and further discussed by T. Kanger, *Mordet på Olof Palme* (1987), 13–22.

6. The evidence of Jeppsson, Nieminen, and Zahir is in CP, III:2, 479–570. On Jeppsson, see also *AB*, April 3, 1986; on Nieminen, see also G. Wall in *Internationalen* 1988 (37), 16; and K. and P. Poutiainen, *Inuti Labyrinten* (1994), 144–45.

2. Blood on the Snow

1. Ljungqvist's evidence is in CP, III:2, 172–204. The telephone operator has refused to comment when approached by journalists and went on sick leave shortly after the murder. By 1996, she had still not returned to work; see Poutiainen, *Inuti Labyrinten*, 79–88; and RA, vol. 20–23, "Poutiainen Questioning," 5–6.

2. On Helin's activities, see Poutiainen, *Inuti Labyrinten*, 29–49; RA, vol. 23, PK 33.

3. It was probably cab driver Hans Johansson or another witness, named Jan-Åke Svensson; see CP, III:2, 291, 305. A less likely candidate is the so-called Skandia Man, who will be discussed later.

4. Poutiainen, *Inuti Labyrinten*, 247–69; E. Magnusson, ed., *Palmerapporten* (1989), 91–92. The evidence of the two officers in the squad car is in PF, vol. 219, appendices to letter dated November 24, 1993.

5. Poutiainen, *Inuti Labyrinten*, 96–101; Magnusson, *Palmerapporten*, 372–74.

6. On the murder chronology, see Poutiainen, *Inuti Labyrinten*, 20–344; NAO, 79–80; GK, 172–84; RA, vol. 17–19, PM 10:4B, and vol. 23, PK 33.

7. These six witness statements are in CP, III:2, 126, 303, 291, 418; CP, III:2, 183; Poutiainen, *Inuti Labyrinten*, 87; and S. Anér, *Polisspåret* (Gothenburg, 1988), 250. It is notable that according to PF, vol. 175, the ambulance sergeant recorded that the vehicle left St. Göran's Hospital at 11:10 and then drove for fifteen minutes before reaching the murder site.

8. Poutiainen, *Inuti Labyrinten*, 72; *AB*, March 2, 1986.

9. GK, 175–78; Poutiainen, *Inuti Labyrinten*, 108; G. Wall in *Internationalen* 1989 (18), 8.

10. Poutiainen, *Inuti Labyrinten*, 203; F. Baude et al., eds., *Mordet på Palme och Polisspåret* (Gothenburg, 1989), 47–50.

11. Poutiainen, *Inuti Labyrinten*, 320–22.

12. Poutiainen, *Inuti Labyrinten*, 271–88; GK, 183–84; RA, vol. 17–19, PM 10:4B, and vol. 23, PK 31.

13. RA, vol. 23, PK 33 vs. vol. 17–19, PM 10:4C, 26.

14. See the interview of Söderström by G. Wall in *Internationalen* 1988 (11), 9–12. Poutiainen presumes that the woman was referring to the phone call from the emergency services operator (*Inuti Labyrinten*, 276).

15. Poutiainen, *Inuti Labyrinten*, 273, 275, 301. Captain Ingemar Krusell, a retired detective with great knowledge of the Palme case, agrees that the first police car arrived at the scene close to 11:25. He attributes the delay at police headquarters to the fact that on a Friday evening, the operators were very busy. When challenged with the "Järfälla hypothesis," both Krusell and fellow detective lieutenant Åke Röst guardedly comment that these are allegations they have heard before.

16. Poutiainen, *Inuti Labyrinten*, 310–16.

3. A Killer on the Loose

1. On the hours after the murder, see JK, vol. 1, 18–26; GK, 46–49; D. Hansén, *The Crisis Management of the Murder of Olof Palme* (2003); and, more incisively, Poutiainen, *Inuti Labyrinten*, 123–244.

2. Poutiainen, *Inuti Labyrinten*, 156–58; and statements by the officers on TV4-CD.

3. Poutiainen, *Inuti Labyrinten*, 169–93; RA, vol. 17–19, PM 10:4C.

4. Poutiainen, *Inuti Labyrinten*, 381; Magnusson, *Palmerapporten*, 63.

5. JK, vol. 1, 41–43; I. Krusell, *Palmemordets nakna fakta* (1998), 79–82.

6. Poutiainen, *Inuti Labyrinten*, 351–80.

7. *Exp*, March 20, 1986.

8. *Exp*, March 1, 1986; I. Carlsson, *Ur skuggan av Olof Palme* (1996), 33–39.

9. Mosey, *Cruel Awakening*, 162–64.

10. E. Winbladh, *Närbilder* (2002), 67–72.

11. U. Dahlsten, *Nirvana kan vänta* (2001), 179–88; *Exp*, February 24, 1987; Poutiainen, *Inuti Labyrinten*, 410–25; *Palme-Nytt* 1995 (2), 16 and 1997 (5), 15–16. The day after the murder, the nurses described Lisbet Palme's injury to a hospital official in exactly the same terms

later used in the newspaper: it was just a reddening across the back that did not require sutures or bandaging.

12. On this farcical story, see *KvP*, March 1, 1986, and H. Holmér, *Olof Palme är skjuten!* (1988), 37.

13. Holmér, *Olof Palme*, 100–101.

14. See the papers by R. Lindahl, *Nyheten om mordet på Olof Palme* (Rapport 10, 1986; Avdelningen för Masskommunikation, Göteborgs Universitet); M. Cronholm and A. Gahlin, *Nyhetsspridningen lördagen den 1 mars 1986* (PUB Informerar, 1986:1); L. Weibull, *Nyhetsspridningen vid mordet på* Olof Palme (Styrelsen för Psykologiskt Försvar, 1986:134), L. Weibull et al., *European Journal of Communication* 2 (1987), 143–70; and O. Möller, *Presshistorisk Årsbok* 1987, 3–19.

15. These U.S. articles are quoted by R. Lindahl and L. Weibull, *Palme i amerikanska ögon* (Arbetsrapport 33, 1986, Avdelningen för Masskommunikation, Göteborgs Universitet).

4. Hans Holmér Takes Charge

1. C. Persson, *Utan omsvep* (1991), 201–6.

2. Krusell, *Palmemordets nakna fakta*, 95; Holmér, *Olof Palme*, 26–28. Welander denied, when interviewed on TV4-CD, that he had ever made the silly remark about the ski race. Another remarkable statement from Holmér, namely that Welander had been drinking whiskey when contacted by the police at midnight, was also indignantly denied by this officer; see Holmér, *Olof Palme*, 20; and *Exp*, November 1, 1988.

3. Their evidence is in CP, III:2, 225–51, 263–76; see also *LO-Tidningen* 1989 (8), 4–6.

4. CP, III:2, 124–31.

5. CP, III:2, 104–23. Björkman had certainly drunk a fair amount of alcohol, but a witness who met him did not think him particularly intoxicated; see interview with J.-Å. Svensson on TV4-CD. It is curious that Björkman later added that he thought Lisbet Palme had been speaking French; see RA, vol. 15, letter from I. Heimer dated November 15, 1994.

6. On Rimborn, see Poutiainen, *Inuti Labyrinten*, 361–76; and Wall, *Mörkläggning*, 59–62.

7. Holmér, *Olof Palme*, 40–42.

8. These six examples are in CP, III:2, 173 vs. 179; 479 vs. 504; 300 vs. 303; 134–35; 440–41; 416.

9. *AB*, March 2, 1986.

10. This section is based on a thorough review of the witness testimony in CP, III:2, 104–570.

11. On Sweden's reaction to the murder, see the articles by H. Persson, *Ord och Bild* 1987 (3), 46–9; M. Scharfe, *Ethnologia Scandinavica* 19 (1989), 142–53; O. Johansson, *Scandinavian Political Studies* 18 (1995), 265–83; and P. Esaiasson and D. Granberg, *British Journal of Political Science* 26 (1996), 429–39.

12. NAO, 41–43; GK, 169–71; Krusell, *Palmemordets nakna fakta*, 115–17; Holmér, *Olof Palme*, 35.

13. On this over-helpfulness of the public, see Holmér, *Olof Palme*, 86–88; *AB*, March 25, 1987.

14. *Arb*, March 14, 1987; Anér, *Polisspåret*, 137–40; GK, 454–55; RA, vol. 17, PM 20.

15. GK, 151–54; Krusell, *Palmemordets nakna fakta*, 80.

16. Namely the witnesses Jan-Åke Svensson and Bengt Palm; see CP, III:2, 290, 406.

17. Krusell, *Palmemordets nakna fakta*, 81–83; interview with Ingemar Krusell. On the marks on the bullets, see *Arb*, May 3, 1986; NAO, app. 2, 3–4.

18. *SDS*, March 3, 1986; *AB*, March 3, 1986; *SvD*, March 3, 1986, vs. *Arb*, March 3 and 4, 1986; *KvP*, March 4, 1986.

19. The original autopsy report is still kept secret, but the discussion of the autopsy before the 1999 commission has been reproduced in *Palme-Nytt* 1999 (11), 13–16, and 1999 (12), 7–13. It is curious that the doctor performing the autopsy was never contacted by the police, and that he was actively prevented from documenting Lisbet Palme's injury; see the articles by E. Amkoff, *Norra Västerbotten*, November 7, 1989, and *Vertex* 1989 (8), 6–7.

20. NAO, app. 2, 4–5, 8–10.

21. RA, vol. 17, PM 6:2; NAO, app. 2, 7–8.

22. NAO, 53–57.
23. *Exp*, March 2, 1986; A.-M. Åsheden, *Jakten på Olof Palmes mördare* (1987), 77–79.
24. Holmér, *Olof Palme*, 147, 160; NAO, app. 8; GK, 247–48. The later police investigation received information that a drunk from Skelleftehamn had written the letters as a prank, but the evidence for this was not conclusive; see PF, vol. 177, 244–50.
25. *KvP*, March 4, 1986; *Exp*, March 4 and 13, 1986; *AB*, March 6, 1986.
26. *AB*, April 5 and 9, 1986. A minor player in this soap opera was Holmér's estranged wife, who claimed to have been knocked down by two masked men saying, "This is the last warning! Tell Holmér!" The claim drew enormous newspaper publicity, and it was suggested that the killer and his accomplice had returned to strike again, this time targeting the police-master and his wife. Holmér was not convinced his wife had been attacked, but nevertheless he ordered police protection for her around the clock; see *AB*, April 9, 1986; *DN*, August 28, 1987; and Magnusson, *Palmerapporten*, 191, 398.
27. On the Phantom, see *AB*, March 7, 1986; *Exp*, March 7, 1986; *DN*, March 7, 1986; *Arb*, March 7, 1986; *KvP*, March 9, 1986.
28. GK, 252–55, 266–67.

5. The First Main Suspect

1. B. Wingren, *Han sköt Olof Palme* (1993), 62–64.
2. Wall, *Mörkläggning*, 84–85; Poutiainen, *Inuti labyrinten*, 541–44. There is more about the Mad Austrian in *Palme-Nytt* 1996 (10), 14–15 and 1999 (3), 12–14.
3. Poutiainen, *Inuti labyrinten*, 539–40; GK, 676–79.
4. Wingren, *Han sköt Olof Palme*, 105–8; Wall, *Mörkläggning*, 87–89. It is curious that in two separate interviews, one of the women alleged she had been shown Gunnarsson's photo *before* the confrontation; see Wall, *Mörkläggning*, 89; and PF, vol. 207, letter from S. Anér dated April 6, 1992.
5. "33-åringen," *Jag och Palmemordet* (1988), 49–50, 58, 60; Magnusson, *Palmerapporten*, 110–11.
6. For a profusion of anti-Gunnarsson anecdotes, see Wingren, *Han sköt Olof Palme*, 240–57; and N. Havu, *Mustachtricket som lurade Lisbet Palme* (2001), 33, 47–48.
7. "33-åringen," 65.
8. Åsheden, *Jakten på Olof Palmes mördare*, 69.
9. Poutiainen, *Inuti labyrinten*, 555–73; Wall, *Mörkläggning*, 91–98.
10. GK, 554–55.
11. Poutiainen, *Inuti labyrinten*, 586–94; GK, 556.
12. GK, 561–64; interview with Åke Röst.
13. Wingren, *Han sköt Olof Palme*.
14. Wingren, *Han sköt Olof Palme*, 204–23; and Havu, *Mustachtricket*, 219–41, make much of the fact that one of the letters was signed "Mr. B.W."—was this Gunnarsson's way of taunting his old enemy Börje Wingren? They ignore, however, that an expatriate right-wing Swede named Bertil Wedin made various confused statements regarding the Palme murder.
15. See journalist Anders Leopold's homepage, www.leopoldreport.com, and Havu, *Mustachtricket*, 186–218.
16. "33-åringen," 73.
17. Krusell, *Palmemordets nakna fakta*, 36, 177–78; GK, 676–79; NAO, 87, 146–47; interview with Zeime in Z 1988 (3), 78–87; Poutiainen, *Inuti labyrinten*, 626–27.
18. *Salisbury Post*, April 29, 2000, and May 7, 2000, and *Exp*, September 23, 2003. Debate concerning Underwood's conviction continues; see the articles by J. Weaver in the *Salisbury Post*, January 11–16, 2004.

6. Red Herrings

1. GK, 429–34; PF, vol. 181, 644–45.
2. GK, 595–98.

3. GK, 194; Åsheden, *Jakten på Olof Palmes mördare*, 37; Holmér, *Olof Palme*, 61.
4. Holmér, *Olof Palme*, 85; PF, vol. 177, 207–18.
5. Hierner's PM is kept in RA, vol. 20.
6. TV4-CD, interview with Karl-Gerhard Svensson. See also Magnusson, *Palmerapporten*, 359–68, and *Örnsköldsviks Allehanda*, June 28, 1994. It is remarkable that according to *Exp*, February 27, 1996, Lisbet Palme was at that time still refusing to show the police her husband's secret notebooks.
7. One version of this story, suggesting the politician was Ulf Dahlsten, was spread by journalist Olle Alsén, a notorious peddler of bogus information in the Palme case; a well-known lawyer told another version, naming the politician as former minister Ove Rainer.
8. On the Rothschild connection, see the London *Times*, December 5, 1986, and C. Isaksson, *Palme privat* (1995), 237–38. The untrue story of the phone call was in *AB*, October 20, 1995, quoting a notoriously unreliable source; see also *Palme-Nytt* 1995 (9), 2–5 and 1997 (11), 8–14.
9. Isaksson is undecided about the MacLaine affair (*Palme privat*, 234–36). He instead points out that Palme had enjoyed a very close and long-standing friendship with artist Ewa Rudling, but this is yet another dubious story, according to Palme's son Mårten (*Exp*, February 10, 1997). See also *AB*, May 17, 2000; and TV4-CD, interview with Harry Schein.
10. On the Harvard case, see H. Hermansson and L. Wenander, *Uppdrag Olof Palme* (1987), 38–53; and K. N. A. Nilsson, *Ondskan Hatet Mordet* (2001), 191–93. The possible link with the murder is discussed by GK, 585–94.
11. A general overview of the Swedish right-wing organizations and their campaign against Palme is provided by Hermansson and Wenander, *Uppdrag Olof Palme*, and Nilsson, *Ondskan Hatet Mordet*; see also GK, 532–45. On the Scientologists as murder suspects, see GK, 518–23.
12. On the European Workers Party as murder suspects, see GK, 512–18. The link with Gunnarsson is discussed in *DN*, March 19, 1986.
13. On Enerström, see GK, 545–50; *Palme-Nytt* 1993 (12), 2–7; *AB*, February 20, 1994; and Nilsson, *Ondskan Hatet Mordet*, 185–88. Enerström's later misfortunes are chronicled in *Exp*, January 27, 2004, and March 15, 2004.
14. On the Skandia Man, see *SDS*, April 7, 1986; *KvP*, April 7, 1986; CP, III:2, 183–84, 242, 328; and CP, TB, 42–72. He is further discussed by J. Arvidsson in *Skydd och Säkerhet* 1992 (5), 6–11; and by S. Anér, *Fyra Nycklar* (1991), C1–C17 and *Cover-up*, 74–115. See also *Palme-Nytt* 1993 (3), 1; 1999 (10), 2–16; and 2000 (14), 2.
15. Interview with Ingemar Krusell, who has knowledge of a secret police file on these matters, written by lieutenant Jerker Söderblom. The witnesses Glantz and Ljungqvist both denied seeing the Skandia Man (CP, III:2, 183, 328); so did the witnesses Ersson and Karin Johansson (TV4-CD).

7. The Kurdish Conspiracy

1. Holmér, *Olof Palme*, 199–246. A more benign view of the PKK is given by Kanger, *Mordet på Olof Palme*, 93–164; and by P. Linde, *Det kurdiska spåret* (1994). An admirably level-headed account is that by Wall, *Mörkläggning*, 116–46. The PKK still exists, although the organization suffered many drawbacks in the 1990s; see M. Radu, *Orbis*, Winter 2001.
2. Hansén, *Crisis Management*, 41; Wall, *Mörkläggning*, 156–57.
3. On Ahlström's story, see Holmér, *Olof Palme*, 183–98; and GK, 624–27.
4. On Baresic, see Holmér, *Olof Palme*, 185–88; and GK, 610–22. Baresic ended a fairly worthless life, mostly spent in various prisons, fighting as a Croat soldier in the Yugoslav civil war in 1991.
5. Åsheden, *Jakten på Olof Palmes mördare*, 157–65; Holmér, *Olof Palme*, 210–18.
6. Wall, *Mörkläggning*, 525–33; *KvP*, July 9, 13, 1988; *AB*, February 13, 1989.
7. The authority on these bugging activities is Wall, *Mörkläggning*, 196–345.
8. Kanger, *Mordet på Olof Palme*, 99–103.
9. Magnusson, *Palmerapporten*, 323–32, 404–11.
10. GK, 637–41.

11. Krusell, *Palmemordets nakna fakta*, 52–55, 167–70; Wall, *Mörkläggning*, 311–15.
12. Holmér, *Olof Palme*, 253–58; Wall, *Mörkläggning*, 180–83.
13. GK, 636–37.
14. He was active there for two years, but his work was pretty worthless, according to *SDS*, November 14, 1989.

8. Ebbe Carlsson's Secret Investigation

1. Wall, *Mörkläggning*, 347–48.
2. On the hospital spy scandal, see Curt Falkenstam, *Polisernas krig* (1983), 216–30; Wall, *Mörkläggning*, 352–73; and L. O. Lampers, *Sjukhusaffären i Göteborg* 1975 (SOU 2002:95).
3. T. G. Peterson, *Resan mot Mars* (1999), 313–42.
4. C. Lidbom, *Ett uppdrag* (1990); and for this entire chapter, Wall, *Mörkläggning*, 346–711.
5. Published as a series in *DN*, and later as Åsheden, *Jakten på Olof Palmes mördare*. Although these articles reflect Holmér's opinions and provide some interesting insights into the early phase of the murder investigation, the chronology of the book and other circumstances have given rise to speculation that it is not based on interviews, or even that it is a falsification, possibly written by Ebbe Carlsson himself (Anér, *Fyra Nycklar*, B1–B24). It seems odd that Holmér would take time off for eighty-one lengthy interviews during such a busy and crucial time in his career. These interviews were alleged to have taken place at police headquarters, but journalist Sven Anér was able to ascertain that the interviewer had been seen there only twice by the security guards and by Holmér's secretaries. Unfortunately for Anér's theory, the truth, as verified by reliable police sources, would appear to be that after these introductory meetings, Holmér met the female journalist at a more convenient place.
6. On this mystery man, see *KvP*, June 7, 1989, and Wall, *Mörkläggning*, 481–92. Edwards seems to have completely disappeared after the Ebbe Carlsson scandal erupted in the media.
7. On these bizarre proceedings, see Wall, *Mörkläggning*, 564–66; *Exp*, April 29 and 30, 1991.
8. The jury is still out on whether Ingvar Carlsson told the truth; see Wall, *Mörkläggning*, 696–703; Peterson, *Resan mot Mars*, 313–42; P. Ahlin and M. Bergstrand, *Den godhjärtade buffeln* (1997), 129–59; interview with Nils-Erik Åhmansson on TV4-CD. In his memoirs, Carlsson claims that he knew about Ebbe's vivid imagination and bad judgment from the start, and that the publisher acted entirely on his own (*Så Tänkte Jag* [2003]).
9. Holmér, *Olof Palme*. This book is alleged to have sold sixty thousand copies in Sweden, an enormous number for such a small country. It was translated into German, Finnish, and Norwegian.
10. On Holmér's later activities, see J. Lindström, *Månadsjournalen* 1993 (7), 44–47. He died in 2002, from a rare and disagreeable disease called primary amyloidosis; see *Exp* and *AB*, October 6, 2002.
11. On Lidbom's scandalous life, see *Exp*, April 21, 1989; *KvP*, April 21, 1989; *Arb*, August 10, 1989; *GP*, August 11, 1989; *Exp*, November 30, 1991. When Lidbom died in July 2004, the obituaries mentioned little about the more sinister aspects of his career.
12. On these two witnesses, see NAO, 97, 154–55; and TV4-CD, interview with Hans Ölvebro.
13. Krusell, *Palmemordets nakna fakta*, 324. Another hypothesis is that the wedding conversations referred to a PKK defector in Germany, who was murdered the day after Olof Palme.
14. Zeime in *Z* 1988 (3), 82; GK, 625.
15. Holmér, PM on TV4-CD; NAO, app. 3.
16. NAO, 97.
17. Helin interviewed on TV4-CD. O. Tunander speculates that Ebbe Carlsson was really a supersleuth, who was following the PKK lead backward to find out who had planted it and thus discover the real leader of the murder conspiracy; this imaginative hypothesis is not supported by any original evidence (*Ord och Bild* 1994 [3], 16).

9. The Second Main Suspect

1. The testimony of the Grand witnesses is in CP, III:1, 7–31, 38–53, 112–27, 142–61, and III:2, 52–86; and has been commented on by Krusell, *Palmemordets nakna fakta*, 65–67; and Wall, *Mörkläggning*, 727–29.

2. The testimony of these two witnesses is in CP, III:2, 87–103.

3. CP, III:2, 7–51; also *AB*, March 14, 1987; and *Exp*, October 5, 1994.

4. *DN*, June 22, 1989; and Krusell, *Palmemordets nakna fakta*, 129–33.

5. *Exp*, December 15, 1988; *AB*, December 19, 1988, and July 28, 1989.

6. The twenty questionings of Sigge Cedergren are in CP, II:1, 74–182. It is curious that several other witnesses referred to his story of the running man as if it were nothing but the truth; see CP, II:1, 187, and II:2, 284, 609, 655–56.

7. Just a few weeks after the murder, Gärdestad was widely rumored to be the hated thirty-three-year-old. He was no fire-breathing rock and roller, but a meek, nervous crooner, whose greatest hit was a ditty about his old teddy bear. Although he had been abroad at the time of the murder, rumors spread like wildfire: people screamed "Murderer!" at him in the streets, and his children were bullied at their school. Gärdestad was a member of an Eastern religious sect led by a guru called Baghwan, and this was of course given a sinister interpretation. It was rumored that Palme had wanted to sell the Swedish fishing waters in the Baltic to the Russians, but Baghwan had decided that this should not happen and ordered his disciple Gärdestad to kill Palme. After several years of persecution, poor Gärdestad committed suicide.

8. The Spinnars questionings are in CP, II:1, 15–72.

9. The Östlund questionings are in CP, III, 201–55.

10. CP, II:3, 864–65, 956, 1071, 1137, 1181.

11. CP, II:3, 1134, 1030–31.

12. CP, III:2, 238–39; *Palme-Nytt* 1998 (3), 6–7.

13. Wall, *Mörkläggning*, 775.

14. Krusell, *Palmemordets nakna fakta*, 189; NAO, 104; NAO, app 4, 5,19; Krusell, interview.

15. CP, II:5, 1304–20.

16. Krusell, *Palmemordets nakna fakta*, 253–57; Krusell, interview.

17. These little-known facts are in RA, vol. 20–23, questioning of Hans Ölvebro, 22, and questioning of Solveig Riberdahl, 5–6, 19.

18. It is recorded that no fewer than 647 photographs were shown. The prosecutors have assured us that Petterson's photo was not among them.

19. For some examples, see CP, II:2, 670–716, and II:3, 764, 787, 923.

20. CP, II:1, 139–40, 245–46; CP, TA 50–55. It is noteworthy, however, that another Oxen habitué claimed to have seen Pettersson there around 11:00 p.m., according to CP, II:2, 311–12.

21. Krusell, *Palmemordets nakna fakta*, 231–36.

10. The Trials of Christer Pettersson

1. Two books discuss the trials: Klami, *Mordet på Olof Palme*; and C. Borgström, *Rättegången om mordet på Olof Palme* (1991).

2. On these two witnesses, see CP, II:3, 1020–28, 1099–101; on the farcical events in court, see Poutiainen, *Inuti labyrinten*, 636–40, 643–46, 657.

3. Borgström, *Rättegången*, 85–87.

4. Poitiainen, *Inuti labyrinten*, 375–80; Krusell, interview. Rimborn's report is in PF, vol. 215, 321.

5. These walkie-talkie observations are reviewed by Wall, *Mörkläggning*, 850–55, 906–12. The remarkable story that some men had conducted transmission tests with walkie-talkies in the shops in the Skandia building, reported in the underground magazine *Grobladet* and later by other, more reputable sources, is an invention, according to Åke Röst.

6. On the phone tap, see Poitiainen, *Inuti labyrinten*, 659–66.

7. Wall, *Mörkläggning*, 736–67. The newspaper rumor about Sigge being bugged was in *Exp*, November 30, 1988.

8. RA, vol. 18, 5b(1) and 5b(3); Krusell, *Palmemordets nakna fakta*, 93; Krusell, interview. It

is curious that the narcotics detectives told the 1999 commission that they went home at 10:00 or 10:30; some said they stayed as late as 11:00. This would have made them excellent defense witnesses, particularly since one detective confidently told the commission that Christer Pettersson had not been seen outside Sigge's apartment by 10:00 p.m. Krusell can well remember, however, that when he reproached these detectives for their neglect of duty—after all, had they remained at work, they might well have caught Palme's killer!—they shamefacedly admitted that they had gone home at 9:00 p.m. This would imply that they lied to the 1999 commission to portray themselves in a better light.

9. On Åsell, see CP, TC, 1–131; and Krusell, *Palmemordets nakna fakta*, 268–69.

10. RA, vol. 20–23, questioning of Anders Helin, 63–67.

11. *DN*, June 20, 1989; *KvP*, June 29, 1989; *SvD*, July 11, 1989.

12. *DN*, September 19, 1989; *Arb*, October 10, 1989.

13. *Arb*, October 4, 1989; Wall, *Mörkläggning*, 788–91.

14. On Holm, see CP, TG, 1–70. Various arguments supporting Åsell and Holm have been advanced by Poutiainen, *Inuti labyrinten*, 666–68; and Wall, *Mörkläggning*, 823–26. It is notable that in their dossier of material to discredit Åsell, the police make much of a confused collection of documents sent to him by a woman who was clearly far from sane and who had meddled in the Palme investigation from an early stage; see CP, TC, 50–67; and Åsheden, *Jakten på Olof Palmes mördare*, 155. But clearly, Åsell could not be blamed for receiving letters from this dubious correspondent. It is also notable that Big Jerka, who was supposed to give evidence against Holm, did not turn up in court.

15. Holgersson's original report is in PF, vol. 178, 348. It was later published as *Forskningsrapport från Vittnespsykologiska Forskningslaboratoriet*, no. 3 (1989). See also A. Gustavsson, *Advokaten* 56 (1990), 142–50; and *Arb*, October 5, 1989.

16. RA, vol. 20–23, questioning of Hans Ölvebro, 39–40.

17. On the press conference, see *AB*, October 13, 1989; *Arb*, October 13, 1989. Ingemar Krusell met Liljeros a few days after the press conference, pulling his leg about his client's imprudent remarks. He got the impression that Liljeros was well aware that Pettersson was the guilty man.

18. *SDS*, October 14, 1989.

11. The Scapegoat Is Never Tarred

1. *DN*, October 13, 1989; *Exp*, October 14, 1989.

2. Pettersson's later life was chronicled in *Exp*, October 1, 2001.

3. *AB*, August 12, 1994.

4. This documentary by journalist Stig Edling gave rise to TV4-CD. His hypothesis, which later reemerged in T. Forsberg, *Spioner och spioner som spionerar på spioner* (2003), 397–417, is less praiseworthy. It is ably criticized by Wall, *Mörkläggning*, 872–74; and when interviewed, Ingemar Krusell agreed that it is entirely untenable.

5. Krusell, *Palmemordets nakna fakta*, 303–17.

6. The appeal documents are held by the Supreme Court of Sweden. They are discussed by Krusell, *Palmemordets nakna fakta*, 339–44; and in an article series in *DN*, April 18, 1998; April 25, 1998; May 9, 1998; and May 16, 1998.

7. Wall, *Mörkläggning*, 874–77. Krusell is adamant that if Sigge had testified in court that he had given Pettersson the revolver, the latter would have been convicted, but this is far from certain given Sigge's habitual untruthfulness.

8. Krusell, *Palmemordets nakna fakta*.

9. P. Svensson, *Sanningen om mordet på Olof Palme* (1998). Unfortunately for this wayward author, he named the wrong foreign minister, and journalist Gunnar Wall was able to seriously shake his hypothesis in *DN*, May 20, 1998. When interviewed, Ingemar Krusell agreed that Pelle Svensson's contributions to the case are entirely worthless.

10. *AB*, November 11, 1999.

11. Dahlsten, *Nirvana kan vänta*, 179–88; also *AB* and *Exp*, October 29, 2001, and October 31, 2001.

12. Mrs. Palme's speculation that the killer was a Croat or Chilean assassin is difficult to rec-

oncile with her statement about the alcoholic. When asked whether her claim that she told the police the killer looked like an alcoholic who had killed before could be true, both Ingemar Krusell and Åke Röst answered in the negative. See also articles in *DN*, October 30, 2001, November 1, 2001, November 23, 2001, and December 1, 2001.

13. On Fylking's activities, see *Exp*, October 30, 2001, and November 3, 2001.

14. On the newspaper publicity surrounding Pettersson's "confession," see H. Elvingdal et al., *Christer Petterssons Erkännande, B-uppsats Södertörns Högskola, HT* 2001.

15. Dahlsten, *Nirvana kan vänta*, 179–88.

16. T. Lindström, *Mitt liv som snut* (1996), 127–30.

17. CP, III:2, 557–61.

18. Ingemar Krusell and Åke Röst agree that Ljungqvist's later testimony is dubious in the extreme and that he had a tendency to regurgitate what he had read in the media as his own observations.

19. Krusell, *Palmemordets nakna fakta*, 210–11.

20. Krusell, *Palmemordets nakna fakta*, 203–4; CP, II:4, 1252–61.

21. CP, II:3, 1071, 1130; Krusell, interview.

22. CP, TA 7–33; Krusell, interview.

23. Namely by professor Elizabeth Loftus (*Palme-Nytt* 1999 [4], 10); and by distinguished Welsh psychologist professor Hadyn Ellis in interview with Jan Bondeson.

24. S. Anér, *Dominoeffekten* (Gothenburg, 1998), 12–43.

25. Wall, *Mörkläggning*, 797–98; Svensson on TV4-CD.

26. Wall, *Mörkläggning*, 791–93; interview with Riberdahl on TV4-CD; RA, vol. 20–23, 6C: 8–9, 6E: 31.

27. S.-Å. Christiansson, *Traumatiska minnen* (1994), 168–72.

28. NAO, app. 5, 6.

29. Tommy Lindström on TV4-CD; Krusell, *Palmemordets nakna fakta*, 251; Krusell, interview.

30. Poutiainen, *Inuti labyrinten*, 688–70.

31. NAO, app. 6, 9.

32. Holmér interviewed in *KvP*, July 27, 1989; and *AB*, October 18, 1992; Lindström, *Mitt liv som snut*, 130–32, and interviewed in RA, vol. 23, PK 13; Persson interviewed in *Slitz* 2002 (11). It is curious that Olof Palme's brother Claës apparently had little trust in his sister-in-law; he declared himself convinced that Pettersson was innocent in *KvP*, January 27, 1990.

33. CP, TF, 24–25; and G. Wall, *Internationalen* 1988 (51), 7.

12. Conspiracy Theories

1. Articles on Palme conspiracies in general include those by N. Granberg, *Folket i Bild* 1986 (6), 4–8,19; J.-O. Sundberg, *Flashback News Agency*, various issues; G. Pettersson, *Ord och Bild* 99 (4) [1990], 9–18, and *Moderna Tider* 1993 (2), 33–37; O. Tunander, *Ord och Bild* 103 (3)[1994], 8–24; H. Hederberg, *Smedjan* 1995 (5), 40–43; and *Året Runt* 1996 (7), 8–10, 79, 1996 (8), 16–9; 1996 (9), 8–10,76; and B. Moelv, *Folket i Bild Kulturfront* 2000 (5), 10–7.

2. On the Palme Detectives, see various articles in *Vi* 1990 (25–34) and 1991 (9); also *Z* 1991 (4), 23–25; *iDag*, October 11, 1993; *Arbetaren* 74 (10) [1995], 2–5.

3. Two early books pointing the finger at the police were Anér, *Polisspåret*, and Baude et al., *Mordet på Palme*.

4. *Arb*, November 6, 1987; Anér, *Polisspåret*, 81–82, 137–40.

5. L. Krantz, *Ett verkligt drama* (1987), is ably criticized by Wall, *Mörkläggning*, 387–92. On the bus driver, see RA, 95–151 and 95–188. In PF, vol. 176, 141, the bus driver wants a ten-million-dollar reward; in PF, 176: 142, he claims that Krantz prompted him by asking some very leading questions before showing him only one photograph, that of the Baseball Gang cop.

6. *DN*, June 26, 1989; August 13, 1989; October 9, 1989.

7. *DN*, February 19, 1990; April 30, 1990; July 29, 1990; *AB*, February 9, 1992; *Vi* 1990 (25/26), 4–6, 37.

8. *DN*, April 18, 1991; May 31, 1991; *AB*, February 9, 1992.

9. On the Dekorima Man, see *DN*, July 27, 1993; February 29, 1994; May 6, 1994; GK, 401–3; RA, vol. 17–19; PM 10 (6), 35–39.

10. Poutiainen, *Inuti labyrinten.*

11. PF, vol. 219, addenda to letter dated November 24, 1993. It is also noteworthy that according to the police archives, two squad cars arrested a drunk and attended to a car break-in just a few minutes before the murder, in the near vicinity of the murder site (PF, vol. 216, documents dated May 17, 1993).

12. GK, 271–424.

13. On the mysterious Östling, see Wall, *Mörkläggning*, 801–17; and GK, 318–30. It is curious that according to a reliable police source, a close business associate of Östling's suffered a nervous breakdown soon after the Palme murder. In 1996, Östling again hit the headlines, after a friend in the military establishment had arranged some lucrative deals between Östling's company, Inoco, and the Swedish military and police; see *DN*, October 19, 22, 1996. All these contracts were cancelled, and Östling later moved to Germany.

14. Grundborg is said to have been away at the time of the murder; still it is amazing that according to the police, he has never been questioned in the Palme inquiry.

15. Sven Anér has published many books on the murder: *Polisspåret* (1988), *Fyra nycklar* (1991), *Affären Chamonix* (1992), *Affären Borlänge* (1995), *Dominoeffekten* (1998), *Cover-up* (1999), and *Palmegåtan—Mot en lösning* (2002). From 1993 until 2003, he also published his journal *Palme-Nytt*, a valuable repository of documents, although suffering from the hot-headed Palme Detective's tendency to see sinister conspiracies everywhere.

16. Anér gives dramatic accounts of the Borlänge conspiracy in *Fyra nycklar*, A1–A14), *Affären Borlänge*, and *Palmegåtan* (9–66). See also *DN*, September 3, 1991; *Palme-Nytt* 2000 (5), 11–15; RA, vols. 17–19, PM 10(6), 15–22; and GK, 388–90.

17. Anér also provides a highly charged account of the Chamonix conspiracy in *Affären Chamonix*; see also *Palme-Nytt* 2000 (4), 9–16 and RA, vols. 17–19, PM 10(6), 22–31.

18. See K.-D. Knapp, *Die Zeit*, February 24, 1995; and *Palme-Nytt* 1996 (2), 2–9.

19. Compare *Arb*, March 2, 1986, to *SvD*, February 25, 1991; see also Magnusson, *Palmerapporten*, 13; and Anér, *Affären Chamonix*, 26–28.

20. On this bizarre incident, see *KvP*, June 9, 10, and 12, 1986; *SDS*, June 10, 1986.

21. L. Krantz, *Ett verkligt drama* (1987) and *Mord i rättan tid* (1996); the same author has a Web site (www.nationalmordet.nu) containing much buffoonery about the murder.

22. The identity of the person who took this photograph is a matter of debate. Ulf Karlsson has been named by some Palme Detectives—see *Palme-Nytt* 2000(9), 2–3, and 2000 (11), 4–10—but he was not at Sabbatsberg at the time Lisbet Palme arrived, according to Baude et al., *Mordet på Palme*, 47–50.

23. E. Lindholm's *Offrets uppdrag*, available online at home.swipnet.se/blodsten, quotes the Alsén manuscript (RA, 93–447) on pages 31–33.

24. www.leopoldreport.com.

25. On the South Africa lead, see GK, 445–81; Wall, *Mörkläggning*, 884–91; A. Hasselbohm, *Vi* 1996 (44), 18–21; E. Wiedemann, *Der Spiegel* 42 (1996), 166–73; Y. Rodny-Gumede, *Daily Mail and Guardian*, June 27, 2001; K. de Jonge on www.totse.com/en/politics; also anonymous articles on www.fecl.org/circular/4701.htm and www.contrast.org/truth/html.

26. *Exp*, October 10, 1996. But the police claimed that these witnesses had really seen a heavyset Spanish tourist with a liking for colorful shirts.

27. GK, 473–78; *Exp*, July 23, 1997; *AB*, July 23 and 24, 1997.

28. *Exp*, January 20, 22, and 24, 2003; *AB*, January 20, 22, 23, and 24, 2003; *DN*, January 20, 2003.

13. The Police Investigation Keels Over

1. The profile is exhaustively reviewed by GK, 844–918.

2. Wall, *Mörkläggning*, 877–80; NAO, 109 and app. 5; GK, 900–12; *Palme-Nytt* 1996 (2), 10–14 and 1999 (13), 11–12; RA, 1–99.

3. On Lundin, see *Exp*, March 12, 1994; and October 5, 1994; also Wall, *Mörkläggning*, 866–70; and GK, 922.

4. On these and other lunatics as murder suspects, see GK, 922–25, 952–54, 961–66.

5. On the Yugoslav, see *AB*, July 5, 1999; February 21, 2000; NAO, 107–25; GK, 955–60, 968–70.

6. NAO, app. 7; GK, 199–211; Krusell, interview.

7. GK, 212–15; interview with Thure Nässén on TV4-CD.

8. *Exp*, October 19, 20, and 21, 2002; November 14, 2002; *AB*, October 19 and 31, 2002; *SvD*, October 19, 2002.

9. GK, 955–60, 968–70; NAO, 113–15, 126–36; *AB*, July 10, 1999; *DN*, August 10, 1999.

10. On Marjasin's downfall, see Wall, *Mörkläggning*, 880–84.

11. *DN*, October 13 and 20, 1999.

14. Did Olof Palme Know His Killer?

1. Åsheden, *Jakten på Olof Palmes mördare*, 101; RA, vol. 23, PK 13; Wall, *Mörkläggning*, 899–905.

2. CP, III:2, 356–86; and Kanger, *Mordet på Olof Palme*, 13–22; also the Morelius testimony in the two Pettersson trials. Ingemar Krusell accepts that the killer waited at the Dekorima corner a few minutes for Palme to arrive; see Krusell, *Palmemordets nakna fakta*, 71; and Krusell, interview.

3. CP, III:1, 61–79; and CP, III:2, 91–103.

4. Krusell, *Palmemordets nakna fakta*, 80–81; and Krusell, interview.

5. For these three witnesses, see CP, III:2, 124–31, 411–23, and 104–23.

6. Interview on TV4-CD.

7. These three witnesses are in CP, III:2, 282–89, 252–62, and 277–81.

8. CP, TH, 438–39, 467, 482.

9. Kanger, *Mordet på Olof Palme*, 12–14; Wall, *Mörkläggning*, 925–30. Wall has gone on to speculate that Palme may not have gone to meet the man outside Dekorima entirely unprotected. Perhaps the walkie-talkie men observed by various witnesses were members of a secret police team protecting the prime minister from a distance? The slow police response to the killing could then be explained as follows: these agents had forewarned police headquarters that they would take care of any incident that occurred near the Dekorima meeting place. This curious hypothesis is unsupported by documentary evidence, however, and no one actually saw any mystery men pursue the killer. A secret police commando would have no authority over the uniformed police, which leaves it unexplained why the officers at police headquarters would keep these matters quiet, when they were in dire need of excuses for their own tardiness.

10. CP, III:2, 93.

11. The murder scene witnesses Björkman, Schödin, Ljungqvist, and Svensson all saw Lisbet Palme standing up after the shots were fired; see CP, III:2, 101, 142, 179, 290. Three young people traveling past the murder scene in a car independently testified that Lisbet Palme was still standing up after the shots were fired. One of them also saw that she had been walking ahead of Olof. See CP, TH, 415, 454, 469–70. The National Audit Office experts clearly distrusted Mrs. Palme's statement that she was dragged down, although they understood not to press the matter; see NAO, app. 2, 11.

12. These include the "lunatic fringe" books by Krantz and others, and also the somewhat more balanced analysis by H. Liljeson, *Palme-Nytt* 2002 (5), 3–13.

13. Palme Detective Ingvar Heimer, who died under somewhat mysterious circumstances in January 2000, was a staunch supporter of this conspiracy theory. See his Web site, home.bip.net/palmemordet, and his articles on members01.chello.se/isotalo/ and in *Palme-Nytt* 1997 (5), 15–16 and 2000 (5), 2–4; also RA, 95–88, 95-160, 96–38, 96–81, 97–16, 97–65; G. Stålbrand, *Lektyr* 1991 (8), 8–11; and I.-L. Rosén, *Vi* 1999 (8), 28. The meeting scenario has also been discussed by journalist Erik Amkoff (*iDag*, February 24, 1992).

14. Kanger, *Mordet på Olof Palme*, 30; Wall, *Mörkläggning*, 933–44. On traumatic memory loss, see also the articles by S.-Å. Christiansson and L.-G. Nilsson, *Memory and Cognition* 12 (1984), 142–55, and S. Porter et al., *International Journal of Law and Psychiatry* 24 (2001), 23–42. It is also reasonable to ask why an educated woman like Lisbet Palme would behave as irresponsibly as she did in the Pettersson trials, enabling the man she had picked out (or been co-

erced to pick out) to walk free. Was this because she had some kind of subconscious awareness of her "repressed memory" from the murder scene? Before the murder, she had been widely admired for her stalwart support of Olof Palme, and was considered an asset for Social Democratic election activities. But after the murder, she became increasingly reclusive. As she herself admitted in the Pettersson trial, she had never once walked past the Dekorima corner after her husband was murdered there. Her later career as chairwoman of the Swedish branch of UNICEF was fraught with controversy, and many of the office staff left in protest against her attitude. See *iDag*, September 19, 1990; *DN*, January 21 and 24, 1991; *Z* 1991 (2), 4–6.

15. CP, III:2, 173, 263, 269–70; interviews with Johansson and Ersson on TV4-CD.
16. CP, III:2, 241–42.
17. *Arb*, March 2, 1986.

15. Who Might Olof Palme Have Met?

1. Interview with Dahl on TV4-CD.
2. GK, 188, 191; and *AB*, April 19, 2003. An individual formerly employed at the Iraqi Embassy says that the ambassador was much more clever than his present-day image would suggest. Baghdad Bob knew Palme and had met him several times before; he was proud of his knowledge of the international arms trade, and had accumulated a dossier on Bofors.
3. Two hostile but largely realistic accounts of the business ethics of Bofors are H. Westander, *Bofors svindlande affärer* (1988); and B. G. Andersson and B. Stenqvist, *Vapensmugglarna* (1988). Four important works on the India deal are H. Westander, *Hemligstämplat* (1990); P. Bhushan, *Bofors: The Selling of a Nation* (New Delhi, 1990); C. Subramaniam, *En personlig dokumentär om Bofors* (1993); and B. Oza, *Bofors: The Ambassador's Evidence* (New Delhi, 1997).
4. Westander, *Hemligstämplat*, 55.
5. Westander, *Hemligstämplat*, 69–70.
6. Westander, *Hemligstämplat*, 58–70; GK, 571–72.
7. Westander, *Hemligstämplat*, 106–8, 135–40; *Exp*, March 22 and 23, 2002.
8. Subramaniam, *Bofors*, 86–89, 170–72. This author hints at links between A.E. Services and the United Kingdom's secret service, and clearly gives the impression there was something very sinister about this company.
9. Two articles about the mysterious Hindujas are in *Forbes*, December 28, 1987; and *Guardian*, February 3, 2001.
10. Worthwhile later articles about the Bofors scandal include those by P. Gupte and R. Singh, *Forbes*, July 7, 1997; V. Sanghvi, *Sunday*, February 2, 1997, *India-Seminar* 2000 (485), and *Mid-Day*, July 24, 2003; R. Singh, *Mid-Day*, February 25, 1998; A. G. Noorani, *Statesman* (Calcutta), December 17, 1999; P. Bhushan, *Frontline* 15 (4), 1998; P. Swami, *Frontline* 15 (9), 1998; S. Muralidharan, *Frontline* 16 (23), 1999; and N. Ram, *Frontline* 16 (24), 1999; also articles in *Hindu*, December 22, 2000; November 20, 2002; and March 16, 2004; and *Indian Express*, October 23, 1999; and December 21, 2000.
11. M. Shankar Aiyar on www.rediff.com.
12. It is interesting that in 2001, Rolf Gauffin was arrested trying to smuggle eleven million Swedish kronor from India to Singapore; see *AB*, May 31, 2002, November 9, 2002; and *Hindu*, October 4, 2002. Gauffin had many times been in India, although he was retired and had no business there. Was this man smuggling out part of the Bofors bribes, as hinted in the interesting articles by H. Westander (*Kapital* 2002 [1], 32–37) and M. Guruswamy (*Tehelka*, September 17 and 18, 2002)? After all, Quattrocchi lived in Malaysia, not far from Singapore. We are unlikely to ever know the truth about the Gauffin connection, since the man was allowed to escape from an Indian prison and take refuge in Sweden.
13. On the Bofors director, see *DN*, February 17 and 18, 1992; and *Exp*, February 18, 1992; on Westander's source, see his *Hemligstämplat*, 65, and *Kapital* 2002 (1), 32–37; on Hökby, see *AB*, August 27, 1998.
14. Salman Rushdie's article was in *Guardian*, February 7, 2001. He is not the only person who has suspected that the murder of Olof Palme is linked to the India deal; see *Exp*, January 8, 1991; and January 20, 1997; the interesting article by Å. Liljefors reproduced in *Palme-Nytt* 1994 (2), 11–12; and P. Gahrton, *Låt mormor bestämma* (1993), 231–37. The crazy Palme De-

tectives have added some sensationalist disinformation, namely that Palme stashed away the Bofors money in a Swiss bank account, and that he bribed Gandhi with plutonium from the Swedish nuclear reactors (for use in an Indian atomic bomb) to secure the deal!

15. GK, 565–69; PF, vol. 183, 812.

16. On the Bäck connection, see GK, 459–61; and *Palme-Nytt* 1994 (2), 8 and 1999 (13), 7–8; and somewhat confused newspaper accounts in *Arb*, June 23, 1988, and *Norrländska Socialdemokraten*, October 1, 1996. Bäck's own articles were in *Civila Försvarstidningen* 1987 (6), 8–9; 1987 (7), 12; 1987 (9), 7; 1987 (10), 7. In Sweden, the letter *I* is pronounced like the English *E*, explaining how Bäck got the company name wrong.

17. M. Shankar Aiyar on www.rediff.com.

18. *Exp*, October 10, 1996; O. Thunander in *Ord och Bild* 1994 (3), 11. Is it just a coincidence that one of Barnett's aliases, perhaps used when in Scandinavia, was Nico Estling?

19. It should be noted that many of the people Palme relied on as political fixers, like Lidbom, Ebbe Carlsson, and Hans Holmér, were away on February 28.

16. The Crime of the Century

1. J. Bondeson, *The Great Pretenders* (New York, 2004). The already vast amount of material on hand will be considerably increased in 2011, when the police register, with eighty thousand names and five hundred thousand documents, is likely to become public access. Unless some latter-day Ebbe Carlsson is assigned to "doctor" these documents, they should prove a very valuable resource for the historian.

2. GK, 690–92.

3. *Palme-Nytt* 1999 (13), 7–8.

SOURCES

A Note on Unpublished and Newspaper Sources

The official police protocols for Christer Pettersson were sought after by journalists and a small edition was photocopied to be sold to them. Concerning Pettersson, there is also the 1996 appeal against him, available from the Supreme Court of Sweden. Three state commissions have been appointed to scrutinize the police investigation of the murder: the first two (SOU 1987:14,72 and SOU 1988:18) can be studied at major Swedish libraries and the third and by far most valuable (SOU 1999:88) can be downloaded via the Internet via www.sou.gov.se. There is also a very interesting un-published analysis of the crime by experts from the National Audit Office, located in the National Archives of Sweden. These archives also hold large amounts of material used by the 1999 commission, some of it very valuable.

I read the relevant newspapers at the University Library of Lund and at the British Newspaper Library, Colindale. I am grateful to the clippings archive of the *Sydsvenska Dagbladet* for allowing me to access its large and well-catalogued collec-tion on the murder of Olof Palme. The Fritz G. Pettersson archive, kept by the Na-tional Archives of Sweden, contains a copious collection of press cuttings about the murder.

A Note on Abbreviations

CP = Police protocols in the Pettersson inquiry. Thus "CP, III:1, 67" refers to volume III:1, page 67, in these protocols. There is also a seried of auxiliary protocols, *Tilläggs-protokoll* A, B, etc. referred to as TA, TB, and so on in the references.

PF = The archives of police files and correspondence relating to the murder, held by the National Police Board, Stockholm.

NAO = The unpublished report of the National Audit Office, held by the National Archives of Sweden, Stockholm.

JK = The report of the 1987 commission (SOU 1987:14 and SOU 1987:72).

GK = The report of the 1999 commission (SOU 1999:88).

RA = The archives of the 1999 commission, held by the National Archives of Sweden. These documents are rather haphazardly organized into various volumes, with bundles of documents divided into a PK and a PM series, as well as dossiers of correspondence referred to by a year and number (for example, 97-16), and other material.

TV4-CD = A CD-ROM about the murder entitled *Vem mördade Olof Palme?* and sold by the television channel TV4 in 1995.

Newspapers: *AB* = *Aftonbladet*; *Arb* = *Arbetet*; *DN* = *Dagens Nyheter*; *Exp* = *Expressen*; *KvP* = *Kvällsposten*; *SDS* = *Sydsvenska Dagbladet*; *SvD* = *Svenska Dagbladet*.

All books are published in Stockholm unless otherwise stated.

INDEX

Figures are indicated by the letter *f*.